EDITORIAL RESEARCH REPORTS ON

CRIME
AND
JUSTICE

Timely Reports to Keep
Journalists, Scholars and the Public
Abreast of Developing Issues, Events and Trends

Published by Congressional Quarterly, Inc.

1414 22nd Street, N.W.

Washington, D.C. 20037

About the Cover

The cover was designed by Art Director Richard Pottern, who also provided many of the graphics in this book.

PRINTED IN THE UNITED STATES OF AMERICA
JULY 1978

Editor, Hoyt Gimlin
Associate Editor, Sandra Stencel
Editorial Assistants, Susan Henry and Lynda McNeil
Production Manager, I.D. Fuller
Assistant Production Manager, Maceo Mayo

Library of Congress Cataloging in Publication Data

Congressional Quarterly, Inc.

Editorial research reports on crime and justice.

Includes index.
1. Crime and criminals — United States.
2. Criminal justice, Administration of — United States. I. Title. II. Title: Crime and justice.
HV6789.C57   1978   364'.973   78-16044
ISBN 0-87187-137-8

Contents

Foreword

"For the first time in this decade, public concern with and perceptions of crime are leveling off, if not subsiding," the American Institute of Public Opinion (Gallup) informed us recently. For years the polling organization has been asking random groups of Americans: "Is there more crime in this area than there was a year ago?" Last November some 43 per cent of the people who were asked said yes. That's a lot, but far less than in years past. Only two years earlier, for instance, 50 per cent said yes. This new perception is reinforced by the FBI's quarterly and annual compilations of national crime statistics, which since 1976 have shown a cumulative decline in the amount of serious crime. The experts have been quite cautious in assessing the underlying meaning of these statistics but now are beginning to voice some optimism that a welcome relief trend may indeed be under way.

However, no one is in a mood to celebrate as long as crime continues to remain so visibly a part of everyday life throughout much of the nation. A recent study by the Ford Foundation surmizes that juveniles are committing more violent crimes than ever. A "troubling conclusion" of this report "concerns the failure of the juvenile justice system to intervene effectively to bring an end to juvenile violence."

The same thing is often said about the entire criminal justice system. Criminal courts tend to be swamped with cases and must rely heavily on plea bargaining rather than trials. Prisons are so overcrowded in some states that judges have decreed them unfit for human habitation. The failure of prisons to rehabilitate has prompted many criminologists to move away from the notion that rehabilitation should even be considered a realistic goal. While pessimism currently pervades much of the thinking about the state of criminal justice, there is — paradoxically — the statistical evidence that the volume of crime is easing off a bit. The experts hesitate to offer their theories as to why this is happening — hesitant because no one explanation seems to satisfy many people.

This book of nine reports issued in the past two years looks at several aspects of crime and justice in the hope that the information they supply may aid public understanding of the problems involved, even if definitive answers are still wanted.

Hoyt Gimlin
Editor

July 1978
Washington, D.C.

CRIME REDUCTION: REALITY OR ILLUSION

by

Suzanne de Lesseps

July 15
1977

Editor's Note: The trend toward a lower crime rate continued in 1977 and the first three months of 1978. Crime in the United States, as measured by the FBI's Crime Index, decreased 4 per cent in 1977 compared with 1976. Violent crimes, however, increased 1 per cent forcible rape increased 10 per cent; aggravated assault increased 5 per cent; murder increased 1 per cent. Robbery decreased 4 per cent while property crimes — burglary, larceny and motor vehicle theft — decreased 5 per cent. During the first three months of 1978 serious crime in the United States fell by 4 per cent compared with the corresponding period in 1977. Violent crimes during this period decreased 1 per cent, while property crimes decreased 5 per cent.

The Criminal Code Reform Act, discussed on p. 19, was approved by the Senate on Jan. 30, 1978. The Senate bill called for establishment of a federal sentencing commission to set guidelines governing the imposition of sentences by judges. The House Judiciary Subcommittee on Criminal Justice, however, rejected this provision. In its place, the subcommittee proposed development of "advisory guidelines" to be issued by the Federal Judicial Center, an arm of the federal courts. Aside from the sentencing changes, the House subcommittee addressed few of the sections of criminal law that the Senate revised.

CRIME REDUCTION

T HE AGE-OLD problem of how to deal with crime continues to plague American society. With the last decade's "war on crime" declared a failure, old truisms such as rehabilitation, probation, parole and indeterminate sentencing are being reexamined and questioned. In searching for new ways to reduce the number of criminal acts committed in this country, criminologists and law-enforcement officials have entered an era of lowered expectations.

"Perhaps the most important thing we have learned in the last few years is that crime is not the kind of problem that is amenable to breakthrough—as in health, with the Salk vaccine, or the technology that put a man on the moon," Gerald M. Caplan, ex-director of the National Institute of Law Enforcement and Criminal Justice, has said. "It is a problem we will be picking away at for a long time to come, and with luck, there should be a little bit of progress here and a little bit there. Cumulatively it may add up to the kind of knowledge and programs that will have a major impact on our crime problem. That is our hope."[1]

Americans have grown so accustomed to hearing about rising crime that it came as a surprise in March when Attorney General Griffin B. Bell announced that the number of reported serious crimes across the country showed no increase in 1976 over 1975. This was the first time since 1972 that the nation's Crime Index, compiled by the Federal Bureau of Investigation (FBI), did not rise. The 1976 figures were bolstered by new FBI figures released July 7, showing a 9 per cent decrease in crime in the United States for the first three months of 1977.

"There is firm ground for hope in the easing of nationwide crime during the past year," FBI Director Clarence M. Kelley said on March 30. "I firmly believe that, while our data are only preliminary at this point, the more thoughtful approaches that are being applied to crime and the more positive public attitude toward this grave social problem are now joining to deter the criminality that has flourished for too long in our society."

The FBI Crime Index statistics are based on police reports of known offenses and arrests in seven types of "serious"

---

[1] Interview in *U.S. News & World Report*, April 11, 1977, p. 82.

crimes—homicide, rape, robbery, aggravated assault, burglary, larceny-theft and auto theft. These crimes are grouped into two categories—violent crimes and property crimes. According to the 1976 figures, the violent crimes of murder, forcible rape, robbery and aggravated assault, as a group, had decreased 5 per cent *(see table, page 7)*. Ninety-seven cities with populations over 100,000, including Baltimore, Chicago, Detroit and Washington, reported decreases. However, New York City recorded its worst rate ever.

Police officials agree that the overall drop in the violent crime rate cannot be explained by any one cause. Rather, they point to a number of reasons which, interacting together, may be responsible. These include (1) citizen awareness and neighborhood crime watch groups, (2) greater use of protective security equipment by private homes and businesses, (3) an increase in the reporting of rape and (4) generally speedier prosecutions and stiffer sentencing. Some FBI officials believe that the extremely cold winter in the East and Midwest may also have contributed to the lower crime rate. Still others think the declining U.S. youth population is a long-term factor.

Emphasis on Prosecuting Repeat Offenders

One crime-fighting program that appears moderately successful is aimed at vigorous prosecution of repeat criminal offenders—"career criminals." Funded by the Law Enforcement Assistance Administration (LEAA), the program is operating in 19 cities and throughout one state, Rhode Island. Although most of the local programs differ in various ways, all have the same general purpose and outline. With money from the federal government, prosecutors are able to hire extra attorneys to help with routine cases and thus devote more of their own time toward developing strong cases against career criminals. When a bail hearing is held, the prosecutor makes it a point to be present and to demand that bail be set high. The prosecutor also tries to bring the case to trial quickly so that witnesses can give fresh accounts of what they saw.

It is not clear how many criminal offenders in this country can be classified as career criminals. One study by the FBI of 256,-000 persons arrested between 1970 and 1975 showed that 64 per cent of them had been arrested two times or more. The group of offenders studied had been accused of more than a million crimes. Another study by the Institute for Law and Social Research in Washington, D.C., found that from 1971 to 1975, only 7 per cent of those arrested for serious crimes in the nation's capital accounted for 24 per cent of all such arrests. Some were arrested as many as 10 times during that period.

To assist prosecutors in handling career criminals, the LEAA

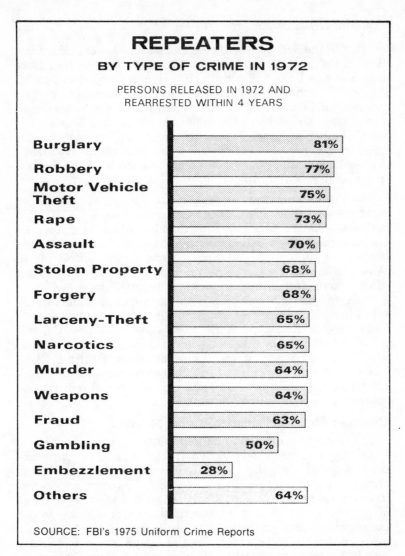

REPEATERS

BY TYPE OF CRIME IN 1972

PERSONS RELEASED IN 1972 AND
REARRESTED WITHIN 4 YEARS

Crime	Percent
Burglary	81%
Robbery	77%
Motor Vehicle Theft	75%
Rape	73%
Assault	70%
Stolen Property	68%
Forgery	68%
Larceny-Theft	65%
Narcotics	65%
Murder	64%
Weapons	64%
Fraud	63%
Gambling	50%
Embezzlement	28%
Others	64%

SOURCE: FBI's 1975 Uniform Crime Reports

has funded the development of a computer-based system for identifying and categorizing important cases according to their seriousness. Known as the Prosecutor's Management Information System (Promis), it enables prosecutors to call up a criminal's arrest and conviction record. Such information is usually available on the criminal's police report. But what is different about Promis is that it lists all other pending cases against the defendant and tells whether he or she is on parole or in violation of bail. Promis also rates a criminal according to how dangerous he or she is.

In eight of the nine cities where the program first started operating in 1975, serious crimes declined the following year, according to the FBI figures. These cities were Boston, Columbus (Ohio), Dallas, Detroit, Indianapolis, New Orleans, Salt Lake City and San Diego. The ninth city, Houston, registered an increase. The robbery rate for these nine cities decreased by 13.4 per cent in 1976, far better than the 9 per cent average for all U.S. cities.[2] Officials who have been studying this data are not sure whether the career criminal program is responsible for these reductions. "Right now it's circumstantial evidence," Sidney Brounstein, director of research for the Institute for Law and Social Research, told Editorial Research Reports.

The FBI also maintains a computerized criminal information system called the Computerized Criminal History (CCH). But states as well as courts and correctional institutions around the country have been reluctant to participate in the system because of the cost of entering records in the central file in Washington. As a result, the information is incomplete and often out of date. Another problem reported by a writer in *Science* magazine is that the computer sometimes makes mistakes in identifying offenders. According to the same account, FBI Director Kelley in April 1976 asked Attorney General Edward Levi to cancel the program altogether, but no action was taken by Levi or, as yet, by his successor, Griffin B. Bell. The Carter administration is reported to be considering a controversial proposal to decentralize the system and redistribute control of its files among the states.[3]

Question About Reliability of Crime Statistics

Criminologists question the reliability of crime statistics, since they are based only on reported crimes. Many have expressed doubt that the figures reflect an accurate picture of criminal activity across the country. Surveys of crime victims have indicated that only about 65 per cent of all robberies and 30 per cent of all burglaries committed are ever reported to the police. Homicides and car thefts are generally almost always reported, but in other categories the actual amount of crime may be far greater than official statistics show. Gary F. Glenn, a statistics officer in the New York City Police Department, has estimated that only about half of the crimes committed annually are ever reported.[4]

Besides the problem of victims not reporting crimes, there is also the question of whether local police officials accurately transmit their statistics to the FBI for its compilations.[5]

---

[2] According to the National Legal Data Center in Thousand Oaks, Calif., robbers account for the largest single group of convicted career criminals in the nine cities.

[3] See Deborah Shapley, "Central Crime Computer Project Draws Mixed Reviews," *Science,* July 8, 1977.

[4] "Crime *Does* Pay!" *The Police Chief,* January 1976, p. 53.

[5] In 42 states, the data are channeled through state-operated uniform crime reporting programs.

Crime Trends in the Seventies

(change from previous year)

Year	All serious* crimes	Violent crimes	Property crimes
1970	up 9%	up 12%	up 9%
1971	up 6	up 11	up 6
1972	down 4	up 2	down 5
1973	up 6	up 5	up 5
1974	up 18	up 11	up 18
1975	up 10	up 5	up 10
1976**	even	down 5	up 1
1977 1st qtr.	down 9	down 3	down 9

* Murder, forcible rape, robbery, aggravated assault, burglary, larceny, motor vehicle theft.
** Preliminary figures.

Source: Federal Bureau of Investigation

Criminologists speak of "the vagaries of police bookkeeping," and it is sometimes hinted that local figures may easily be manipulated to make the community or its police officials look good. Patrick V. Murphy, a former big-city police chief and former director of the LEAA, has said: "When I was a rookie in the 72nd Precinct in Brooklyn, no police commander worth his salt would admit he couldn't control crime and he proved it by controlling crime statistics."[6] An additional shortcoming of the FBI's compilation of crime statistics is that they do not include such "white-collar crimes" as antitrust violations. Embezzlement, however, is included in the list of 29 offenses that make up the FBI's Uniform Crime Reports.

A recent study by the LEAA has contradicted one set of FBI-compiled crime figures. In a report released May 24, 1977, the agency published the results of a poll indicating that nationwide rates for violent crimes remained unchanged from 1974 to 1975.[7] FBI figures portrayed a rise in crime in 1975. Last year, the Department of Justice began drafting a proposal to create a new Bureau of Criminal Justice Statistics that would consolidate the statistical programs now scattered throughout federal law enforcement agencies. The proposal is now awaiting the consideration of Attorney General Bell.

An important element in the crime situation is the citizen's perception of how much crime is being perpetrated in the local

---

[6] Quoted by David Burnham in *The New York Times*, Jan. 2, 1969.

[7] "Criminal Victimization in the United States," February 1977.

community. A drop in the crime index is small comfort to persons who continue to be afraid to walk their own streets. According to a Louis Harris Survey, the public's fear of crime appears to be diminishing somewhat. In 1975, 70 per cent of the adults who responded to a Harris public-opinion poll said they thought that crime in their area was increasing. In March 1977, only 58 per cent expressed this belief. The polling organization also reported that for the first time in 10 years, less than half of the people surveyed felt "more uneasy on the streets" than they did the year before.

Surprisingly, the Harris interviews were conducted after a well-publicized spate of terrorist acts had occurred in February and March. These included the seizure of three buildings in Washington, D.C., by 12 American black members of the Hanafi Muslim sect who held 134 hostages for 38 hours before finally agreeing to release them. One person was killed and 19 others were wounded in the takeover. In the final surrender agreement, Abdul Khaalis, the leader of the terrorist band, was released without bail, causing a flurry of local criticism.[8]

Controversy Over Bail, Pre-trial Detention

Whether to confine or release arrested persons prior to trial is a question that has aroused particularly strident debate in recent years. It is not uncommon for individuals with long records of past criminal activity to be rearrested for new crimes while they are free on bail or some other form of release. But pre-trial release has another side as well—something that Congress recognized in enacting the Federal Bail Reform Act of 1966. Until passage of the act, poor defendants unable to raise bail were often incarcerated for days. In signing the bail reform bill into law, President Johnson described the case of a man who spent 101 days in jail because he could not raise bail on a false complaint. The law stated its purpose was to "assure that all persons, regardless of their financial status, shall not needlessly be detained pending their appearance to answer charges...when detention serves neither...justice nor the public interest."

The act said that to the extent possible, defendants should be released on their own recognizance—also referred to as personal surety or nominal bond—if the court determined that they were reliable enough to show up for subsequent court appearances. Special provisions apply to murder cases and cases on appeal to higher court. Judges are expected to gather sufficient information about defendants to determine the risk of releasing them. But critics of the law say the judges' information gathering is laborious and their decision making subjective.

---

[8] Khaalis was jailed on March 31 for allegedly violating the terms of his release agreement. On June 1, he and 11 of his followers went on trial in District of Columbia Superior Court on charges of murder and armed kidnapping.

Past Efforts to Control Crime

THE PROBLEM of crime has been with this country since its very beginnings. In 1762 a New York printer named John Holt wrote of "so many robberies...within the circuits of this city, both day and night; it is becoming hazardous for any person to walk in the latter."[9] In the American colonies, police forces as we know them today did not exist; a good deal of policing had to be done by ill-trained and poorly equipped volunteers. Sometimes these "officers" might be assaulted by strangers on the streets.

In colonial days, 160 offenses were punishable by death, ranging from treason, piracy and murder to arson, burglary and housebreaking. So-called "minor" offenses were punishable by whipping, dunking, maiming or pillorying. The U.S. Constitution's prohibition against "cruel and unusual punishments," as stated in the Eighth Amendment, came in reaction to some of these colonial practices. Nevertheless, punishment remained the popular method of deterring crime until prison reformers in the 19th century waged their campaign to rehabilitate rather than punish the offender. First with children[10] and then with adults, the reformatory idea was applied in institutions throughout America.

Reformatory "cures" were to be tailored to the individual criminal, who was not to be released until rehabilitated. Over the years, prisons began to develop what is now often referred to as the "medical model." Crime became associated with disease and inmates were, in a sense, viewed as patients. Psychiatrists, psychologists and social workers were added to prison staffs, and prison administrators began to use medical terminology, implying that criminals could be "cured" with the proper diagnosis and treatment.

Although criminal behavior was not systematically researched until the 20th century, it was the subject of study during the 1700s and 1800s. A famous criminologist of the 18th-century Enlightenment, Cesare Beccaria, thought the Italian penal system barbaric and repressive and called for a more uniform system that punished all persons equally with no regard to their social or economic status. He viewed capital punishment as a useless deterrent, and argued instead for punishment "as

---

[9] Quoted in "Two Hundred Years of American Criminal Justice," published by the Law Enforcement Assistance Administration as a bicentennial study. See also "Violence in American Life," *E.R.R.*, 1968 Vol. I, pp. 405-424.

[10] Under English Common Law, children at age seven were treated as adults in criminal proceedings. Until the 19th century, little distinction was made between adults and children in U.S. courts.

minimal in severity as possible" that would convince the offender to do no further wrong.

Jeremy Bentham, the English political theorist, also believed that the purpose of punishment was to educate the offender and thereby prevent further criminal behavior. In criminology, Bentham is perhaps best remembered for his proposal to build a model, utopian prison. According to his design, the prison was to be built in a circular fashion with the cells placed along the outer wall and an inspector's station in the center. Prison managers would be responsible for reforming the inmates. If any prisoner, after being released, later committed another offense, then that prisoner's manager would be required to pay a fine. Two prisons were built later in the United States along the pattern suggested by Bentham.

Early Theories About Causes of Crime

With the publication of Charles Darwin's *Origin of Species* in 1859, a new era in criminal research began. Basing his theory on the concept of the survival of the fittest, Darwin argued that there existed superior and inferior beings. The idea was quickly seized upon by others to offer a scientific explanation for the existence of a criminal class. Criminal researchers began to work under the assumption that offenders were born with criminal traits and concentrated their efforts toward identifying and classifying these characteristics.

In 1896, the Italian physician Cesare Lombroso attempted to prove that some persons were "born criminals." He studied the physical characteristics of 5,900 inmates in Italian jails, measuring their skulls and facial features. From this information, Lombroso drew up a list of the physical characteristics that he believed marked members of the criminal class. These included "outstanding ears, frontal sinuses, voluminous jaws and zygomas (prominent cheekbones), a ferocious look and a thin upper lip." Lombroso concluded that criminals were primitive men who through some quirk had not been "selected out" through the Darwinian process of natural selection.

At the same time that Lombroso was conducting his research, an American named Robert Dugdale was in the midst of what has since come to be thought of as a classic criminal research project. Dugdale studied a criminally addicted family, whom he called the Jukes, and concluded in 1877 that environment, in close connection with heredity, was responsible for criminal behavior.[11] Many persons, however, used the study to buttress

---

[11] Dugdale titled his book *The Jukes: A Study in Crime, Pauperism, Disease and Heredity*. Jukes was a fictitious name Dugdale applied to the family to protect its privacy.

at all levels and compilation of more accurate and comprehensive crime statistics.

Johnson responded by proposing a "Safe Streets" act to channel federal funds to local police departments and correctional agencies. Congress passed the act in 1968[12] but loaded it with amendments that the President opposed. For example, a section permitted police wiretapping in a wide variety of criminal cases, in direct contradiction to administration proposals that electronic surveillance be limited to national security cases. Congress also weakened the President's proposed gun-control provisions by making controls applicable only to handguns. Congress also imposed "block grants"—providing the federal funds to state governments rather than directly to local communities as Johnson had proposed.

The 1968 act established the Law Enforcement Assistance Administration (LEAA) within the Department of Justice to administer the grant programs. Congress authorized approximately $100-million in fiscal 1969—$25-million for state planning grants, $25-million for training, education and research programs and $50-million to recruit and train police officers. States were required to provide some matching funds in order to receive the federal grants.

Contrast Between Nixon and Johnson Policies

The Nixon administration, taking office in January 1969, had a different approach to the crime problem. In Johnson's view, the war on crime could not be separated from the war on poverty. His Great Society programs were aimed at reducing the "root causes" of crime, such as poverty, racial discrimination and unemployment. To President Nixon, however, crime was primarily a law-enforcement problem. During the 1968 campaign he pledged to reduce crime by strengthening the "peace forces" and refusing to coddle criminals. "The truth is," he said, "that we will reduce crime and violence when we enforce our laws—when we make it less profitable, and a lot more risky, to break our laws." The year 1970 was a high-water mark for Nixon anti-crime legislation. Four major administration bills were approved by Congress: an extension of the 1968 Safe Streets Act, a drug-control law that expanded federal support for drug treatment, an act to curb large-scale organized crime[13], and a bill authorizing policemen to enter homes in the District of Columbia and make searches and arrests without notice.

Today, both the Great Society approach and the Nixon-Ford "get tough" approach appear to be incapable of dealing with the nation's crime problem. Criminologists are having second

---

[12] Signed into law on June 19 as the Omnibus Crime Control and Safe Streets Act of 1968.
[13] See "Drive on Organized Crime," *E.R.R.*, 1970 Vol. I, pp. 181-202.

thoughts about what used to be conventional wisdom and are trying to find new ways to deter criminal action. One practice that has fallen out of favor in recent years is indeterminate sentencing. Opponents assert that it results in longer sentences than most judges would give, gives administrative authorities undue control over prisoners' lives, permits disparities in sentencing, and is psychologically damaging to prisoners who never know when they will be released and who are forced to play games with the system.[14] With the realization that rehabilitation may no longer be a feasible goal in criminal corrections, the elements of parole and indeterminate sentencing may soon be eliminated from the correctional system. Legislation now before Congress, for example, would establish a federal sentencing commission to set federal sentencing standards and guidelines for judges to follow. Under this new approach emphasis on rehabilitation and parole would be greatly decreased.

Directions of Future Efforts

IT IS TOO early to tell whether the crime figures for 1976 and early 1977 are an aberration or represent the beginning of a trend. "I would like to wait a little bit longer, possibly another year, to say a significant trend is taking place," Paul A. Zolbe, chief of the FBI's Uniform Crime Reporting Section, told Editorial Research Reports. Marvin Wolfgang, director of the Center for Studies in Criminology and Criminal Law at the University of Pennsylvania, believes that the 1976 figures reflect a leveling off that will continue through the early 1980s. After that will come a decrease in crime, he predicts, to be followed by another increase beginning about 1990.

Wolfgang's reasoning is based on demographics—specifically on an expected shrinkage and then another expansion in the size of the nation's youth population, which accounts for a disproportionate share of crime in America *(see table, p. 553).* According to projections by the U.S. Census Bureau, today's unusually large youth population is entering a period of decline. The great number of Americans who were born in the postwar "baby boom" are growing out of their teens—some out of their twenties. Persons of ages 14 through 24 made up 20.8 per cent of the U.S. population in 1975 but are expected to form only 15 to 16 per cent in 1990.

However, the drop in actual numbers of 14-24 year olds may be as little as 3.9-million or as great as 5.4-million, depending

---

[14] See "Criminal Release System," *E.R.R.*, 1976 Vol. I, pp. 439-460.

U.S. Population Projections

For Ages 14-24

(add 000; % of total in parentheses)

Year	Projection 1*	Projection 2*	Projection 3*
1975**	44,520 (20.8)	44,520 (20.8)	44,520 (20.8)
1980	45,194 (20.0)	45,194 (20.3)	45,194 (20.5)
1985	42,222 (17.5)	42,222 (18.0)	42,222 (18.5)
1990	38,700 (15.1)	38,103 (15.6)	40,625 (16.0)
2000	51,154 (17.9)	43,080 (16.4)	36,732 (15.0)

*Each set of projections ("series") is based on a separate set of assumptions about future fertility rates
** Estimate

Source: U.S. Bureau of the Census

on which of three sets of Census Bureau assumptions about future fertility rates that a demographer chooses to accept. Moreover, by 1990 the youth population will be on the increase again, according to two of the three sets of assumptions. University of Michigan demographer Ronald Lee, for one, has predicted that women will start bearing more children than they do now, bringing on a new baby boom whose effects will be felt fully by the end of the century.[15] There are other demographers who think that the fertility rate, which has been dropping since 1957, will continue on its downward course.

Crime is definitely a problem associated with youth. Arrests of young people for serious crimes have risen about 200 per cent in the past 15 years, according to FBI statistics, while arrests for lesser crimes have doubled. "The crime of the 1960s was the worst we ever had and probably ever will have unless we have another baby boom," James Alan Fox, assistant professor of criminal law at Northeastern University in Boston, has surmised. "The baby boom generated a lot of children over a relatively short time span. One generation later there will be another bunch of kids, but it will be spread out more. Eventually the impulse created by the first baby boom will disappear, barring another war...or something else that creates a perturbation in the fertility rate."[16]

Crime is also associated with urban America, even though the incidence of crime in suburban and rural areas has increased in recent years. Crime still tends to be highest in the inner city and decreases as the distance from the inner city increases. The larger the city, the higher its crime rate is likely to be, according to the FBI's Crime Index. The following table from the 1975 in-

---

[15] For the views of Lee and like-minded demographers, see "The Changing American Family," *E.R.R.*, 1977 Vol. I, pp. 430-431.

[16] Quoted by Lawrence Mosher in *The National Observer*, May 9, 1977.

dex, the latest for which complete statistics have been published, shows the number of crimes per 100,000 population:

Area	Crime Rate	Area	Crime Rate
Cities over 250,000	8,202.5	Cities 10,000-25,000	4,763.6
Cities 100,000-250,000	7,699.2	Cities under 10,000	4,112.5
Cities 50,000-100,000	6,361.0	Suburban areas	4,614.4
Cities 25,000-50,000	5,591.3	Rural areas	2,229.0

Whether or not the crime rate is in fact leveling off, criminal justice officials are continuing to look for new ways to fight crime. "Inasmuch as there has been such a drastic increase in violent crime over the past 10 or 15 years, even though there was a reported reduction last year, we have to be careful not to be complacent and not feel that somehow we have found the answers," Alvin Zumbrun of the Maryland Crime Investigating Commission has said.[17] While mandatory sentencing probably will continue to be popular in many areas, there is also a movement toward "decriminalizing" so-called "victimless" crimes such as gambling, prostitution and marijuana smoking. By placing control of such crimes in the hands of regulatory agencies rather than the police or the courts, prosecutors hope to be able to concentrate on more serious crimes such as robbery, rape and murder.

Programs to Compensate Victims of Crime

Many citizens have long complained that the criminal justice system pays too much attention to the needs of the criminal and too little to the needs of the victim. But this appears to be changing with the emergence of victim compensation programs in many states. California was the first state to institute such a project in 1965. Since then 19 other states, which account for two-thirds of all reported crimes in the country, have set up victim compensation programs.[18] Under a typical program, crime victims are compensated for medical bills and lost wages. Persons who staff the victim compensation program usually are available to counsel victims during any courtroom proceedings and to offer such social services as transportation when necessary.

On May 16, the House Judiciary Committee approved a bill authorizing the Department of Justice to subsidize state victim compensation programs that meet certain standards. In the right circumstances, the subsidy could cover the entire amount of the victim's compensation. However, no federal money could

---

[17] Quoted by Richard Egan in *The National Observer*, Feb. 5, 1977.

[18] Alaska, Delaware, Hawaii, Illinois, Kentucky, Maryland, Massachusetts, Michigan, Minnesota, Nevada, New Jersey, New York, North Dakota, Ohio, Pennsylvania, Tennessee, Virginia, Washington and Wisconsin.

Arrests By Age Group, 1975

	Total Arrests	Under 15	Under 18	Under 21	Under 25
Criminal homicide	19,526	3.7%	21.6%	57.2%	95.5%
Forcible rape	21,963	3.9	17.6	37.0	58.0
Robbery	129,788	9.6	34.3	57.7	77.0
Aggravated assault	202,217	5.2	17.6	32.3	49.6
Burglary	449,155	20.1	52.6	72.6	85.2
Larceny-theft	958,938	20.1	45.1	62.8	75.4
Motor vehicle theft	120,224	14.4	54.5	73.1	84.6
Total Crime Index Offenses	1,901,811	17.0%	43.1%	61.5%	75.2%

Source: FBI Uniform Crime Reports, 1975

be used to pay victims for property losses or for "pain and suffering"—only for medical expenses and lost wages. The state must also reduce any claim when the victim is found to be partly responsible, as in a barroom brawl.

While the idea of compensating victims of crimes has attracted wide interest, it is not unanimously endorsed. Skeptics maintain that, even with safeguards, fraudulent claims of compensation often will go undetected. Moreover, critics of the bill approved by the House Judiciary Committee argue that the federal government has no responsibility for enforcing a state's criminal laws and, therefore, has little or no responsibility for compensating its victims. In a written dissent, nine committee members said the proposed federal compensation program "is essentially selective largesse."

Dissatisfaction Over LEAA's Performance

Another matter that Congress is considering this year is the restructuring of the LEAA. Despite some success with the career criminal program, the agency's overall usefulness has been questioned. Separate studies conducted last year by the Twentieth Century Fund and the Center for National Security Studies concluded that the agency has had little impact on crime. "LEAA is unclear as to its mission, and what it has attempted it has done poorly," the report by the Center for National Security Studies stated. The 13-member study group of the Twentieth Century Fund declared: "State and local justice systems remain as fragmented as ever. The courts are still overloaded; jails are still crowded; prosecutorial offices are generally underfunded and sentencing and parole procedures...remain arbitrary and uncoordinated. Nor do we

17

know any more about the causes of crime than we did before LEAA came into being."

A third report, by the Advisory Commission on Intergovernmental Relations, was also highly critical of LEAA activities. The report said that the agency had not established meaningful standards for judging the performance of the state criminal justice planning agencies that distribute federal grants to local police. In addition, the report noted that LEAA has had five administrators in seven years. "In the opinion of almost all officials interviewed," it stated, "the effects of this rapid turnover of top leadership, at the least, have been harmful to the agency's mission." LEAA has spent nearly $6-billion on crimefighting programs since it came into existence.

Both President Carter and Attorney General Bell have expressed their displeasure with the agency, charging it with wasting money on poorly conceived projects. Bell was reported to have been especially upset when he learned upon assuming office that the agency had allocated $2.5-million to produce a pamphlet telling local police departments how to apply for its grants. On June 30, a Department of Justice study group appointed by Bell recommended that the LEAA place more emphasis on research and that it channel money more directly to the states and ease the requirements on how they spend it. In releasing the report, Bell said that he had come to no conclusions on the future of the agency. However, in an interview with the Associated Press on June 21, Bell said he favored eliminating virtually all of the agency and having the Treasury Department give out federal crime-fighting grants.

According to *Science* magazine writer Constance Holden, a new report by the National Academy of Sciences on the research arm of the LEAA—the National Institute of Law Enforcement and Criminal Justice—recommends that it be separated from the agency and established as an autonomous body within the Justice Department. The report, scheduled to be formally released this fall, was written by the Academy's Committee on Research on Law Enforcement and Criminal Justice. "So distressed was the committee with the quality of the institute's work that it gave some thought to proposing that it be put out of business altogether," Holden wrote. "It concluded, however, that a central national research effort on crime is desirable." According to Holden, the report stated the institute should concentrate on developing a reliable body of knowledge on crime, but should not be used as an instrument for solving the crime problem.

While the debate over LEAA continues, Congress is resuming its decade-old effort to reform and codify the nation's criminal laws, which are spread throughout the U.S. statutory code. The current recodification bill is given a better chance of passage than its predecessor, S 1, which died in committee last year after several wrangles between liberals and conservatives on the Senate Judiciary Committee. This year, however, John L. McClellan (D Ark.), chairman of the Senate Judiciary Subcommittee on Criminal Laws and Procedures, and fellow subcommittee member Edward M. Kennedy (D Mass.) have agreed to join forces and support the new bill which is free of last year's disputed provisions. The bill, known as the Criminal Code Reform Act of 1977, has been introduced in the Senate as S 1437 and in the House as HR 6869.

Proposal for Federal Sentencing Commission

A key feature of this year's bill calls for establishment of a federal commission that would set guidelines for sentencing. Federal judges would be bound to sentence offenders in keeping with these guidelines unless they could justify another sentence. In the event an offender was sentenced below the specified range of years, the government could appeal the case. If the offender was sentenced above the range, he or she would have the opportunity to appeal. "This system provides an ingenious means of assuring sentences that are not only fair to individual defendants but fair to the public as well," Bell testified June 8 before McClellan's subcommittee.

Although indeterminate sentencing would be kept to a minimum under the newly proposed system, parole would not be eliminated entirely. In some instances, a sentencing guideline might call for "four to six years, with parole after four." Under such a sentence, an offender would be assured of release in four years, assuming that his conduct was good while in prison. Evidence of "rehabilitation" would not be required for release.

Government officials are becoming much more realistic in the fight against crime. "[T]he ability of government—federal, state or local—to do something about crime is far less than we thought back in 1965, when the federal government launched its war on crime," Gerald M. Caplan has said. Echoing this thought, Norval Morris, dean of the University of Chicago Law School, has said: "I don't think there is going to be any dramatic change made in crime problems in America over the next few years. The best we can hope for is to set out with more responsibility toward more efficient police work, a larger capacity to process cases, and larger justice in sentencing."[19] For the time being, government officials appear to be concentrating their efforts on just those goals.

---

[19] Interview in *The Washington Star*, March 5, 1977.

Selected Bibliography

Books

Clark, Ramsey, *Crime in America*, Simon & Schuster, 1970.

Frankel, Marvin E., *Criminal Sentences: Law Without Order*, Hill and Wang, 1973.

Morris, Norval, *The Future of Imprisonment*, The University of Chicago Press, 1974.

Ohlin, Lloyd E. (ed.), *Prisoners in America*, Prentice-Hall, 1973.

Von Hirsch, Andrew, *Doing Justice: The Choice of Punishment*, Hill and Wang, 1976.

Wilson, James Q., *Thinking About Crime*, Basic Books, 1975.

Articles

"A War on Career Criminals Starts to Show Results," *U.S. News & World Report*, Nov. 22, 1976.

Adler-Mueller, Freda, "Crime, An Equal Opportunity Employer," *Trial*, January 1977.

Cowger, Nancy, "LEAA: Restructuring Alone Won't Do the Job," *American Bar Association Journal*, April 1977.

Judicature, journal of the American Judicature Society, selected issues.

Maltz, Michael D., "Crime Statistics: A Historical Perspective," *Crime & Delinquency*, January 1977.

Miller, Walter, "The Rumble This Time," *Psychology Today*, May 1977.

Mosher, Lawrence, "Are We 'Outgrowing' Crime?" *The National Observer*, May 9, 1977.

"The Youth Crime Plague," *Time*, July 11, 1977.

Studies and Reports

Advisory Commission on Intergovernmental Relations, "Safe Streets Reconsidered: The Block Grant Experience 1968-1975," January 1977.

Editorial Research Reports, "Criminal Release System," 1976 Vol. I, p. 439; "Reappraisal of Prison Policy," 1976 Vol. I, p. 185; "Police Innovation," 1974 Vol. I, p. 283.

General Accounting Office, "War on Organized Crime Faltering—Federal Strike Forces Not Getting the Job Done," March 17, 1977.

Institute for Law and Social Research, "Curbing the Repeat Offender: A Strategy for Prosecutors," 1977.

President's Commission on Law Enforcement and Administration of Justice, *The Challenge of Crime in a Free Society*, February 1967.

U.S. Bureau of the Census, "Population Estimates and Projections," October 1975.

U.S. Department of Justice, Law Enforcement Assistance Administration, "Criminal Victimization in the United States," February 1977.

INTERNATIONAL TERRORISM

by

Sandra Stencel

**Dec. 2
1977**

INTERNATIONAL TERRORISM

A MONG the 86 hostages freed in a West German commando raid on a hijacked Lufthansa airliner in Somalia last October were a woman and her five-year-old son from Santee, Calif. A number of Americans were aboard a Japan Air Lines jet hijacked to Bangladesh earlier that month. On Sept. 10, 1976, a New York-to-Chicago jet was commandeered by five Croatian nationalists. Although none of the 81 passengers was injured, a New York City police officer was killed by a bomb left by the hijackers in Grand Central Station. On Sept. 21, 1976, Ronni Karpen Moffit, a 25-year-old fund-raiser for the Institute for Policy Studies in Washington, D.C., was killed along with co-worker Orlando Letelier, a former Chilean ambassador to the United States, when a bomb exploded under their car. A month earlier, three American employees of Rockwell International Corp. were assassinated while being driven to work at an Iranian air force base in Tehran.

These Americans were recent victims of a spreading wave of international terrorism. In the past most terrorist attacks against U.S. citizens were directed at diplomats or other government officials. American business executives stationed overseas also were frequent targets, especially in Latin America. But as recent terrorist incidents indicate, political extremists at home and abroad are no longer restricting their attacks to the wealthy or influential. Today's terrorists have, Michael Waltzer wrote in 1975, "emptied out the category of innocent people."[1]

Between 1968 and the end of 1976, there were 1,152 international terrorist incidents, according to a recent CIA report.[2] These included 137 kidnapings, 35 "barricade and hostage situations," 501 bombings, 119 armed assaults or ambushes, 63 assassinations and 146 hijackings.[3] U.S. citizens or property were victimized in 391 of these incidents. Last year alone there were 61 terrorist attacks on Americans or American property.

Terrorism has increased in recent years. In 1968 the CIA recorded only 37 international terrorist incidents; last year there were 239. This upsurge is attributable in part to the continuing conflict in the Middle East. Over 15 per cent of all terrorist in-

---

[1] Michael Waltzer, "The New Terrorists," *The New Republic,* Aug. 30, 1975, p. 13.
[2] Central Intelligence Agency, "International Terrorism in 1976," July 1977, p. 15.
[3] Excludes skyjackings that did not have a political motive.

cidents in the past eight years were perpetrated by Palestinians or others espousing the Palestinian cause.

But according to the CIA, "terrorism would not have mushroomed to its present dimensions were it not for the concurrent convergence and acceleration of a number of changes in the global environment."[4] These changes included (1) technological advances that provided terrorists with new mobility, new weaponry and worldwide publicity, (2) the growth of global and regional ties that provided terrorists with a host of new targets for attack, including transportation, communication and commercial centers, and (3) a 'revolutionary' turn in the overall political environment.

Seán Mac Bride, a member of the Irish Republican Army (IRA) in the 1920s and 1930s and winner of the 1974 Nobel Peace Prize, linked the recent upsurge in terrorism to a general escalation of violence and cruelty in the world. In his Nobel Prize acceptance speech, Mac Bride said, "If those vested with authority and power practice injustice, resort to torture and killing, is it not inevitable that those who are victims will react with similar methods? This does not condone savagery or inhuman conduct, but it does provide part of the explanation for the increasing violence and brutality of our world."

Social and political observers are particularly perplexed by the outburst of political violence in Western Europe in recent years. Unlike the Palestinians, the Irish or the South Moluccans, Europe's youthful terrorists are not motivated by nationalism. Fred Luchsinger, editor of the *Swiss Review of World Affairs,* suggested that the wave of kidnapings, bombings and assassinations might be "the inevitable price of more than 30 years of peace—or at any rate, absence of war—in Europe. Aggressive instincts and destructive energy which previously exhausted themselves in the generation-to-generation cycle of European wars are now held to be breaking out in this way."[5] Others attribute the increase in terrorism to Europe's slow recovery from the 1974-75 recession, which has left large numbers of European youth unemployed.[6]

Media's Role in Popularizing Terrorism

Many experts contend that press and television coverage of terrorist incidents may itself be a contributing factor in the growth of terrorism. "The willingness and capability of the news media to report and broadcast dramatic incidents of violence throughout the world enhances and even may encourage

---

[4] "International and Transnational Terrorism: Diagnosis and Prognosis," April 1976, p. 2.
[5] Fred Luchsinger, "Europe's Young Barbarians," *Swiss Review of World Affairs,* September 1977, p. 4.
[6] See "World's Slow Economic Recovery," *E.R.R.,* 1977 Vol. II, pp. 745-764 and "Youth Unemployment," *E.R.R.,* 1977 Vol. II, pp. 765-784.

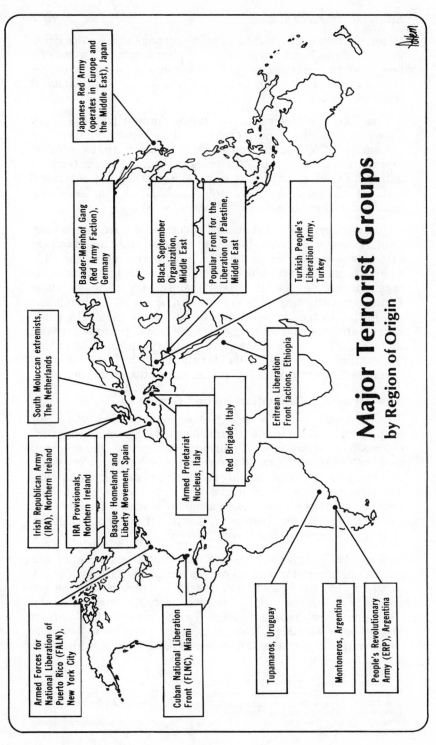

Major Terrorist Groups
by Region of Origin

Japanese Red Army (operates in Europe and the Middle East), Japan

Baader-Meinhof Gang (Red Army Faction), Germany

Black September Organization, Middle East

Popular Front for the Liberation of Palestine, Middle East

Turkish People's Liberation Army, Turkey

South Moluccan extremists, The Netherlands

Eritrean Liberation Front factions, Ethiopia

Irish Republican Army (IRA), Northern Ireland

IRA Provisionals, Northern Ireland

Basque Homeland and Liberty Movement, Spain

Armed Proletariat Nucleus, Italy

Red Brigade, Italy

Armed Forces for National Liberation of Puerto Rico (FALN), New York City

Cuban National Liberation Front (FLNC), Miami

Tupamaros, Uruguay

Montoneros, Argentina

People's Revolutionary Army (ERP), Argentina

terrorism as an effective means of propaganda," said Brian Jenkins of the Rand Corporation.[7] Walter Laqueur, author of a new book on terrorism, said, "The success of a terrorist operation depends almost entirely on the amount of publicity it receives."[8]

The Law Enforcement Assistance Administration's Task Force on Disorders and Terrorism, in a report published in December 1976,[9] found "considerable evidence that contagion and imitation are significant factors in the incidence of terrorist activity. Often, after the use of novel and seemingly successful terrorist techniques has been widely publicized, they have been imitated and embellished by other terrorists."

Some experts say that media coverage of terrorism is particularly excessive given the actual material and human toll exacted by terrorists. From 1967 to 1975, according to the CIA, some 800 persons were killed and 1,700 wounded in terrorist attacks—including the terrorists themselves. Although these figures are disturbing, they are dwarfed by the 20,000 homicides committed in the United States in 1975 alone. The CIA study also pointed out that although the total cost of terrorist activity, including ransom payments and property damage, has never been tallied, it probably falls "far short" of the $500-million in damages that vandals inflict on U.S. school buildings each year.

New Trends; Collaboration Among Groups

Terrorism is not a new phenomenon *(see p. 31)*. But despite historical precedents and parallels, recent terrorist incidents have shown some disturbing new trends. One source of concern has been the trend towards bolder and more dramatic actions, with an accompanying escalation of casualties, damage and demands. "In all strategies of terror," wrote author and critic Irving Howe, "there is an inherent tendency to go beyond the limits previously accepted.... It is just this 'one step further' that makes terror momentarily effective."[10]

Since 1967 there has been a substantial increase in the number of terrorist groups as well as in the number of countries in which they are operating. The CIA has identified some 140 groups that have been linked to international terrorism. Of the 53 groups which the agency deemed most "noteworthy," only 20 existed prior to 1968. Of equal concern have been the links between terrorist groups. There is a growing body of evidence to

[7] Brian Jenkins, "Terrorism Works—Sometimes," April 1974, p. 5.

[8] Walter Laqueur, *Terrorism* (1977), p. 109.

[9] "Disorders and Terrorism: Report of the Task Force on Disorders and Terrorism," 1976, p. 9. The task force was set up in the spring of 1975 as part of the LEAA's National Advisory Committee on Criminal Justice Standards and Goals.

[10] Irving Howe, "The Ultimate Price of Random Terror," *Skeptic*, January-February 1976, p. 15.

show that terrorists are providing each other with arms, information, "safe" housing, and other forms of support. This trend is "extremely important," said Brian Jenkins, because it provides small terrorist organizations with the resources to undertake far more serious operations than they would be capable of otherwise and because it makes identification of terrorists more difficult.[11]

For example, the October hijacking of the West German jetliner was carried out by four Arabs proclaiming solidarity with West German terrorists who, the previous month, had kidnaped West German industrialist Hanns Martin Schleyer. Both groups of terrorists demanded the release of 11 persons being held in West German jails, including the most prominent survivors of the notorious Baader-Meinhof gang—Andreas Baader, Jan-Carl Raspe, Gudrun Ensslin and Irmgard Moeller. Hours after West German commandos freed the hostages in the hijacked jet, the four attempted suicide—three successfully.

This was not the first time West German and Arab terrorists had worked together. Support rendered by members of the Baader-Meinhof gang is said to have facilitated the attack on Israeli athletes at the 1972 Munich Olympics. The attack was carried out by members of the Palestinian terrorist group Black September. Two Germans were among the seven pro-Palestinian guerrillas who hijacked an Air France jet in June 1976, forcing it to land at Entebbe Airport in Uganda. The links between the two terrorist factions—German and Palestinian—are thought to have been cemented in 1970 when many of the original members of the Baader-Meinhof gang went to the Middle East to study guerrilla warfare at training camps run by the Popular Front for the Liberation of Palestine.

Another example of collaboration was the 1972 Lod Airport massacre in Israel, in which three members of the Japanese Red Army terrorist gang, acting for the Palestinians, gunned down 26 people. According to Ovid Demaris, author of a new book about the international terrorist network, "no one more fully epitomizes the interlocking...nature of worldwide terrorism" than Ilich Ramirez Sanchez, the 28-year-old Venezuelan commonly known by his code name, "Carlos." Carlos remains a man of mystery, but, according to Demaris, he and his polyglot band of Germans, Arabs, Japanese and Latin Americans have been linked to the Lod Airport attack, the firing of two rockets at an El Al airliner at Orley Airport in France in January 1975, the bombing of Le Drugstore in Paris in September 1974, the murder of two French intelligence officers and a Lebanese informer in Paris in June 1975, and the attack on 11 ministers of

[11] Brian Jenkins, "International Terrorism: A New Mode of Conflict," California Seminar on Arms Control and Foreign Policy, January 1975, p. 19.

the Organization of Petroleum Exporting Countries (OPEC) in Vienna in December 1975.[12] The CIA has predicted that the trend toward greater international contact and cooperation among terrorist groups will gain further momentum.

Attacks on Businessmen and Companies

An increasing number of terrorist attacks has been directed at business executives rather than government officials. The CIA has estimated that 60 per cent of the terrorist incidents involving American citizens or facilities abroad in 1976 were directed at U.S. businesses or their employees. The agency's report went on to say that "because of the tighter security measures that have been introduced at U.S. military and diplomatic installations, the continuing lure of potentially lucrative ransom or extortion payments, and the symbolic value of U.S. firms...there is a real danger that terrorist attacks on the U.S. business community abroad will become even more frequent in the future."[13]

The danger to American companies and their employees is not just overseas. In the San Francisco Bay area alone, there have been more than 60 successful bombing attacks by a group known as the New World Liberation Front. One man, a passer-by, died in one of the explosions and three others have been injured. Nearly half of the attacks, according to bomb expert Arleigh McCree, were directed against the Pacific Gas & Electric Corp.[14] The Weather Underground, the best-known terrorist group in the United States, has claimed responsibility for at least 30 bombings.[15] Its targets have included the Capitol, the Pentagon, the State Department, police stations and multinational corporate offices. In New York, Puerto Rican terrorists have claimed credit for at least 65 bombings in the past three years. A group known as the Armed Forces of Puerto Rico's National Liberation (FALN) was responsible for the 1974 bombing of the historic Fraunces Tavern in Manhattan's financial district in which four people were killed and 50 injured.

Attacks against European and Latin American businessmen have been much more frequent than those against their American counterparts. In Italy, kidnapings of businessmen or members of their families have become almost daily occurrences. At least 10 persons have been killed by West German terrorists so far this year, including industrialist Hanns Martin

---

[12] Ovid Demaris, "Carlos: The Most Dangerous Man in the World," *New York*, Nov. 7, 1977, p. 35.

[13] "International Terrorism in 1976," p. 4.

[14] Quoted by James Grant in "White-Collar War," *Barron's*, Oct. 31, 1977, p. 3.

[15] The Weather Underground was formed in 1969 as a faction of the Students for a Democratic Society (SDS). The group was originally called the Weathermen, from a line in Bob Dylan's song "Subterranean Homesick Blues": "You don't need a weatherman to know which way the wind blows." In 1970 members of the Weathermen disappeared from public view and later changed their name to the Weather Underground.

Counterterror Commando Units

Many governments have responded to the growing terrorist threat by forming their own anti-terror commando teams. The usefulness of these special units was demonstrated last October, when West German commandos stormed a hijacked jet at Mogadishu, Somalia, killing three terrorists, wounding another and rescuing 86 hostages. The West German group—known as *Grenzschutzgruppe Neun* or Border Protection Group 9—was created in 1972 following a bungled attempt to rescue Israeli hostages at the Munich Olympics.

Britian's Special Air Service (SAS) is the oldest commando unit in the world. Formed during World War II, the SAS fought behind the lines in North Africa and Italy. Since then it has battled Communist guerrillas in Malaya, Mau Mau insurgents in Kenya and IRA gunmen in Ulster. Probably the most experienced commando unit is Israel's General Intelligence and Reconnaissance Unit 269, best known for its 1976 raid on Entebbe Airport in Uganda. The French police have a 30-man team called the Gigene and the Italians have a 50-man anti-terrorist squad.

The U.S. Department of Defense has acknowledged that it, too, has a special strike force. It is made up of about 50 volunteers from all branches of the service. Some have suggested that the United Nations establish its own "flying squad" to deal with terrorist activities around the world. But at a press conference on Sept. 16, 1976, Secretary General Kurt Waldheim said, "We have no money for that."

Schleyer and banker Jurgen Ponto. Attacks on businessmen by politically motivated terrorists frequently spawn imitations by ordinary criminals who mimic the tactics of terrorists for profit. One of the latest victims of these "quasi-terrorists" was Dutch real estate tycoon Maurits Caransa, kidnaped on Oct. 28 and released a few days later after paying a $4-million ransom.

As the number of politically motivated bombings, kidnapings and murders grows, corporations are taking steps to protect their property and their employees. Many companies have installed elaborate security and alarm systems, including closed-circuit television systems which enable guards to monitor the movements of anyone in lobbies or hallways. Some firms have even been working closely with the police to try to anticipate trouble. Edward Foley, chief of the criminal division at the FBI's New York office, said that "ITT [International Telephone & Telegraph Corp.] regularly touches base with us and the CIA to get information on who might be out to get them."[16]

As for business executives themselves, they are taking the advice of professional security consultants and avoiding the public limelight, adopting less conspicuous life-styles, using personal bodyguards, buying watchdogs and handguns, learning evasive

---

[16] Quoted in *Newsweek*, Nov. 14, 1977, p. 89.

driving techniques, installing electronic surveillance devices and other security products in their homes, and doing whatever else they can to reduce their vulnerability to terrorist attack.

Factors Motivating Political Extremists

Although scores of books, articles and scholarly studies have been written about terrorism, only recently have experts begun to examine in-depth the various individuals involved in such activities and those factors motivating their behavior. In an attempt to draw a sociological profile of the modern urban terrorist, counter-intelligence experts Charles A. Russell and Capt. Bowman H. Miller of the U.S. Air Force studied more than 350 individuals from 18 urban guerrilla groups. Russell and Miller found that generally terrorists have been single men aged 22 to 24 (although the leaders tend to be older) who have some university education if not a college degree. Women terrorists—except for those in the West German groups and an occasional leading figure in the underground Irish Republican Army, Japanese Red Army or Popular Front for the Liberation of Palestine—tend to occupy support rather than leadership roles.

Russell and Miller found that well over two-thirds of the terrorists they studied came from the middle or upper classes.[17] Trying to explain why individuals from this socio-economic background would turn to terrorism, they wrote:

> Although [their] parents were part of the existing social and economic systems, many of them had been frustrated in their efforts to use them as vehicles for upward social and economic mobility. Liberal in political outlook, they frequently advocated significant social and political change. When these parental views were coupled with the radical socioeconomic doctrines so popular in most university circles during the 1960s, this combination of forces—added to general student distrust of 'democratic institutions' as effective media for implementing social change—may have moved some young people toward terrorism...as methods of achieving the desired change or obtaining the power to implement such changes.[18]

According to Brian Jenkins of the Rand Corporation, the Russell-Miller study does not go far enough in explaining why certain individuals are attracted to terrorism. Jenkins told Editorial Research Reports that the person drawn to terrorism is likely to be a fanatic, an impatient, action-prone individual and quite possibly a "gun-freak." Jenkins said that a number of people who have been held hostage by terrorists have mentioned the constant assembling and disassembling, oiling and cleaning

---

[17] The major exception to this rule was among members of the Provisional Wing of the Irish Republican Army.

[18] Charles A. Russell and Capt. Bowman H. Miller, "Profile of a Terrorist," *Military Review*, August 1977, p. 29.

of weapons. "Guns seem to be almost a fetish with these people," Jenkins said. While most terrorists are not insane or suicidal in a medical sense, he added, "they do undertake unnecessary risks not needed to accomplish the job." Jenkins has found that many of the young people who join terrorist groups lack any coherent ideological or political goals. For them, he said, "the act of terror itself is an ideology."

Harvey Schlossberg, a psychiatrist who trains the New York City Police Department's anti-terrorist unit, contends that many terrorists are compensating for inadequate personalities. "If they cry and stamp their feet, no one pays attention," Schlossberg explained. "But by taking hostages, in a matter of minutes the whole world is watching. This helps overcome their ego deficit."[19]

According to Walter Laqueur, "generalizations about the 'terrorist personality' are of only limited assistance.... Throwing bombs and firing pistols does not necessarily prove that [terrorists] had more in common with one another than have rose growers or stamp collectors.... All that can be said with any degree of confidence is that terror was (and is) a pursuit of young people, and that in most other respects the differences between terrorists are more pronounced than the features they may have in common."

Origins and Uses of Terrorism

THE EXECUTION OF Marie Antoinette in 1793 may not seem like a terrorist act by today's definition. But in fact, it was one of the first acts of terrorism in history, or at least one of the first incidents that was actually called terrorism. In this instance the terrorists were not trying to overthrow the government; they were the government. The Committee of Public Safety, led by Robespierre, chief spokesman of the Jacobin Party, governed France during the tumultuous period known as the Reign of Terror (September 1793-July 1794). It is from this period that the word "terrorism" is derived.

The Jacobins maintained their political power through terror; in the 19th century, terrorism was used to destroy governments more often than to sustain them. The most notorious 19th century terrorists were Russian revolutionaries who employed terror to weaken the Czarist regime. Terror tactics first were used dur-

---

[19] Quoted in *Time*, Oct. 31, 1977, p. 33.

ing the wave of political repression that swept Russia during the 1860s. Although there was an attempt to kill Czar Alexander II as early as 1866, the "first generation" of Russian terrorists generally resorted to violence only to punish traitors and police spies or to retaliate against the brutal treatment of political prisoners.

A split in the Russian revolutionary movement in 1879 led to the formation of an extremist group, Narodnaya Volya (Will of the People). Its followers believed that terrorism should be used offensively as well as defensively. The aim of terrorism, according to their program, was "to compromise the prestige of governmental power, to give constant proof that it is possible to fight the government, to strengthen thereby the revolutionary spirit of the people and its faith in the success of the cause, and finally to form capable cadres trained in the struggle."

Terrorism in czarist Russia usually took the form of selective assassination. The targets were either key policymakers, policemen or other government officials. The top priority target was the Czar himself. After several unsuccessful attempts, the Narodnaya Volya finally killed Alexander II in 1881 with a bomb thrown at his carriage. The victory was short-lived, however. Within a week nearly all of the leading members of the group were arrested and most were executed.

What distinguished Narodnaya Volya from later terrorist groups was its acknowledgement of the moral dilemmas associated with the use of political violence. Its members argued that they had been forced to murder because the regime had closed all possibilities of peaceful reform. Their leaders even promised that if they ever saw signs of "even the possibility of an honest government" they would abandon the use of terror. Indeed, their principles were revealed through these comments on the assassination of President James Garfield in 1881:

> In a land where the citizens are free to express their ideas, and where the will of the people does not merely make the law but appoints the person who is to carry the law into effect...political assassination is the manifestation of a despotic tendency identical with that to whose destruction in Russia we have devoted ourselves.

Second Generation of Russian Terrorists

The "second generation" of Russian terrorists appeared in 1901 when the Socialist Revolutionary Party came into existence and proceeded to carry on the tradition of the Naradnaya Volya. Its victims included the Grand Duke Sergius, two ministers of the interior, and an impressive list of high police officials and provincial governors. The group's morale was seriously undermined when it was discovered that the chief of its combat organization, Evno Azev, had been planted in the party as an *agent provocateur* by the Okhrana, the Czar's secret police force.

This discovery, together with the opening of the Duma (parliament) after the uprising of 1905, led the party to abandon terrorism in 1906, according to J. Hardman in the *Encyclopedia of the Social Sciences.* Three years later this decision was revoked and terrorist activity continued until World War I. The Social Revolutionaries resorted to selective assassination again after the revolution of 1917 to combat Bolshevik repression. The assassination of the German ambassador to Russia—calculated to create an international incident embarrassing to the Bolsheviks—and an attempt upon Lenin's life were their last important acts.

Like the Narodnaya Volya, the Socialist Revolutionaries took special pains to avoid endangering innocent bystanders. For example, the poet Ivan Kaliaiev, who assassinated the Grand Duke Sergius on the night of Feb. 2, 1905, passed up an opportunity to throw the bomb earlier in the evening because the grand duchess and some of her nieces and nephews also were riding in the grand duke's carriage.

The Russian terrorists inspired the wave of anarchist terrorism that swept across Europe between 1880 and the outbreak of World War I, and eventually spread to the United States. The anarchist doctrine of the "propaganda of the deed" claimed the lives of at least four heads of state: President Carnot of France (1894), Empress Elizabeth of Austria (1898), King Umberto of Italy (1900) and President William McKinley (1901). But the old moral strictures of the Russians fell into disuse; increasingly, the victims of anarchist violence were innocent bystanders.

Campaigns Against Colonial Governments

Most of the more recent terrorist developments originated in former colonial possessions, such as Ireland, Israel, Cyprus and Algeria. Native terrorist groups did not expect to win military victories over occupying colonial powers. Instead, they set out to provoke repressive measures that would stir up controversy and ultimately convince the occupiers that it had become too expensive to hold on. These movements were all at least partially successful in persuading colonial powers to withdraw.

Terrorism has plagued Ireland at least since the mid-19th century. The terrorist group known as the Irish Republican Army was founded in 1918, and it can trace its ancestry back to the Irish Republican Brotherhood, a secret society established in 1858 to fight for Irish independence. But H.H.A. Cooper of

American University's Institute for Advanced Studies in Justice pointed out, "the current activities of the Irish Republican Army [in Ulster] and particularly what has come to be known as the Provisional Wing are very much a child of the present times and have more in common with other, similar movements in the world today than they do with the earlier history of the Irish self-determination movement."[20]

The four-year campaign against the British waged by EOKA (the National Organization of Cypriot Fighters) between 1955 and 1959 is one of the best examples of the successful use of terror against a colonial regime. But while the Cypriot terrorists influenced Britain's decision to pull out, they failed to achieve their original objective: union with Greece. In Palestine, the Irgun and its more militant offshoot, the Stern Gang, conducted terrorist campaigns against the Arabs and the British before, during and after World War II. For the most part, the Irgun limited their terrorist activities to attacks against property.

As long as the war in Europe continued they directed their attacks primarily against government buildings, but once the war was over, military installations became the primary targets. These attacks culminated in July 1946 when a part of the King David Hotel in Jerusalem containing British government and military offices was blown up, killing more than 90 persons. The strategy of the Stern Gang relied heavily on the use of selective assassination. The murder of Lord Moyne, the British minister of state for the Near East, in November 1944 in Cairo attracted worldwide attention.

The Algerian insurrection (1954-1962) spawned not one but several varieties of political terrorism. "In the last months of French rule," wrote Robert Moss, "when Moslems and Europeans were being machine-gunned from moving cars in the winding streets of Algiers, or blown up by plastic bombs in cafes or bazaars, it became impossible to predict whether the next outrage would be the work of the National Liberation Front (FLN), the (anti-Moslem) Secret Army Organization (OAS) or the barbouzes (a paramilitary group organized with police backing to out-terrorize the OAS). Confused spectators spoke not only of terrorism and counter-terrorism, but of counter-counter-terrorism as well."

Skyjacking Epidemic in the 1960s and 1970s

One of the terrorist acts most associated with the late 1960s and early 1970s was skyjacking.[21] Two brief flurries of plane hijacking had already drawn attention to the problem. The first,

---

[20] H.H.A. Cooper, "The International Experience With Terrorism: An Overview," Appendix 1 of the "Report of the Task Force on Disorders and Terrorism," p. 420.

[21] See "Control of Skyjacking," *E.R.R.*, 1973 Vol. I, pp. 65-84.

in the early 1950s, had been composed almost entirely of East European aircraft commandeered solely for escaping to the West. The second period, which extended from the late 1950s to the early 1960s, primarily involved Cubans seeking political asylum in the United States. But on May 1, 1961, a man armed with a knife and pistol ordered a National Airlines Convair en route from Miami to Key West to fly to Cuba. The plane was detained briefly and then permitted to return to Florida. Three months later an Eastern Air Lines plane was forced to make an unscheduled trip to Havana. In all, there were four skyjackings to Cuba that year.

There was a lull in plane hijacking during the mid-1960s, followed by a new surge toward the end of the decade, as shown in the following table:

	1968	1969	1970	1971	1972
Skyjacking Attempts	35	87	83	60	61
Successful Skyjacking	30	70	56	23	25
Terrorist Skyjackings	6	25	47	14	16

In July 1968 a new element was added to the hijacking problem when Arab terrorists hijacked an Israeli airliner on a flight from Rome to Tel Aviv. This was the first time Arabs had extended their guerrilla warfare against Israel to the air routes.

Terrorist skyjackings reached near epidemic proportions in 1970. The most dramatic incident occurred on Sept. 6, when Arab commandos seized three airliners in three different parts of the world—a Pan American B-747, a Swissair DC-8 and a Trans World Airline B-707—and three days later seized a British Overseas Airways Corp. VC-10 jetliner.[22] The Pan Am plane, one of the first "jumbo jets," was flown to Cairo where it was blown up minutes after the passengers scrambled off. The other three planes were taken to a desert site in Jordan where the passengers were held hostage. Eventually the passengers were released, but the three remaining planes were destroyed on the desert airstrip.

National and Global Responses

T HE RECENT UPSURGE in terrorist incidents in Europe has prompted calls for greater international co-operation in the fight against terrorism. West German President Walter Scheel, for example, said that if the international com-

---

[22] An Arab commando attempt to seize an El Al B-707 on Sept. 6 was thwarted by an Israeli guard on board. He killed one skyjacker and wounded the other.

munity did not show solidarity in this struggle, terrorism "would spread like a brush fire all over the world."[23] But if past history is any indication, the nations of the world are likely to have great difficulty reaching a consensus on the terrorism issue.

The primary problem is one of definition. There is as yet no universally accepted definition of terrorism. Just four years ago, a special United Nations committee was established to formulate such a definition but it gave up after four weeks of acrimonious debate.[24] The heart of the problem lies in differing moral perspectives and priorities. "Terrorist" is a relative term almost always used pejoratively. Terrorists refer to themselves as revolutionaries or members of liberation movements. Stated simply, what is terrorism to some is heroism to others.

Despite problems of terminology, the international community has taken some joint action against terrorism. Several agreements have been negotiated among various nations pertaining to crimes against civil aviation. The most recent was the U.N. General Assembly's Nov. 3 resolution condemning air piracy and calling on governments to take steps to tighten airport security and to prosecute or extradite hijackers. Among those who assented to the resolution were several nations that have in the past provided havens for hijackers, including Algeria, Libya, and South Yemen.[25] The resolution called on governments to approve three treaties drafted by the International Civil Aviation Organization. The three are:

1. The Tokyo Convention of 1963 on Offenses and Certain Other Acts Committed Aboard Aircraft. It provides that participating states (1) take "all appropriate measures to restore control of the [hijacked] aircraft to its lawful commander" and (2) see that passengers, crew and cargo are allowed to proceed on the rightful journey as soon as practicable. As of Oct. 26, 1977, 88 countries had ratified it.

2. The Hague Convention of 1970 on Unlawful Seizure of Aircraft. It provides that each participating nation will extradite a skyjacker or submit his case to competent national authorities for prosecution. This convention came into force on Oct. 14, 1971, after the United States became the tenth nation to ratify it. So far 79 countries have ratified it.

3. The Montreal Convention of 1971 for the Suppression of Unlawful Acts Against the Safety of Civil Aviation. It extends the provisions of the Hague Convention to cover sabotage, bombing

---

[23] Remarks made Oct. 25, 1977, at a ceremony honoring slain West German industrialist Hanns Martin Schleyer.

[24] The 35-member U.N. Special Committee on International Terrorism met in New York from July 16 to Aug. 11, 1973. It was established by a U.N. resolution adopted on Dec. 18, 1972.

[25] Cuba was the only nation to voice opposition to the resolution.

and other acts endangering aircraft in flight. It came into force in January 1973 and has been ratified by 75 nations.

Several other multinational agreements pertaining to terrorism have been negotiated in recent years. In 1971, following a rash of diplomatic kidnapings, 13 members of the Organization of American States signed a Convention to Prevent and Punish Acts of Terrorism Taking the Form of Crimes Against Persons and Related Extortion that are of International Significance. So far six members of the OAS have ratified it. Like the Hague convention, the OAS treaty requires participatory nations to extradite or prosecute terrorists. A 1973 U.N. convention, which has been ratified by more than 22 nations, required contracting states to establish as crimes under international law certain specified acts against diplomats or their official residences, private accommodations or means of transport.

The December 1975 raid on the OPEC ministerial meeting in Vienna and the July 1976 Entebbe hijacking both played a role in inspiring the European Convention on the Suppression of Terrorism that was adopted by the Council of Europe on Nov. 10, 1976. The treaty, which has not yet come into force, makes prosecution or extradition mandatory for individuals responsible for a wide range of terrorist acts.

According to the CIA, "these conventions...do not singly or in combination constitute much of an effective constraint on terrorist activity."

> In the first place [the agency noted] many states—including a high percentage of those that have been particularly active in supporting revolutionary or national liberation groups—are not yet parties thereto. Secondly, the conventions lack teeth in that all make the extradition or prosecution of terrorists subject to discretionary escape clauses and none provides for the application of punitive sanctions against states that simply refuse to comply at all.

The weakness of the existing agreements was demonstrated last January when the French government released Palestinian terrorist Abu Daoud—the man widely suspected of masterminding the 1972 massacre at the Munich Olympic Games—even though both West Germany and Israel had submitted requests for his extradition. Daoud was held for four days and then allowed to fly to Algeria. Daoud's release illustrated yet another obstacle to more effective international action against terrorism—the reluctance on the part of many countries to commit themselves to any course of action that might invite retribution, either by terrorists or persons sympathetic to their cause.

Lacking international cooperation, nations have been compelled to deal with terrorism on their own. Many countries are adopting a hard-line approach. There appears to be a growing tendency to fight fire with fire. The German commando raid on the hijacked Lufthansa jetliner in Somalia, was just the latest in a series of counter-terror attacks. Israel led the way in 1976 with its daring rescue of 104 hostages from a hijacked French jet at Entebbe Airport in Uganda. Two months later Egyptian commandos disguised as mechanics boarded a hijacked Egyptian jet at Luxor and disarmed three gunmen. Last June Dutch troops stormed a hijacked commuter train, killing six South Moluccan terrorists and rescuing 55 hostages who had been held for 19 days.

Adoption of Tough, Hard-Line Policies

The new get-tough tactics are not universally applauded. In an article in the *Bulletin of the Atomic Scientists* in 1976, Samuel H. Day Jr. questioned the wisdom of the Entebbe rescue. "Rather than deter terrorism," Day wrote, "the Entebbe raid is more likely to facilitate it in the long run. It does this by deluding the public into believing that unilateral, national, preemptive force is the most effective answer to the problem, rather than a cooperative, international approach based on peaceful non-violent solutions."[26]

Also coming under attack in recent years has been the U.S. government's "no concessions" policy. President Nixon explained the rationale for the policy in March 1973 at a State Department ceremony honoring two American diplomats—George Curtis Moore and Cleo A. Noel Jr.—who were killed after Black September terrorists seized the Saudi Arabian Embassy in Khartoum.

> All of us would like to have saved the lives of these two brave men [Nixon said]. But they knew and we knew that in the event we paid international blackmail, it would have saved their lives, but it would have endangered the lives of hundreds of others all over the world, because once the terrorist has a demand...that is satisfied, he then is encouraged to try it again; that is why the position of your government has to be one...of not submitting to international blackmail....

Similar thoughts were expressed recently by Heyward Isham, the State Department's director for combating terrorism. "It may seem cold-blooded," Isham said, "but the minute they think they can blackmail you, it leads to an endless chain of demands."[27]

---

[26] Samuel H. Day Jr., "Some Questions About Entebbe," *Bulletin of the Atomic Scientists,* September 1976, p. 7.

[27] Quoted in *Time,* Oct. 31, 1977, p. 31.

Negotiating With Terrorists

The possible advantages of a flexible negotiating policy were revealed on March 9, 1977, when black American members of a religious sect known as the Hanafi Muslims, led by Hamaas Abdul Khaalis, attacked three District of Columbia buildings, including the B'nai B'rith headquarters in Washington. Nearly 40 hours later the 134 hostages being held at the three sites were released after police and federal officials acceded to some of the Hanafis' demands. The FBI refused to hand over to the Hanafis the five men convicted of the 1973 murders of seven women and children at Hanafi headquarters in Washington.

But officials did agree to repay Khallis the $750 he had been charged for a contempt of court citation at their trial. They also arranged to have a movie the Hanafis found offensive— "Mohammed, Messenger of God"—removed from theaters— at least temporarily. As another condition for the release of the hostages, federal prosecutors agreed to allow Khaalis to be freed without bail on his own recognizance. His freedom was short-lived, however. He was jailed on March 31 (after making murder threats in a wiretapped telephone call), convicted July 23 along with the other 11 Hanafis and sentenced Sept. 6 to a minimum of 41 years in jail.

Walter Laqueur defended the government's hard-line approach. "If governments refused to give in to terrorists' demands, terrorism would be much reduced in scale," he wrote. On the other hand, the LEAA's Task Force on Disorders and Terrorism advocated a more flexible approach to negotiations with terrorists. "Under certain circumstances, it may well be unwise or inappropriate to make any concessions whatsoever to terrorists...," the task force said. "But it serves little useful purpose to announce such a policy in advance, and such an announcement may indeed have an adverse effect."[28]

The government's "no-concessions" policy also has been questioned by Brian Jenkins. He contends that there is little evidence to support the assumptions that (1) refusing to negotiate, pay ransom or make political concessions deters terrorists or (2) that any deviation from such a policy would lead to a proliferation of such incidents. The wringing of concessions is only one objective of terrorism, Jenkins pointed out. A "no-concessions" policy will do little to stop terrorists whose primary objective is to secure publicity for their cause. What would really deter terrorists, Jenkins said, is not a hard-line policy during the crisis, but determined action afterward to capture and convict the terrorists.[29]

---

[28] "Report of the Task Force on Disorders and Terrorism," p. 413.
[29] Quoted by Judith Miller in "Bargain With Terrorists?" *The New York Times Magainze*, July 18, 1976, p. 39.

State Department records show that terrorism involves remarkably few risks. For example, a terrorist involved in a kidnaping has about an 80 per cent chance of escaping punishment or death. Of the approximately 115 successful terrorist hijackings between March 1968 and the end of 1975, less than a dozen are known to have ended in the death or imprisonment of the terrorists. All told, only 267 individuals associated with international terrorism were caught between 1970 and 1975. Of these, 39 were freed without punishment, 58 escaped punishment by getting safe conduct to another country, 16 were released from confinement on the demand of fellow terrorists, 50 were released after serving out their prison terms and 104 were still in jails as of mid-September 1975. The average sentence handed out to those terrorists who actually stood trial was 18 months.[30]

Countermeasures and Civil Liberties

Many people fear that anti-terrorist efforts may turn out to be as bad as terrorism itself. They worry that increased terrorism might force democratic governments to adopt countermeasures that could threaten civil liberties. Some people already feel, for example, that many of the security measures designed to stop airplane hijackings violate the Fourth Amendment ban against unreasonable searches and seizures. Dr. Frederick J. Hacker, one of the world's leading experts on the psychology of terrorism, has written that "counterterrorist activities can, by use of electronic surveillance, clandestine infiltration, illegal searches, and similar actions, compound the violation of the values that they intend (or pretend) to protect. Inadvertently or by design, counter-terrorist campaigns often adopt the tactics they presumably abhor and for the sake of efficiency become as terroristic as the activities against which they fight."[31]

This problem bothers conservatives as well as liberals. James Burnham of the *National Review* wrote in 1974: "Effective anti-terror action requires methods normally considered incompatible with democratic principles and civil rights, and—if the terrorism is both serious and long continued—apparently also requires a certain amount of counter-terror." Burnham went on to say, "Sensible people understand that a constitutional republic must occasionally resort to undemocratic and normally illegal means to meet an emergency.... But sensible people also realize that the use of normally illegal undercover and terrorist methods is always a danger to the integrity of the republic and a

---

[30] See Interview with Robert A. Fearey, Special Assistant to the Secretary of State and Coordinator for Combatting Terrorism, *U.S. News & World Report*, Sept. 29, 1975, p. 79.

[31] Frederick J. Hacker, *Crusaders, Criminals, Crazies: Terror and Terrorism in Our Time* (1976), p. 4.

fatal danger when the methods become routine and pervasive."[32]

West Germany is among the democratic European nations that now faces the delicate problem of trying to limit opportunities for terrorists and, at the same time, preserve essential freedoms. Many Germans have voiced opposition to two controversial laws enacted this year in reaction to terrorist campaigns. The first permits the monitoring of all written communications with jailed terrorists. The second, passed after the kidnaping of industrialist Hanns Martin Schleyer, allows the temporary isolation of jailed terrorists from all contact with each other and the outside world—including their lawyers—for renewable periods of 30 days in emergencies. The government considered this necessary to deal with radical lawyers alleged to be in conspiracy with their clients.

"If governments refused to give in to terrorists' demands, terrorism would be much reduced in scale."

Walter Laqueur, *Terrorism* (1977)

The West German parliament is debating a bill that would allow court-appointed monitors to listen to private conversations between lawyers and their imprisoned clients who are convicted or suspected terrorists. The bill is opposed by the West German Lawyers Association because (1) it would allow courts to appoint people to monitor conversations merely upon the suspicion of conspiracy, (2) it would not establish any specific guidelines under which judges may give such an order, and (3) it would not require evidence that would support the claim of suspicion. Even more controversial is a bill introduced by the opposition parties to allow keeping convicted terrorists in jail beyond the expiration of their original sentences if there is evidence that they will commit similar crimes.

Threat of Nuclear-Armed Terror Groups

Looking to the future, several studies have raised the possibility of terrorism being employed by one nation as a means of surrogate warfare against another. The CIA is more concerned about the possibility of terrorist groups acquiring weapons of mass destruction, including nuclear weapons. Stolen nuclear material does not have to be fashioned into a bomb to cause serious damage. Plutonium is one of the most toxic substances known to man.

---

[32] James Burnham, "Antiterror Problems, *National Review,* March 29, 1974, p. 365.

Dr. Edward Martell, a nuclear chemist with the National Center for Atmospheric Research has stated: "In the not too unlikely event of a major plutonium release, the resulting contamination could require large-scale evacuation of the affected area, the leveling of buildings and homes, the deep plowing and removal of topsoil and an unpredictable number of radiation casualties."[33] Terrorists who threated the release of plutonium oxide on a population center would have to be negotiated with seniously.

How real is the danger of nuclear terrorism? The experts disagree. Some, like physicists Theodore B. Taylor, a former designer of nuclear weapons, argue that it would be comparatively easy for terrorists to steal nuclear material and make a bomb from it. In 1972 Taylor and Mason Willrich, a law professor at the University of Virginia, were given a grant by the Ford Foundation's Energy Policy Project to do a thorough study of the nuclear safeguard problem. In their book, *Nuclear Theft: Risks and Safeguards*, they wrote that "under conceivable circumstances a few persons, possibly even one person working alone, who possessed about ten kilograms of plutonium oxide and a substantial amount of chemical high explosive could, within several weeks, design and build a crude fission bomb." Taylor and Willrich insisted such a bomb could be constructed "using materials and equipment that could be purchased at a hardware store and from commercial suppliers of scientific equipment for student laboratories."[34]

Others say people like Taylor underestimate the difficulties of manufacturing a bomb or acquiring sufficient quantities of weapons-grade nuclear material. According to some estimates there is a 50 per cent death risk in stealing nuclear material and about a 30 per cent risk in bomb manufacturing.[35] While the prospect of nuclear-armed terrorists cannot be dismissed, a more likely scenario would seem to be a terrorist seizure of a nuclear power plant or a nuclear weapons storage facility. Attempts have already been made by terrorist groups to use precision guided weapons such as the Soviet SA-7 or the American Redeye missile.

Some experts say there is a very real threat that one day terrorists will employ chemical or biological weapons.[36] In contrast to nuclear devices, many of these weapons are relatively easy to acquire. Moreover, since small quantities are usually all

---

[33] Edward H. Martell, quoted in Roger Rapport, *The Great American Bomb Machine* (1972), p. 47.

[34] Mason Willrich and Theodore B. Taylor, *Nuclear Theft: Risks and Safeguards* (1974), pp. 20-21. See also "Nuclear Safeguards, *E.R.R.*, 1974 Vol. II, pp. 865-884.

[35] See Laqueur, *op. cit.*, p. 229.

[36] See "ChemicalBiological Warfare," *E.R.R.*, 1977 Vol. I, pp. 393-412.

International Terrorist Attacks
on U.S. Citizens or Property in 1976

Target	Number of Incidents
U.S. officials (civilian or military) or their property	7
U.S. installations or property	15
U.S. businessmen	3
U.S. business facilities or commercial aircraft	21
Foreign employees of U.S. firms	12
U.S. private citizens	3
Total	61

SOURCE: Central Intelligence Agency

that is needed for potentially devastating effects, such agents also tend to be easy to conceal, easy to transport and easy to disperse into a target area. Whether or not such weapons of mass destruction will actually be added to the terrorist arsenal is uncertain. What is certain is that terrorism in one form or another will plague civilization for a long time to come.

Selected Bibliography

Books

Becker, Jillian, *Hitler's Children: The Story of the Baader Meinhof Terrorist Gang*, J.B. Lippincott, 1977.

Hacker, Frederick J., *Crusaders, Criminals, Crazies: Terror and Terrorism in Our Time*, W.W. Norton, 1976.

Hyams, Edward, *Terrorists and Terrorism*, St. Martin's Press, 1974.

Laqueur, Walter, *Terrorism*, Little, Brown, 1977.

Lineberry, William P., ed., *The Struggle Against Terrorism*, The H.W. Wilson Company, 1977.

Mallin, Jay, ed., *Terror and the Urban Guerrillas*, University of Miami Press, 1971.

McKnight, Gerald, *The Terrorist Mind*, Bobbs-Merrill, 1974.

Moss, Robert, *The War for the Cities*, Coward, McCann & Geoghegan, 1972.

Watson, Francis M., *Political Terrorism: The Threat and the Response*, Robert B. Luce, 1976.

Articles

"Businessmen and Terrorism," *Newsweek*, Nov. 14, 1977.

Krieger, David, "What Happens If...? Terrorists, Revolutionaries, and Nuclear Weapons," *The Annals of the American Academy of Political and Social Science*, March 1977.

Miller, Judith, "Bargain With Terrorists?" *The New York Times Magazine*, July 18, 1976.

"Psyching Out Terrorists," *Medical World News*, June 27, 1977.

Russell, Charles A., and Capt. Bowman H. Miller, "Profile of a Terrorist," *Military Review*, August 1977.

Skeptic, January-February 1976 issue.

"The New War on Terrorism," *Newsweek*, Oct. 31, 1977.

"War Without Boundaries," *Time*, Oct. 31, 1977.

Reports and Studies

Central Intelligence Agency, "International Terrorism in 1976," July 1977.

——"International and Transnational Terrorism: Diagnosis and Prognosis," April 1976.

Editorial Research Reports, "Control of Skyjacking," 1973 Vol. I, p. 65; "Political Terrorism," 1970 Vol. I, p. 338.

Jenkins, Brian, "International Terrorism: A New Kind of Warfare," The Rand Corporation, June 1974.

——"International Terrorism: A New Mode of Conflict," California Seminar on Arms Control and Foreign Policy, January 1975.

——"Terrorism and Kidnapping," The Rand Corporation, June 1974.

——"Terrorism Works—Sometimes," The Rand Corporation, April 1974.

National Advisory Committee on Criminal Justice Standards and Goals, "Disorders and Terrorism: Report of the Task Force on Disorders and Terrorism," Law Enforcement Assistance Administration, 1976.

COMPUTER CRIME

by

Marc Leepson

Jan. 6
1 9 7 8

Editor's Note: The Senate Judiciary Subcommittee held hearings, June 21-22, 1978, on a bill introduced by Sen. Abraham Ribicoff, discussed on p. 48, to authorize long prison terms and heavy fines for nearly all unauthorized uses of government-owned computers and privately owned computers involved in interstate commerce.

COMPUTER CRIME

T HE ANNALS of crime are recording a new and growing type of criminal activity: crimes involving computers. Fraud, embezzlement, blackmail and other crimes committed by the manipulation or misuse of computers cost Americans more than $100-million a year, according to the U.S. Chamber of Commerce.[1] "Today business and government are more vulnerable to white-collar crime through use of computers than they were ever before or probably ever will be in the future," according to Donn B. Parker, senior management systems consultant at SRI International (formerly Stanford Research Institute) in Menlo Park, Calif. Parker, an expert on computer fraud, said a basic reason for this vulnerability is "the lack of progress in recognizing the threat and taking protective action in a period of rapid transition from manual, paper-based business activities" to fully computerized systems.[2]

There are other reasons why computer-related crime is on the increase. For one thing, the number of computers and persons who work with them is rising steadily. International Data Corp., a publishing and market research consulting firm with headquarters in Waltham, Mass., reported that 86,314 general-purpose computers were installed in American businesses as of Jan. 1, 1977—the latest date for which figures are available. The company also reported that 176,315 minicomputers—small, relatively inexpensive units—are in use. In addition, the U.S. government uses some 10,000 computers.

Computers touch the daily lives of nearly all Americans. They are used in nearly all business and governmental functions that are particularly susceptible to monetary theft. They are used by banks, public utilities, consumer credit companies and by financial offices in large corporations and in state, local and federal governments. Along with this increasing use of computers is a parallel rise in the number of persons who work with the machines—operators, programers and technicians. SRI International estimated that 2,230,000 Americans worked directly with computers in 1975. The figure is believed to be substantially higher today.

---

[1] Figure published in the U.S. Chamber of Commerce's 1974 report, "Handbook on White-Collar Crime." Other estimates run as high as $300-million a year.
[2] Donn B. Parker, *Crime by Computer* (1976), p. 298.

In many organizations, management supervisors have only faint knowledge of computer operations. That fact, combined with the near impossibility of checking the extremely complicated computer operating procedures, makes computers infinitely more vulnerable to misuse than the manual paper-based systems they replaced. "It is almost universally conceded in the electronic data processing industry that...it is extremely difficult to detect acts of embezzlement, fraud or thievery in which computers...are used as the principal tools of crime," Thomas Whiteside wrote in a recent *New Yorker* magazine series on computer crime.[3] For example, a bank teller with access to the bank's computer makes transactions that are fundamentally different from those that are written on paper. The ease of access to computers leaves virtually no trails for auditors or other investigators to follow.

Difficulty of Detection and Conviction

August Bequai, a criminal lawyer who served as chairman of a Federal Bar Association subcommittee on white-collar crime, told Editorial Research Reports that the chance of an electronic crime being discovered is only one in a hundred. "And the likelihood of being convicted of a computer crime is one in five hundred and of going to jail one in a thousand. The odds for avoiding a stiff sentence are even more favorable."

Bequai and others have pointed out that the criminal justice system was set up to deal mainly with crimes of violence. But most white-collar criminals, especially computer culprits, are middle-class citizens who typically have no past record of criminal activity. Some 40 statutes are used to prosecute computer crimes but none of these laws was written specifically to cover these crimes. That situation contributes to the difficulties of administering justice to computer criminals.

Sen. Abraham Ribicoff (D Conn.) has introduced a bill in Congress to authorize long prison terms (up to 15 years) and heavy fines (up to $50,000) for nearly all unauthorized uses of government-owned computers and privately owned computers involved in interstate commerce. Ribicoff introduced the bill June 27, 1977, and a similar measure subsequently was introduced in the House of Representatives. No hearings had been held by the Judiciary Committees of either house when Congress ended its 1977 session in December but there was a prospect of action early in the 1978 session, possibly in February. One reason for the slow progress to date is the complex process of integrating the measures into the U.S. criminal code.

---

[3] Thomas Whiteside, "Dead Souls in the Computer," *The New Yorker,* Aug. 29, 1977, p. 34.

Sabotage and Vandalism by Employees

The many types of computer crime fall into two broad categories: (1) vandalism and sabotage, and (2) theft, fraud and embezzlement. Vandals and saboteurs have physically attacked computers on several occasions and for varied reasons. Some attacks have been politically motivated; some have come for personal reasons. A good number of vandalism cases involve disgruntled employees who steal or destroy computer equipment and tapes. Unhappy employees have attacked company computers with shotguns, screwdrivers and gasoline bombs. Malicious workers have deliberately mislabeled, misfiled or erased computer tapes.

A computer operator for Yale Express System in New York City, for example, thought he was being worked too hard and took revenge by destroying billing information he was supposed to enter into the trucking company's computer. He destroyed some $2-million worth of bills. A small business on the West Coast was hit even harder. An unhappy employee programed the company's computer to destroy all accounts receivable six months after he quit his job. This left no record of who owed the company money. It placed a newspaper advertisement asking its customers to pay what they owed. When only a few responded, bankruptcy followed.

Several instances of politically motivated attacks on computers occurred during the Vietnam War. A group of protestors erased computer tapes containing data on napalm production at Dow Chemical Co. offices in Midland, Mich., in 1970. Students attacked Department of Defense research computer centers at the University of Wisconsin and Fresno State College in 1970. The attacks caused millions of dollars in damage at both schools and, in the Wisconsin attack, resulted in the death of a researcher.

August Bequai said recently: "What will prevent a politically motivated group from locking itself into a key computer section of a large multinational or American company and threatening to blow themselves up unless a ransom is paid?" And new ways to apply crimes of sabotage and vandalism to computers may develop. Small, accurately guided weapons, so-called "smart bombs," conceivably could be used to destroy a computer operation or computer tapes from areas many miles away.

It is even possible to commit a murder by computer. Such a crime can take place because computers are capable of controlling life-support systems in hospitals. If a hospital computer guiding a patient's life-support system is tampered with to function incorrectly, the result could be death for the patient. What worries law-enforcement authorities about computer crimes involving vandalism and sabotage is that no special knowledge of computers may be needed. "If technical expertise is lacking," Arthur R. Miller wrote, "a match, or a hammer in the case of a disc or a data cell, will do the same job...in a minute or two."[4]

Electronic Theft, Fraud and Embezzlement

There are many kinds of computer theft, including theft of data, services, property and financial theft. "Time-shared" systems, in which several companies make use of the same computer, offer a particularly tempting target for the theft of services. One of the soft spots in such systems occurs when computerized information moves from the central processing unit *(see p. 10)* through communications links to customers. In addition to the relatively simple task of bugging the transmission line and recording the electronic communications passing over it, the wiretapper might attach his or her own computer terminal to the line and join the group sharing the system's ser-

---

[4] Arthur R. Miller, *The Assault on Privacy* (1971), p. 28.

Reported Cases of Computer Misuse

Year	Vandalism	Information or Property Theft	Financial Fraud or Theft	Unauthorized Use or Sale of Services	Total
1965	—	1	4	3	8
1966	1	—	1	—	2
1967	2	—	—	2	4
1968	2	3	7	1	13
1969	4	6	3	2	15
1970	8	5	10	10	33
1971	6	19	23	6	54
1972	15	18	16	17	66
1973	11	20	26	11	68
1974	7	15	25	12	59
1975	6	7	26	4	43
Total	62	94	141	68	365

SOURCE: SRI International

vices. A bookmaker was caught using a college computer in this manner to run an illegal bet-taking operation.

One of the most publicized cases of computer-abetted property theft occurred in Los Angeles. Jerry Neal Schneider masterminded a scheme which resulted in his conviction for stealing an estimated $1-million worth of telephone equipment from the Pacific Telephone & Telegraph Co. in 1970-1972. Schneider accomplished what author Gerald McKnight called "one of the most amazing robberies in the history of crime"[5] by using stolen computer information to order equipment through the Los Angeles telephone company's own computer. Before he was discovered, Schneider employed 10 persons to gather and sell the pirated equipment.

Confidential business information attracts thieves because it is likely to be very valuable. Large volumes of paper material can be boiled down and stored on small reels of magnetic tape, making it comparatively easy to steal. Thieves stole two reels of Bank of America tape at the Los Angeles International Airport in 1971 and threatened to destroy them if the bank did not pay a large ransom. In January 1976, the head programer of the computer department of Imperial Chemical Industries in Rotterdam, the Netherlands, took all the company's computer tapes that dealt with European operations. He asked for the equivalent of $200,000 in cash for their return.

[5] Gerald McKnight, *Computer Crime* (1973), p. 33.

Computer theft also lends itself to blackmail. Persons with access to computers have retrieved private data and threatened to make the information public. Such potentially damaging information includes poor college performance, erratic employment history, crime conviction or mental hospitalization. In one case, computer-room employees in Manchester, England, threatened to destroy their company's records if it did not give large salary increases.

The most costly, and perhaps the most common, computer crimes involve fraud and embezzlement. There are many cases of clerks with knowledge of their company's computers who have transferred money from customer accounts to their own pockets. But computer fraud does not always involve company clerks or bank tellers or persons working in computer rooms. Some schemes involve perpetrators with no access to computers or computer terminals. One such fraud has taken place in several major cities across the country.

It works like this: The criminal opens a small checking account in a bank and then steals some blank checking deposit slips—the ones that banks provide for depositors who do not have premarked checking deposit forms. The criminal takes the blank forms to an unscrupulous printer who adds the criminal's magnetic-ink checking account number to all the slips. The doctored deposit forms are slipped back into their usual place at the bank. Everyone using them is therefore depositing money into the criminal's checking account. Within days, hundreds of thousands of dollars are sent by the bank's computer into the perpetrator's account. The thief withdraws the money and moves on.

By far the biggest computer-related crime on record involved a nationwide investment firm, the Equity Funding Corporation of America. The Equity Funding scandal first came to public attention in 1973. Computer crime was but one part of a widespread illegal financial fraud masterminded by the highest officers of the now-bankrupt company. Equity's president and 21 other executives were convicted in 1975 of setting up life insurance policies for some 56,000 fictitious persons and selling the policies to other insurance companies. The bogus insurance policies existed only inside Equity Funding's computer. A bankruptcy trustee's report calculated that the total value of the fraudulent policies was $2.1-billion.

Computer fraud is by no means relegated to private enterprise. The federal government, too, has been the victim of computer crime. The General Accounting Office, Congress's investigating arm, reported in 1976 on 69 instances of improper use of computers in the U.S. government. The 69 cases resulted in losses of some \$2-million. The report said that the 69 cases "do not represent all the computer crimes involving the federal government since agencies do not customarily differentiate between computer-related and other crimes."[6] The GAO investigation further revealed the distinct possibility that a large number of computer crimes in the federal government have yet to be detected or reported. Computer-related crimes were documented at all levels of the government.

In one case, an Internal Revenue Service programer fed information into an IRS computer to funnel unclaimed tax credits into a relative's account. Another IRS programer used a computer to take checks being held for those whose mailing addresses could not be located and deposit the checks into his own account. Concern about the vulnerability of the federal government's computers is high because the government pays tens of billions of dollars by computer every year. The crimes documented by the GAO ranged from those involving hundreds of dollars to those involving hundreds of thousands of dollars.

Potential for Computer Misuse

R ESEARCH initiated during World War II led to development of the first electronic computer, the Electronic Numerical Integrator and Calculator—commonly known as Eniac—at the University of Pennsylvania in 1946. The Eniac, which took two-and-one-half years to build, solved its first problem, an equation involving atomic physics, in two hours. The machine contained 18,000 vacuum tubes and could carry out 5,000 additions a second. Computers today use transistors or microcircuits instead of tubes and can make as many as several billion computations a second. The intricacies of computers magnify their potential for misuse. Computer operation may be broken down into five principal segments—*input, programing, central process, output* and *communications*. Each is vulnerable to certain kinds of crime.

Input is the feeding of information into the computer, usually at a terminal keyboard. The input phase is vulnerable to criminal activity in two different ways. A computer operator can either introduce false data into the computer or alter the computer's records by removing vital data. The heart of the computer fraud involved in the Equity Funding case was based on

---

[6] General Accounting Office, "Computer Related Crimes in Federal Programs," April 27, 1976.

false input—that is, 56,000 phony life insurance policies. Payroll accounts are especially vulnerable to manipulation at this stage.

Programing consists of detailed instructions given to the computer to solve problems. Programs are placed in storage where the information to be processed and the rules to be used in processing it are kept until needed. Law-enforcement officials have reported dozens of cases involving illegal tampering with computer programs. Many crimes of this type occur in banks. Computer operators, bank officers or other employees with access to a bank's computer have wrongfully programed instructions to take money from accounts and transfer it to others.

The "round down fraud" is one type of programing crime. It has been used with computer systems in institutions such as large savings banks that have large numbers of financial accounts. A crime of this sort involves a computer program that rounds down an amount such as $59,11544 to $59.11, thus leaving a remainder of .00544 cents. While that figure is infinitesimal, the constant rounding down of thousands of figures adds up quickly. In normal circumstances round-down remainders are distributed to all the accounts in a bank, but a computer program can be altered to place them in a separate account —where the money can be withdrawn.

"Experienced accountants and auditors indicate the round down fraud technique has been known for many years, even before the use of computers," Donn Parker has written. "But to what extent is this done in the complex environment of computer technology?"[7] The answer is that no one knows because of the ease with which such crimes can be accomplished.

Access to Stored and Transmitted Data

Central Processing Unit is the computer's "brain" or "memory bank" where the processing of information actually takes place. It acts on instructions from the program. Writing in *Barrister,* an American Bar Association magazine, August Bequai maintains that the central processing unit is "extremely vulnerable" to "attack from wiretapping, electro-magnetic pickups or browsing."[8]

Knowledgeable persons have been able to gain access to central processing units to steal secrets, such as corporate data, or personal information. Information stolen from computers has been sold to rival companies, used for ransom or blackmail, and for setting up complicated programs without the expense of planning and writing them. Jerry Schneider, who stole nearly $1-million of telephone equipment in Los Angeles, did so by

---

[7] Parker, *op. cit.,* p. 117.
[8] August Bequai, "The Electronic Criminal," *Barrister,* winter 1977, p. 11.

tapping into Pacific Telephone & Telegraph's computer. Many crimes of this sort involve a persons working for the victimized company. But the computer tampering in Schneider's crime was carried out by Schneider alone after he surreptitiously learned several of the telephone company's computer codes. "It was very easy to do," Schneider said. "...I did it myself from the outside. I just called up on the telephone and placed the orders inside the computer."[9]

Output is the processed information provided by the computer. Output may consist of mailing lists, payroll checks or private, secret or other sensitive information. Output data, like any other valuable commodity, is subject to theft.

Communication is transference of output data between computers. It usually is accomplished by telephone or teleprinter. This aspect of computer operations is subject to electronic interception either to change or to steal data. Communications crimes are particularly difficult to detect and are attractive to criminals because the perpetrator often is far from the scene of the crime.

One such case involved an illegal transfer of funds between two banks some 3,000 miles apart. A man opened a large account at a New York bank, informing bank officials that he was a West Coast manufacturer about to open a new factory in the East. He instructed the New York bank to expect the transfer of a large sum of money from his West Coast bank to finance the new business venture. Subsequently $2-million was transferred to the New York bank by computer instruction—a standard procedure among major financial institutions.

In this instance, the "manufacturer" received his money and fled. Police investigations revealed that he had conned a woman computer operator at the West Coast bank into sending a message to transfer the $2-million in the belief she was helping him play a joke on a friend. "Since the missing...pseudo-manufacturer was not available for questioning by the police," Thomas Whiteside wrote, "the two banks involved in the two-million-dollar transfer were left with the computerized message as a souvenir."[10]

Virtual Absence of Computer Security

One reason why computer crimes occur is that there is virtually no security at most computer operations. Moreover, a foolproof method of protecting computers has yet to be developed. "Fundamentally, we do not know how to protect large-scale, multi-access computer systems," Donn Parker said

---

[9] Quoted by McKnight, *op. cit.*, p. 38.
[10] Whiteside, *op. cit.*, Aug. 22, 1977, pp. 49-50.

recently.[11] The 1976 GAO report said that the problem is the same in the federal government. Every incident of computer misuse reviewed by the agency was "directly traceable to weaknesses in system controls...the result of deficient systems designs, improper implementation of controls by operating personnel or a combination of both."

Of the computer criminals who are caught, many are tripped up only because of some unrelated activity. The head teller of the Park Avenue branch of the Union Dime Savings Bank in New York City was convicted in 1974 of embezzling $1.5-million by raiding depositors' accounts and covering up the crime by manipulating the bank's computer. The losses were not uncovered until police raided an illegal gambling emporium. They found receipts indicating that the teller bet as much as $30,000 a day on horse races and other sporting events. The teller's annual salary was $11,000. When police questioned the teller, he confessed that he had been stealing from the bank for three years.

Jerry Schneider was brought to justice only after one of his employees became angry at being refused a raise. The disgruntled employee called the police. Informants' tips have uncovered many other computer-related crimes, including the Equity Funding scandal. First word of the scandal came when a former Equity employee informed the New York State Insurance Department that he suspected wrongdoing by his former employer.

Efforts to Improve Safeguards, Training

This is not to say, though, that computer supervisors are not aware of security problems and are doing nothing about it. The Federal Bureau of Investigation recently opened a special course at its Quantico, Va., training center to train FBI agents and state and local police for investigating consumer fraud and other white-collar crimes. But the course has come in for criticism. Thomas Whiteside wrote: "...[A]ccording to commercial computer-security people I have talked with, the training so far offered is not of a very advanced type in relation to all the ramifications of the existing criminal problems."[12] August Bequai said of the FBI training program: "It's not enough to train a person on what a computer can do. You have to train him in the sophisticated and complicated frauds that a complex computer is capable of performing."

International Business Machines, the leading manufacturer of computers, recently came up with recommendations to prevent computer crime. IBM studied computer security for several years and is reported to have spent $40-million on the effort.

---

[11] Quoted in *Business Week*, Aug. 1, 1977, p. 44.

[12] Whiteside, *op. cit.*, Aug. 29, 1977, p. 40.

Volume of Annual Transactions
Affecting Data Processing

Type of Transaction	1955	1970	Increase 1955-70
Checks written	2.1 billion	7.2 billion	243%
Telephones in use	56.2 million	120.2 million	114
Individual social security payments	8 million	26.2 million	228
Individual federal tax returns	58.3 million	77 million	32
Public welfare recipients	5.6 million	13.3 million	137
Airline passengers	42 million	171 million	307
Persons entering hospitals for treatment	21.1 million	31.7 million	50
Persons covered by private hospitalization insurance	107.7 million	181.5 million	69
Motor-vehicle registrations	62.7 million	108.4 million	73
Passports issued	528,000	2.2 million	317
Students enrolled in colleges and universities	2.6 million	6.9 million*	165
Applications received for federal employment	1.7 million	2.9 million	71
New York Stock Exchange transactions	820.5 million	3.2 billion	290
Pieces of mail handled, U.S. Post Office (all classes)	55.3 billion	84.9 billion	52

SOURCE: Donn B. Parker, *Crime by Computer* (1976), pp. 242-244.
*1969

The company recommends four basic measures to help prevent computer abuse: (1) rigid physical security, (2) new identification procedures for keyboard operators, (3) new internal auditing procedures to keep a fuller record of each computer transaction, and (4) new cryptographic symbols to scramble information. Even with those and other precautions, security problems remain. "The data security job will never be done— after all, there will never be a bank that absolutely can't be robbed," IBM's director of data security, John Rankine, has said.[13]

Brandt Allen, a professor of business administration at the University of Virginia, analyzed 150 cases of computer fraud

---

[13] Quoted by Whiteside, *op. cit.*, Aug. 29, 1977, p. 58.

and concluded that most computer crime "can often be prevented by a tight system of internal control."[14] Allen recommended: (1) stricter controls of input transactions, (2) rigorous audits, (3) improved management supervision, and (4) tighter program and file controls. Controls such as those recommended by Allen and IBM have one consequence that is not popular with many business executives. They involve significant outlays of money. "Operating efficiency and [internal security] controls are counterproductive," Carl Pabst, a computer expert with the New York accounting firm of Touche, Ross & Co., said recently.[15] Pabst said that many companies do not install elaborate security systems in the hope that losses from theft will not be higher than the costs of setting up security measures.

Even the most complex security system can be broken—simply through the dishonesty of someone involved in the security itself. Donn Parker wrote, "Why go to all the trouble of technically compromising a computer center when all [one has] to do is con one of the trusted people into doing anything [one wants] him to do?"[16] One other factor compounds the problem. Most businesses and the federal government do not screen employees who work directly with computers. Nor are computer operators, programers and the like licensed or compelled to abide by a standard code of conduct. Until such a system is implemented, some experts believe, the inefficient security at today's computer centers will add to the continuing increase in computer crime.

Criminal Justice and Technology

MOST OBSERVERS of the computer crime scene agree on one thing: computer crime is growing and will continue to grow before there is any improvement. "There are going to be a lot of shocks and horror stories out there," Carl Pabst of Touche, Ross & Co. said recently, predicting more and larger computer crimes in the future.[17] One factor that has been of prime importance in the rising rate of computer crime is the inadequacy of the criminal justice system in dealing with it.

"Criminologists, lawyers, judges—the entire legal

---

[14] Brandt Allen, "The Biggest Computer Frauds: Lessons for CPA," *The Journal of Accountancy*, May 1977, p. 52.

[15] Quoted in *The Wall Street Journal*, Oct. 5, 1977.

[16] Parker, *op. cit.*, p. 282.

[17] Quoted in *The Wall Street Journal*, Oct. 5, 1977.

system—concentrate on violent crimes such as arson, rape and murder," August Bequai said recently. "But the technological revolution has hit the area of crime and the traditional legal system has proven incapable of handling it."[18] The rules of evidence make it especially difficult to try most computer crime cases, for stolen computer material often consists not of cash or securities but of a series of invisible electronic impulses.

This situation is made worse by what Bequai called "serious procedural and evidentiary handicaps built into the legal system." He maintains that the overall inefficiency of the legal system also adds to the problem. "Right now," he said, "it takes one year to dispose of a simple shoplifting case. A complicated, sophisticated computer crime can tie up the legal system for years. The situation challenges the whole legal apparatus."

Adding to the problem of prosecution is the fact that many police investigators, prosecuting attorneys, judges and juries have only scant knowledge of the simplest computer operations. This makes the uncovering of a crime, its presentation before a jury and the sentencing of a convicted criminal extremely complicated and time-consuming. Even if a computer thief gets caught, is tried and then convicted, chances are that the sentence will be a light one. One reason is that probation officers and others who prepare pre-sentencing reports on computer criminals tend to stress the non-violent nature of the crime.

Leniency for White-Collar Offenders

Most computer criminals are white and middle class and have no prior criminal record. As a result, criminals convicted of computer crimes often wind up with light sentences. Jerry Schneider, who stole some $1-million worth of telephone company equipment, was sentenced to 60 days in jail. He served 40 days and was released. The head teller of the Union Dime Savings Bank branch in New York City, who embezzled $1.5-million, was sentenced to two years in prison and served 20 months. The pre-sentencing report on one convicted computer criminal said: "Computer-program theft is the crime of the future. As such it has not been referred to this office at the felony level in prior instances. Thus, there is no ready frame of reference for determining a proper sentence."[19]

Some computer criminals have received extremely lenient treatment from their victims. "It's like rape," commented Gary Keefe, a computer expert with the accounting firm of Peat, Marwick, Mitchell & Co. "Management feels it's been beaten and doesn't want people to know about it."[20] Banks, for ex-

---

[18] Interview, Dec. 2, 1977.
[19] Quoted by Whiteside, *op. cit.*, Aug. 29, 1977, p. 42.
[20] Quoted in *The Wall Street Journal*, Oct. 5, 1977.

Cashless and Checkless in America

The cashless, checkless society may be upon us in the not too distant future. If current progress continues, most Americans will be using electronic funds transfer (EFT) systems to pay all their bills and make store purchases and bank transactions.

Today, EFT systems are in use in bank teller machines, automatic bill payment plans and direct sales in stores that require no cash, checks or credit cards. In these point-of-sale transfers, customers make purchases using nothing more than their debit cards. These cards resemble credit cards but really are automatic checkbooks. Through computers, the amount of the sale instantly is deducted from the buyer's bank account and added to the retailer's account. No cash is exchanged, no check written, no bill sent, and often no receipt given.

The largest and most common EFT systems in use today are bank-to-bank account transfers. These systems handle billions of dollars daily and do not involve the physical movement of money. Other EFT systems are used to deposit funds or withdraw cash from automated teller machines that remain in operation when the banks are closed. Bank customers usually use a combination of their checking account card and a confidential code to dial transactions. Other EFT conveniences include automatic deposits of paychecks into checking or savings accounts and automatic payment of regular bills such as rent, car payments, mortgages and insurance. Many banks will handle bill payments after receiving telephone calls from their customers.

It is predicted that eventually a national EFT system will have some 40 million computer terminals attached to thousands of computers connecting consumers and retail stores with banking functions. Computers, of course, are at the heart of EFT systems. Some of the factors that make computers vulnerable to fraud, embezzlement and theft exist in EFT systems.

But the EFT transactions are traceable, recordable and revocable. Still, adequate security measures have yet to be developed and the criminal justice system is poorly equipped to handle litigation involving EFT systems. If these cashless transactions spell the end of street robberies and traditional bank holdups, will these crimes be replaced by electronic ones?

ample, fear publicity about large thefts involving computers. The worry is that depositors will lose confidence when they learn the vulnerability of their banks to computer crime. Publicly held corporations, too, tend to keep computer-crime losses quiet. They do not want to lose the confidence of stockholders. Gerald McKnight has written: "Because of what competitors, shareholders and loan providers such as banks might do if they found out that the company's costly computer had been broached, those in the know hush up scandal after scandal."[21]

Some offenders have been merely reprimanded. Some have been fired, but without being forced to make restitution. Others have even been given good references for future employment. An extreme example came in the case of a young executive in England who, when confronted with evidence, admitted he had been stealing from his company's computer. For fear of bad publicity, the company gave the man a letter of recommendation to help him find a new job. He soon went to work for another company as executive director and proceeded to raid the new company's computer, embezzling some $2,000 a week for three-and-a-half years. For a second time, the embezzler was uncovered but not prosecuted. Again the victimized company did not ask for restitution and provided the thief with a good employment reference.

"A million dollars from a computer crime is considered respectable but not an extraordinary score."

The nature of computer crime lends itself easily to thefts of large amounts of money. Brandt Allen, in his analysis of 150 cases of computer fraud *(see p. 58),* found that the average loss was $621,000 among corporations, $193,000 among bank and savings institutions, $329,000 among state and local governments, and $45,000 among federal government agencies. "A million dollars from a computer crime," Thomas Whiteside wrote, "is considered a respectable but not an extraordinary score."[22]

With such large sums of money involved, law-enforcement authorities have become concerned that organized crime groups may be getting involved in computer crimes. Terry Knoepp, U.S. Attorney in San Diego, Calif., said in 1976: "My guess is that any time you have large amounts of money involved...that can be transferred without any sort of audit or tracing, you're

[21] McKnight, *op. cit.,* p. 47.
[22] Whiteside, *op. cit.,* Aug. 22, 1977, p. 38.

Case of the Missing Boxcars

The time: October 1971. The place: Pennsylvania. The case: the disappearance of 217 boxcars owned by the bankrupt Penn Central Railroad.

FBI agents eventually found the cars, which were worth several million dollars. They were sitting on sidings owned by the La Salle and Bureau County Railroad, 100 miles west of Chicago. The L&BC is a tiny rail company that has only 15 miles of track. The boxcars were painted over to appear to be owned by the L&BC, but the Penn Central logo was visible under some of the paint.

A federal crime task force set up to investigate the incident concluded that the boxcars were sent to Illinois through manipulation of the Penn Central's computer. The task force never fully ascertained who misrouted the cars or why. But investigators strongly suspected the cars were sent on their journey by an organized crime syndicate which planned either to sell or rent the boxcars to another railroad.

going to get organized crime interested.... I think that that's certainly a potential...."[23]

Predictions of Rise in Computer Crimes

Computer crime, Donn Parker has written, "is expected to continue to rise merely from the proliferation of computers."[24] Not only will computer crime continue to rise, but new and different forms of computer abuse likely will be developed. One new field, international computer data communication, involves large corporations and enormous amounts of money. Parker wrote that unless strict measures are developed to safeguard those international transactions, "Equity-Fund" type scandals could easily occur on an international scale.

The potential for computer abuse multiplies as computers control more and more functions. Certain aspects of city subway systems, air traffic control, hospital intensive-care monitoring, and even police and fire department functions are being computerized across the nation. In addition, the 500,000 computers that Parker predicts will be in operation by 1980 will be installed in places where white-collar crimes have been prevalent in the past.

Those who study computer crime do so from a judicial, technological or security perspective. But all agree that computer crime will continue to rise in the near future. Donn Parker does not see any improvement in the situation until the early 1980s. And his prediction of improvement then is based on the

---

[23] Interviewed on "60 Minutes" (CBS-TV), Oct. 10, 1976.
[24] Parker, *op. cit.*, p. 293.

Computer Misuse in Industry and Government Among 372 Cases Studied*

Breakdown	Number of Cases	Per Cent of Totals
Banking	70	19
Education	66	18
Government	61	16
Local	22	
State	14	
Federal	13	
Foreign	12	
Manufacturing	46	12
Insurance	28	8
Computer Services	24	6
Transportation	9	2
Retail Stores	8	2
Dating Bureaus	6	2
Trade Schools	5	1
Utilities	5	1
Communications	5	1
Credit Reporting	5	1
Securities	4	1
Petroleum	4	1
Other	26	8

*Through October 1975, by SRI International

Percentages do not add to 100 because of rounding

assumption that the development of security systems will keep pace with other technological advances in computerization. Others, including Thomas Whiteside, have painted an even gloomier picture. Whiteside wrote that the designers of future computer systems "seem no more able to promise absolute solutions to problems of data security than chess players are able to foresee games in which White can never be beaten." Until a foolproof system is developed, computer crime is likely to perplex the people that computers are intended to serve.

Selected Bibliography

Books

Adams, J. Mack and Douglas H. Haden, *Social Effects of Computer Use and Misuse,* Wiley, 1976.

Ellison, J.R. and F.E. Taylor, *Where Next for Computer Security?* International Publications, 1974.

Kemeny, John G., *Man and the Computer,* Scribner's, 1972.

McKnight, Gerald, *Computer Crime,* Walker and Co., 1973.

Parker, Donn B., *Crime by Computer,* Scribner's, 1976.

Sobel, Ronald L. and Robert E. Dallos, *The Impossible Dream: The Equity Funding Scandal,* Putnam, 1975.

Van Tassell, Dennis, *Computer Security and Management,* Prentice Hall, 1972.

Articles

Allen, Brandt, "The Biggest Computer Frauds: Lessons for CPAs," *The Journal of Accountancy,* May 1977.

Bequai, August, "The Electronic Criminal," *Barrister,* winter 1977.

—"White Collar Crime: The Losing War," *Case & Comment,* September-October 1977.

Cameron, Margaret, "Crime In, Crime Out," *Canadian Banker,* May-June 1977.

Computerworld, selected issues.

Congressional Quarterly Weekly Report, Sept. 17, 1977, pp. 1955-56.

Davis, James R., "Computer Controls—A Different Emphasis," *The National Public Accountant,* June 1977.

Infosystems, selected issues.

"The Growing Threat to Computer Security," *Business Week,* Aug. 1, 1977.

Turn, Rein, "Privacy Protection and Security in Business Computer Systems," *Atlanta Economic Review,* November-December 1976.

Whiteside, Thomas, "Dead Souls in the Computer," *The New Yorker* (2 parts), Aug. 22, 29, 1977.

Reports and Studies

Chamber of Commerce of the United States, "Handbook on White Collar Crime," 1974.

Editorial Research Reports, "Approach to Thinking Machines," 1962 Vol. II, p. 537; "Reappraisal of Computers," 1971 Vol. I, p. 347; "Crime Reduction: Reality or Illusion," 1977 Vol. II, p. 537.

General Accounting Office, "Ways to Improve Management of Federally Funded Computerized Models," Aug. 23, 1976.

—"Computer-Related Crimes in Federal Programs," April 27, 1976.

U.S. Senate Governmental Affairs Committee, "Computer Security in Federal Programs," Feb. 2, 1977.

—"Problems Associated with Computer Technology in Federal Programs and Private Industry," June 18, 1976.

Mar. 12
1976

R EAPPRAISAL OF PRISON POLICY

by

Suzanne de Lesseps

No. 10
Vol. I

Editor's Note: The Criminal Code Reform Act, discussed on p. 70, was approved by the Senate on Jan. 30, 1978. The bill established fixed rather than indeterminate prison terms, virtually eliminating parole and time off for good behavior from the sentencing process. For a discussion of House action this year on criminal code reform see the editor's note preceding "Crime Reduction: Reality or Illusion."

The trend toward rising crime rates, discussed on p. 73, was reversed starting in 1976. Updated crime statistics are contained in the report on "Crime Reduction."

On the question of prisoners' legal rights, discussed on p. 78, the U.S. Supreme Court ruled April 27, 1977, that prisoners have a constitutional right of access to the courts, and states are required to furnish prisoners with law libraries or alternative sources of legal knowledge in order to protect this right *(Bounds v. Smith)*. In another case *(Jones v. North Carolina Prisoners' Labor Union Inc.)*, the Supreme Court ruled June 23, 1977, that the First Amendment does not preclude state prison officials from forbidding inmates who are members of prisoners' labor union to solicit other inmates to join or to otherwise take an active part in the operation of the union.

According to the annual *Corrections Magazine* survey of prisons populations, the number of individuals in state and federal prisons increased by 5 per cent during 1977. In numerical terms, the increase was from 281,439 on Jan. 1, 1977, to 294,896 on Jan. 1, 1978.

REAPPRAISAL OF PRISON POLICY

G OVERNMENT officials across the country are currently reevaluating the purpose of the prison. Many of the basic assumptions about prisoner rehabilitation are being questioned. After extensive interviews with leading opinion makers in the field of criminal justice, *Corrections Magazine*, a journal of prison affairs supported by the American Bar Association, has reported that substantial agreement exists on several points:

> There is little or no evidence that correctional "treatment" programs work.

> The gradual restructuring of the American correctional system over the last 50 years around the notion of individualized and enforced treatment for all offenders was a mistake.

> A radically new approach is needed that will provide both better protection for the public and incorporate a more realistic view of what can and cannot be done to reduce recidivism.[1]

It is often said that the primary purposes for sentencing a criminal to prison are retribution, rehabilitation and deterrence. Before the 19th century, society placed greater emphasis on the first and last goals. Then came successive waves of penal reform that stressed reforming the offender rather than punishing him. The philosophy behind prison corrections became "let the sentence fit the individual" instead of "let the sentence fit the crime." Now, there appears to be a movement back in the other direction.

One of the reasons for the swing toward retribution is the growing body of opinion that rehabilitation has failed to reform criminals and reduce crime. The nation's prison populations are currently at an all-time high, and states are grappling with the problem of how to ease dangerous overcrowding. "The correctional institutions of the United States are on the threshold of a population explosion," U.S. Bureau of Prisons Director Norman A. Carlson said last fall. "The most important reason why the number of inmates is rising is that crime itself is on the increase."[2]

---

[1] Michael S. Serrill, "Is Rehabilitation Dead?" *Corrections Magazine*, May-June, 1975, p. 29.

[2] Speech delivered Oct. 28, 1975, to the Kiwanis Club in Birmingham, Ala.

One prison official who believes that rehabilitation has been ineffective is Allen Ault of the Georgia state prison system. "Rehabilitation, as currently applied, is a myth," he has said. "The responsibility to rehabilitate is placed on the state rather than the offender. We have assumed that all offenders are 'sick' and we have tried to force treatment on them. This has not worked...."[3] Those who believe that efforts to rehabilitate criminals have been futile, have found support in a study by sociologist Robert Martinson of the City University of New York. After examining the results of 231 rehabilitation programs conducted around the country from 1945 to 1967, Martinson concluded: "With few and isolated exceptions, the rehabilitative efforts that have been supported so far have had no appreciable effect on recidivism."[4]

Support for Punitive Theory of Criminal Justice

James Q. Wilson in his well-publicized book *Thinking About Crime* has argued against the standard liberal notion that society should fight crime by getting at its root causes—poverty, unemployment, poor family relationships, and so forth. He said society should concentrate on more practical ways of reducing the crime rate. Government, he suggested, should accept the idea that the main purpose of prisons is not to rehabilitate but rather to isolate and punish. "It is a measure of our confusion," he wrote, "that such a statement will strike many enlightened readers today as cruel, even barbaric. It is not. It is merely a recognition that society at a minimum must be able to protect itself from dangerous offenders and to impose some costs...on criminal acts; it is also a frank admission that society really does not know how to do much else."[5] Wilson wants probation abolished so that anyone convicted of committing a serious crime would have to spend some time in prison. He contends that the certainty of prison would deter many would-be offenders.

Several studies support this thesis. According to Gordon Tullock, a crime-research analyst at Virginia Polytechnic Institute: "There is no question any longer. Economists in the U.S., Canada and England have shown conclusively that punishment does cut down on crime."[6] One of the most comprehensive studies was done by economist Isaac Ehrlich of the University of Chicago. He calculated the effect of imprisonment and length of imprisonment on the rates of seven major types of crimes in 1940, 1950, and 1960. Ehrlich concluded that the prospect of go-

---

[3] Quoted in *The Atlanta Constitution*, Oct. 28, 1975.
[4] Robert Martinson, "What Works?—Questions and Answers About Prison Reform," *The Public Interest*, spring 1974, p. 23.
[5] James Q. Wilson, *Thinking About Crime* (1975), pp. 172-173.
[6] Quoted in *Business Week*, Sept. 15, 1975, p. 92.

ing to prison and longer sentences both reduced crime.[7] Ehrlich, in a separate study, has also indicated that capital punishment serves as a deterrent against murder.[8]

Surprisingly, support for stricter methods of sentencing is also coming from the prisoners themselves. "Criminals should be punished," said Willie Holder, a former convict who heads the "Prisoners' Union," a San Francisco-based organization representing prisoner interests. "Society ought to admit that punishment is a form of retribution and not pretend that prisons are for any other purpose. I've heard many prisoners say they'd rather be beat in the head with a shovel than have their brain constantly examined like they do."[9] Holder has supported voluntary rehabilitation programs and the abolition of probation, parole and indeterminate sentencing. It is ironic that parole and indeterminate sentencing were two of the most important practices arising from 19th-century prison reform.

Dissatisfaction With the Indeterminate Sentence

The reformers advanced the belief that sentences should not be fixed when the offenders entered prison but should be based on how well they "progressed" while in confinement. Gradually, most states adopted the concept of "indeterminate sentencing." This is a general term used to describe a system in which an offender's specific term of imprisonment is left to the discretion of administrative authorities, based on the offender's behavior and performance in prison. The basic philosophy behind the indeterminate sentence is that no two prisoners are alike, and some may take more time to achieve rehabilitation than others.

Indeterminate sentencing became the watchword of prison reformers. As late as 1970, Ramsey Clark, the former Attorney General, wrote: "If rehabilitation is the goal, only the indeterminate sentence will be used.... The sentence contemplates a rehabilitation program specifically designed for each individual convicted. Professionally trained correctional authorities can then carefully observe a prisoner and release him at the earliest time within the limits fixed...."[10] Today, however, the concept of indeterminate sentencing has fallen out of favor with many leading criminologists. They assert that it (1) results in longer sentences than most judges would give, (2) gives correctional officials too much control over a prisoner's life, (3) permits disparity in sentencing, and (4) is psychologically damaging to the prisoners because they can never be sure when they will be released.

---

[7] See "The Deterrent Effect of Criminal Law Enforcement," *Journal of Legal Studies*, Vol. I, 1972.

[8] "The Deterrent Effect of Capital Punishment: A Question of Life and Death," *The American Economic Review*, June 1975.

[9] Quoted by Leroy Aarons, *The Washington Post*, Aug. 17, 1975.

[10] Ramsey Clark, *Crime in America* (1970), p. 222.

Some criminologists also argue that indeterminate sentencing weakens the effect of rehabilitation programs. They say many prisoners volunteer only to improve their chances of being paroled. The prisoners, in effect, are forced to play games with the system. The author Jessica Mitford quoted a convict as saying: "From the vindictive guard who sets out to build a record against some individual to the parole board, the indeterminate sentence grants corrections the power to play God with the lives of prisoners."[11] According to federal Judge Marvin E. Frankel, "indeterminate sentencing, as thus far employed and justified, has produced more cruelty and injustice than the benefits its supporters envisage."[12]

The concept of equal punishment imposed by inflexible sentences has already received support from the Ford administration. In his message to Congress on crime, June 19, 1975, President Ford said: "I propose that incarceration be made mandatory for (1) offenders who commit offenses under federal jurisdiction using a dangerous weapon; (2) persons committing such extraordinarily serious crimes as aircraft hijacking, kidnapping, and trafficking in hard drugs; and (3) repeat offenders who commit federal crimes—with or without a weapon—that cause or have a potential to cause personal injury." He went on to say, "There should be no doubt in the minds of those who commit violent crimes...that they will be sent to prison if convicted...."

In a speech to Wisconsin correctional officials in Milwaukee on Feb. 2, 1976, Attorney General Edward H. Levi proposed that the federal parole system be abolished and the sentencing power of federal judges be reduced. In addition, Levi suggested the creation of a permanent federal commission to set sentencing guidelines for judges in cases not covered by Ford's proposals. "If a judge decided to impose a sentence inconsistent with the guidelines," Levi said, "he would have to accompany the decision with specific reasons for the exception, and the decision would be subject to appellate review." In November 1975, Sen. Edward M. Kennedy (D Mass.) introduced a bill to create a federal sentencing commission. The Kennedy bill is expected to be incorporated in an omnibus Senate bill (S 1) to reform and revise the federal criminal code. S 1 is being considered by the Senate Judiciary Committee.

Problems Caused by Overcrowding of Facilities

Ironically, the "get tough" policy of the Ford administration has come at a time when prison officials around the country are being forced to release minor offenders because of overcrowd-

---

[11] Jessica Mitford, *Kind and Usual Punishment* (1970), p. 83.
[12] Marvin E. Frankel, *Criminal Sentences* (1972), p. 88.

American Prison Population

State	Number of Inmates Jan. 1, 1975	Number of Inmates Jan. 1, 1976	Per Cent Change
Alabama	4,260	4,420	4
Alaska	322	349	9
Arizona	2,072	2,534	22
Arkansas	2,007	2,338	17
California	24,780	20,007	−20
Colorado	1,968	2,104	7
Connecticut	2,805	3,060	9
Delaware	555	701	27
District of Columbia	1,321	1,538	16
Florida	11,420	15,709	38
Georgia	9,772	11,067	13
Hawaii	310	366	18
Idaho	536	593	11
Illinois	6,672	8,110	22
Indiana	4,360	4,392	1
Iowa	1,520	1,857	22
Kansas	1,421	1,696	19
Kentucky	2,958	3,257	10
Louisiana	4,759	4,774	0.3
Maine	527	643	22
Maryland	6,128	6,606	8
Massachusetts	2,047	2,278	11
Michigan	8,702	10,882	25
Minnesota	1,370	1,724	26
Mississippi	2,117	2,429	15
Missouri	3,754	4,150	11
Montana	344	377	10
Nebraska	1,254	1,259	0.4
Nevada	854	893	5
New Hampshire	285	302	6
New Jersey	4,824	5,277	9
New Mexico	979	1,118	14
New York	14,387	16,056	12
North Carolina	11,997	12,486	4
North Dakota	173	205	19
Ohio	9,326	11,451	23
Oklahoma	2,867	3,435	20
Oregon	2,001	2,442	22
Pennsylvania	6,768	7,054	4
Rhode Island	550	594	8
South Carolina	4,422	6,100	38
South Dakota	277	372	34
Tennessee	3,779	4,569	21
Texas	16,833	18,934	12
Utah	575	696	21
Vermont	387	393	2
Virginia	5,635	6,092	8
Washington	2,698	3,063	14
West Virginia	940	1,213	29
Wisconsin	2,591	3,055	18
Wyoming	222	384	73
States and D.C.	203,431	225,404	
U.S. Bureau of Prisons	22,361	24,134	8
Total	**225,792**	**249,538**	**11***

* Average state and federal

SOURCE: *Corrections Magazine*

Parole and Probation Defined

Parole and probation are probably two of the best known but least understood concepts in the correctional system. *Parole* is the release of a prisoner to serve the remainder of his sentence in the community, under certain restrictions and requirements. *Probation* is a substitute for prison custody. A person granted probation does not have to serve any part of his sentence, but is returned to the community immediately after conviction.

Although the same agency usually supervises both parolees and probationers, the two processes have different origins. Parole is the administrative act of an executive agency, while probation is a function of the courts.

ing. In October 1975, the Georgia Board of Pardons ordered the immediate release of 427 prisoners convicted of simple theft or burglary and moved up the release dates of over 4,000. Georgia prisons have been so crowded that some inmates have had to sleep on mattresses on the floor. In South Carolina, another state suffering from prisoner overpopulation, officials have had to make greater use of early parole for young offenders. And in North Carolina, the legislature has acted to ease overcrowding by allowing the early release of prisoners serving less than a one-year sentence.

The worst crowding problems have occurred in southern states. Arkansas has had to house prisoners in house trailers. Virginia plans to convert a warehouse into a prison facility, and South Carolina is considering the use of abandoned schools and factories. For a while, Louisiana corrections officials thought of buying a mothballed Navy ship to house inmates. However, according to Richard Crane, an attorney for the Louisiana Department of Corrections, the state has abandoned the idea. Instead, state officials are planning to renovate a mental hospital and construct two new prisons. The new prisons are scheduled to be completed in about one year.

Several court rulings in the South have focused attention on the seriousness of prison overcrowding. In May 1975, Judge Charles R. Scott of the U.S. District Court in Jacksonville, Fla., ordered Florida officials to reduce the state's prison population to normal levels within one year. In 1965, Florida's prison population was less than 7,000. By December 1975 it had reached almost 16,000. Prisoners have been housed in tents and converted warehouses. "A free domocratic society cannot cage inmates like animals or stack them like chattels in a warehouse and expect them to emerge as decent, law-abiding, contributing members of the community," Scott said. Louisiana and Mississippi are also under federal court order to relieve overcrowding and improve prison living conditions.

72

On Jan. 13, 1976, U.S. District Judge Frank M. Johnson Jr. declared Alabama's state prison system "barbaric and inhumane" and ordered state officials to implement 44 major changes. These included giving every prisoner at least 60 square feet of living space and "three wholesome and nutritious meals per day." Alabama Gov. George C. Wallace said the state would appeal the federal ruling. The governor indicated that $50 million to $100 million would be necessary to implement the order, and that the state legislature would probably have to increase taxes. "Federal judges are very good about telling you how to spend money, but they don't tell you how to raise the money," Wallace said. The governor also accused the federal government of trying to create a "resort like" atmosphere in the Alabama prison system—a charge Judge Johnson denied.

Similar court orders have been issued to city officials in charge of municipal jails. In Washington, D.C., U.S. District Court Judge William B. Bryant has repeatedly urged authorities to ease overcrowding at the 100-year-old District of Columbia Jail, where teams of inspectors have found over 1,000 housing violations. In November 1975, Judge Bryant ordered the appointment of a compliance officer to implement a reduction in the inmate population and upgrade the physical facilities. In New York City, a series of rulings by U.S. District Court Judge Morris E. Lasker led to the closing of the Manhattan House of Detention, popularly known as the Tombs, in December 1974. On Jan. 6, 1976, Judge Lasker ordered an end to the practice of confining two inmates in one-man cells for more than 30 days at the House of Detention for Men on Rikers Island. In November 1975, the prisoners at Rikers Island had staged a 17-hour riot in protest of living conditions there.

Rise in Crime and the Demand for Punishment

Carlson, the U.S. Bureau of Prisons director, said in his Birmingham speech, that until recently, penal experts had expected the prison population decline of the late 1960s and early 1970s to continue. But, he said, the prison population is climbing and is expected to go even higher in the immediate future. The nation's leading barometer of serious crime, the Crime Index[13] compiled by the Federal Bureau of Investigation from local police reports, rose 38 per cent from 1969 through 1974. The trend continued upward during the first nine months of 1975, the latest period for which crime statistics have been compiled. Crime was 11 per cent higher than in the same nine months a year earlier.

According to a recent survey by *Corrections Magazine*, the

---

[13] The index takes into account what the FBI considers "serious" crimes—murder, rape, robbery, aggravated assault, burglary, larceny, and motor vehicle theft.

combined population of state and federal prisons reached a record high of 249,538 at the beginning of 1976, an 11 per cent increase over a year earlier *(see table, page 71).* The only state that did not report an increase was California. Its decrease was caused by new, more liberal parole guidelines. The magazine attributed the overall increase in prison population to public demand for harsher sentencing. Commenting on the survey, Lloyd Ohlin, professor of criminology at Harvard Law School, said that "what we're seeing is a massive counterattack" against programs, like probation, that allow offenders to remain in the community. "The climate has shifted in favor of punishment," he added.

In an article written for the *American Journal of Correction,* John J. Flanagan, professor in the School of Social Work at the University of Wisconsin, listed several reasons why he thought the prison population would continue to increase. They included hardening public attitudes and rising crime caused by unemployment and inflation. Flanagan also noted that the number of persons in the 20 to 30 age bracket, which includes a disproportionately high share of criminal offenders, is expected to peak in 1985.[14]

Changing Philosophy of Corrections

HISTORICALLY, the idea of imprisonment as a form of punishment is fairly new. Before the 19th century, floggings, brandings and executions were much more common than incarceration. In early Roman law, imprisonment as a form of punishment was forbidden. The Roman jurist Ulpian wrote: "Prison ought to be used for detention only, but not for punishment." During the Middle Ages, this legal principle was accepted throughout Europe, although it was violated in some instances. By the late 16th century, governments began placing juveniles, beggars and vagabonds in workhouses and houses of correction.

The word "penitentiary" is derived from the word "penitent" and reflects the 18th century notion that solitary confinement, rather than corporal punishment, would cure offenders of their criminal tendencies. The enlightened reformers professed the belief that mankind possessed the ability to change for the better and could be reformed through religious meditation. The

---

[14] "Imminent Crisis in Prison Populations," *American Journal of Correction,* November-December 1975, p. 20.

tenets of this philosophy were outlined in America in 1787 when Dr. Benjamin Rush delivered a paper on the modern prison system to a small group gathered in the Philadelphia home of Benjamin Franklin.

Rush proposed: (1) that prisoners be classified according to housing assignments and treatment plans, (2) that the prison be supported by inmate labor, and (3) that prisoners be confined for an indeterminate period and released upon showing evidence of their progress toward rehabilitation.[15] In 1790, the Philadelphia Society for Alleviating the Miseries of Public Prisons, now known as the Pennsylvania Prison Society, was instrumental in obtaining passage of state legislation to reorganize the Walnut Street Jail in Philadelphia on the basis of hard labor and isolation. The Walnut Street Jail became the first penitentiary in the United States.

"...The degree of civilization in a society can be judged by entering its prisons."

—Dostoyevsky, 1862.

The principle of solitary confinement was emphasized even more strongly by the creators of the Eastern State Penitentiary which opened on Cherry Hill in Philadelphia in 1829. Here, prisoners were detained in small cells and completely isolated except for an occasional visit. Prisoners were allowed to work in their cells on weaving, carpentry, shoemaking or other crafts.

In New York, state officials formulated a different philosophy of prison management, and allowed the prisoners to work with each other during the daytime. Under this Auburn system—named for the prison where it went into effect—the inmates were still required to remain silent at all times. The Boston Prison Discipline Society endorsed the Auburn Prison system by noting, "The unremitted industry, the entire subordination and subdued feeling of the convicts, has probably no parallel among any equal number of criminals." The report continued: "In their solitary cells, they spend the night, with no other book but the Bible; and at sunrise they proceed in military order, under the eye of turnkeys, in solid columns, with the lock

---

[15] Alan M. Dershowitz, "Criminal Sentencing in the United States: An Historical and Conceptual Overview," *The Annals*, January 1976, p. 125.

march, to their workshops; thence in the same order, at the hour of breakfast, to the common hall...."[16] Although the Pennsylvania and Auburn systems of prison management ultimately failed because of high operational costs and a high rate of insanity among the prisoners, both systems had wide influence.

Emergence of Modern Concept of Rehabilitation

One of the earliest forerunners of the modern parole system was developed at Norfolk Island, an English penal colony off the east coast of Australia, between 1840 and 1844. This "mark" system emphasized training and study rather than solitude. Prisoners worked toward their release by earning marks or credits through good behavior and hard work. The system was refined later in the 1800s by Sir Walter Crofton, director of prisons in Ireland. Irish prisoners served the first part of their sentence in isolation and then were given the opportunity to work with other prisoners. Six months before their scheduled release, inmates spent time in smaller institutions with unarmed guards and were given more freedom and responsibility. A prisoner who misbehaved during this period could be sent back to confinement. The Irish system was imitated in many ways by the reformatories that emerged in the United States during the late 19th century for juveniles and first offenders.

One of the leaders of this reformatory movement was Zebulon Brockway, superintendent of the Elmira Reformatory in New York and a staunch advocate of the indeterminate sentence. In an address to the first Congress of the National Prison Association[17] in 1870, titled "The Ideal of a True Prison System," Brockway rejected the punitive purposes of prisons in favor of reformation and rehabilitation. If prisons were to concentrate on these goals, he said, society would be better protected from crime. In accordance with his thinking, the congress adopted a Declaration of Principles calling for a variety of reforms. Reformatory "cures" were to be tailored to the individual criminal, who was not to be released until rehabilitated.

A year earlier, in 1869, Brockway had succeeded in persuading Michigan to enact the nation's first indeterminate sentencing law, although it applied only to prostitutes. New York followed in 1877 with a broader law, and by 1922 a total of 37 states had adopted indeterminate sentencing. The rehabilitative ideal, as expressed by the 1870 congress, formed the basis of prison management in the 20th century until now. Training and education for employment, not penitence in solitary confinement, were to be the means of reform. Whereas

---

[16] Quoted by Kenneth Lamott, "Is Prison Obsolete?" *Horizon*, summer 1975, p. 44.
[17] Now the American Correctional Association.

before, criminals were viewed as evil sinners who chose a life of crime of their own free will, after 1870 they came to be seen as individuals lacking certain qualities, opportunities and advantages.

Gradually, prisons began to develop what is now often referred to as the "medical model." Crime became associated with disease and inmates were viewed as patients. Psychiatrists, psychologists and social workers were added to prison staffs. Prison administrators began to use medical terminology, implying that criminals could be cured with the proper diagnosis and treatment. Criminologists Norval Morris and James Jacobs have written:

> The search for a "cure" for the criminal has sometimes even taken us beyond the bounds of civilized treatment. Drugs, electroshock therapy, sterilization, and even psychosurgery have all been used to "reform" the prisoner's behavior. What little evidence there is has shown that behavior is seldom changed for the better and that the prisoner's hostility and aggression are often increased when subjected to such treatments. In addition, such techniques have often been misused for purposes of punishment in order to reinforce prison rules, rather than for genuine rehabilitative purposes.[18]

Inmate Protests in Past Decade; Attica Uprising

In the 1960s and early 1970s, the rehabilitative approach to criminal corrections began to show obvious signs of breaking down; riots in protest of prison life erupted across the country.[19] The most famous occurred at the Attica (N.Y.) Correctional Facility on Sept. 9, 1971, when about 1,200 out of 2,245 prisoners overwhelmed 39 guards and held them as hostages. The rebelling inmates demanded 28 specific reforms of prison conditions, all of which the correction commissioner agreed to seek or implement. But the negotiations bogged down on three demands. They were the ouster of the warden, a guarantee of legal amnesty for the rebellious inmates and their free passage to a "non-imperialistic" country.

The negotiations reached an impasse on these points Sept. 12, and those involved in the talks, warning that bloodshed was likely, urged Gov. Nelson A. Rockefeller to come to the scene. The governor refused, saying his appearance at the prison would do no good. Early the next morning, an assault force of 200 state troopers with helicopter support and National Guardsmen in reserve, stormed the facility and quelled the rebellion.

This action brought death, either immediately or later, to 43 persons. It was the highest death toll in an American prison riot

---

[18] Public Affairs Committee, "Proposals for Prison Reform," Public Affairs Pamphlet No. 510, 1974, p. 13. The Public Affairs Committee is a non-profit educational organization.

[19] See "Racial Tensions in Prisons," *E.R.R.*, 1971 Vol. II, pp. 801-820.

since 1930, when 317 inmates who were locked in their cells at the Ohio State Penitentiary perished in a fire set by other rioting inmates. The Ohio State Penitentiary was again the scene of disorder in 1968. Five convicts were shot to death there when 500 National Guardsmen and policemen charged the prison to quell a riot by 500 prisoners.

One result of the prison riots during this period was that prison officials began to pay more attention to the importance of individual prisoner rights. Pennsylvania, for example, in 1971 issued a "bill of rights" for prisoners, insuring their right to be treated with fairness and dignity. Patterned after the Standard Minimum Rules for the Treatment of Prisoners adopted by the United Nations in 1955, the administrative directive provided for the separation of tried and untried prisoners, and the prohibition of corporal punishment.

Judicial Expansion of Prisoners' Legal Rights

The idea that prisoners have rights has found legal expression only in recent years. A Virginia court ruled in 1871 that a prisoner was a "slave of the state" who "not only forfeited his liberty, but all his personal rights except those which the law in its humanity accords to him." As late as 1948, the Supreme Court held that "lawful incarceration brings about the necessary withdrawal or limitation of many privileges and rights, a reaction justified by the considerations underlying our penal system."[20]

In contrast, the Supreme Court during its 1971-72 term ruled that (1) formal proceedings must be followed in revoking parole, (2) inmates are entitled to be given legal materials, (3) prison administrators must provide inmates with opportunities for religious worship, and (4) a person who is not mentally competent to stand trial for a criminal offense cannot be confined indefinitely. In 1974 the Court ruled that although a prisoner's rights "may be diminished by the needs and exigencies of the institutional environment, [he] is not wholly stripped of constitutional protections.... There is no iron curtain drawn between the Constitution and the prisons of this country."[21]

The National Advisory Commission on Criminal Justice Standards and Goals reported in 1973 that most judicial action expanding the rights of prisoners has come in the lower courts, particularly in federal district courts. "[I]t is in these courts that the 'hands off' doctrine has been either modified or abandoned altogether."[22] Several prisons have been held in violation of the

---

[20] *Price v. Johnston* (1948), 334 U.S. 266.
[21] *Wolff v. McDonnell* (1974), 418 U.S. 539.
[22] *Corrections,* National Advisory Commission on Criminal Justice Standards and Goals, Jan. 23, 1973, p. 19.

Major Prison Disturbances in the 1970s

Site	Date	Action
Soledad Prison (Salinas, Calif.)	Jan. 13, 1970	3 black convicts shot to death in racial fight between prisoners; white guard killed Jan. 16
Essex County Jail (Newark, N.J.)	April 27, 1970	200 inmates riot to protest prison conditions; about 90 rioted again on Nov. 27, 1970
Holmesburg Prison (Philadelphia)	July 4, 1970	29 guards and 84 inmates injured in riot with racial overtones
Tombs (New York City)	Oct. 2-5, 1970	Prisoners hold 26 hostages to protest overcrowding
Cummins Prison Farm (Grady, Ark.)	Nov. 20-22, 1970	Some 500 inmates riot, demanding separate quarters for black and white prisoners
San Quentin (near San Rafael, Calif.)	Aug. 21, 1971	6 persons, including black militant George Jackson and 3 guards, killed in alleged escape attempt
Attica Correctional Facility (Attica, N.Y.)	Sept. 9-13, 1971	43 persons, including 11 prison employees, killed in riot over prison conditions
Rahway State Prison (Woodbridge, N.J.)	Nov. 24-25, 1971	Inmates take six hostages in rebellion over prison conditions

Eighth Amendment ban on "cruel and unusual punishment," as were the overcrowded prisons in Alabama. In December 1975, for example, U.S. District Court Judge Alfonso J. Zirpoli ruled in San Francisco that the conditions and practices in San Quentin Prison's maximum security adjustment section amounted to cruel and unusual punishment.

Zirpoli ordered that the use of tear gas and neck chains be stopped unless the prisoner presented a "clear and immediate danger" of escaping or inflicting bodily harm. The judge also ordered that the outdoor exercise periods for the inmates be expanded. The federal ruling came as the result of a civil suit filed by six San Quentin inmates accused of murdering three guards and two inmates in the 1971 escape attempt at San Quentin in which black militant George Jackson was killed.

Critical Issues Facing Penologists

THE ACTIVE interest and involvement of prisoners in inmates-rights issues is a notable development. Today, prisoners are alerting the public to prison conditions through newspaper stories, books and lawsuits. One of the most revolutionary concepts to emerge is that of a prisoners' union. According to C. Ronald Huff, a social scientist at the University of California at Irvine, the most extensive union type of activity inside a prison was the "Ohio Prisoners' Labor Union." At its peak in 1973 and 1974, the union has since ceased to exist. Huff said this was partly because of conflicts between staff members outside the prison and union members inside.

The California Department of Corrections refused in early 1976 to let inmates organize "Inmate Representing Organizations," staffed by persons outside of prisons who would help prisoners prepare complaints and legal papers. The California Correctional Officers Association, an organization of prison guards, warned that they might strike if the plan was approved. California corrections officials had spent several months discussing the idea of an inmates union with "Prisoners' Union," the San Francisco organization which claims to represent approximately 20,000 convicts and ex-convicts around the country. Staff members perform a lobbying service for inmates by testifying on criminal legislative matters and acting as spokesmen for prisoners' rights. The organization supports three major goals: (1) an end to indeterminate sentencing, (2) establishment of labor rights for working prisoners, including the right to organize and bargain collectively, and (3) recognition of civil and human rights for all prisoners.[23]

The first goal—abolition of indeterminate sentencing—appears to be one on which most penologists agree. "The era of the indeterminate sentence...is quickly drawing to a close," wrote Alan M. Dershowitz, professor at Harvard Law School, in January 1976. "Reaction is beginning to set in."[24] Dershowitz served on the Committee for the Study of Incarceration, composed of liberal lawyers, scholars and social scientists, and funded by the Field Foundation and the New World Foundation.

After four years of study, the committee concluded that rehabilitation was no longer a realistic goal of sentencing. In its

---

[23] John Irwin and Willie Holder, "History of the Prisoners' Union," *The Outlaw: Journal of the Prisoners' Union*, January-February, 1973, p. 1. Reprinted by C. Ronald Huff, "The Prisoners' Union: A Challenge for State Corrections," *State Government*, summer 1975, p. 147.

[24] Dershowitz, *op. cit*, p. 130.

Arkansas Prison Scandal

One of the nation's most disturbing prison scandals erupted in January 1968 when three human skeletons buried in crude coffins were unearthed at the Cummins Prison in Arkansas. A prison inmate, Reuben Johnson, identified one of the skeletons as that of Jake Jackson, a prisoner who had been listed in prison records as a 1946 escapee. Johnson told news reporters that he had helped bury Jackson and that he had witnessed the murders of 12 prisoners during his term at Cummins. Other Cummins inmates also reported they had witnessed beatings and killings.

A few weeks before the three bodies were discovered, Arkansas Gov. Winthrop Rockefeller had appointed Thomas O. Murton, a professor of criminology, state prison superintendent with instructions to reform the Arkansas penitentiaries. Murton publicly reported that political corruption existed in the state prison system, and that whips and an electrical torture device had been used to subjugate prisoners. Following the discovery of the skeletons, the governor dismissed the new superintendent and charged him with staging a publicity stunt.

A federal grand jury in 1969 indicted 15 former Arkansas prison officials on charges of torturing inmates. The former superintendent of the state's Tucker Intermediate Reformatory, Jim Bruton, was acquitted on eight counts of brutality but in 1970 pleaded no contest to the charge that he tortured inmates with electrical shocks. That same year, a federal district court in Arkansas declared that conditions in the state's penitentiary system were "so bad as to be shocking to the conscience of reasonably civilized people."

final report, published in February 1976 under the title *Doing Justice*, the committee recommended that instead of sentencing an offender according to his need for treatment, he should be sentenced according to the severity of his crime. The parole system would be abolished and the offender would be required to serve the full sentence. In this respect, the committee's plan echoes President Ford's proposal for mandatory sentencing in his 1975 message to Congress on crime.

The committee proposed that only those who commit serious crimes be sent to prison, and then only a few for more than three years. Most first offenders and petty thieves would be let go with only a warning from the judge. "We do not have inflated hopes about working wonders on the crime rate," said Charles Goodell, the chairman, a former member of Congress from New York. "If we're lucky, we may succeed in a modest reduction, but the main advantage of our proposals is that they produce a fairer system of punishment." Goodell said he believed that increasing the certainty of punishment is a greater deterrent to crime than increasing the severity.[25]

---

[25] Interview with Philip Nobile, *Midwest*, Chicago *Sun-Times* magazine, Jan. 11, 1976.

Not everyone in government or corrections work has given up on the idea of prisoner rehabilitation. The Task Force Committee on Correctional Problems, composed of prison officials from southern states, reported to the Southern Governors' Conference on Jan. 23, 1976:

> We acknowledge that the advocates of a "correctional," as contrasted with a "punitive," approach to offenders, often have oversold the case in the past; but we continue to be firmly of the conviction that the essential validity of a rehabilitative approach remains applicable.

In a survey of 84 of the nation's top correctional administrators, conducted by *Corrections Magazine*, 63 per cent of those responding said that some rehabilitation programs do have a positive effect on inmate behavior. Seventy-two per cent were opposed to eliminating indeterminate sentences.

It is generally agreed that correctional programs achieve their immediate objective; that is, they do teach illiterate inmates how to read and write, and they do turn out competent mechanics, welders, plumbers, electricians and other skilled workers. According to tests given to inmates after they underwent counseling and therapy, some offenders showed less hostility and more constructive attitudes. None of this has been disputed. The controversy is whether rehabilitation programs reduce recidivism.

Several corrections administrators have criticized Robert Martinson's conclusion *(see p. 68)* that rehabilitation has not reduced the rate at which released offenders return to criminal activity. They point out, for example, that his study includes only those programs conducted before 1967—before many rehabilitation projects were properly staffed and administered. They have noted that the Law Enforcement Assistance Administration, a federal agency that allocates money for rehabilitatiion programs of law enforcement and criminal justice, was not created until 1968. Martinson has acknowledged that his information was limited.

Testing of Revised Ideas in New Federal Prison

Regardless of whether rehabilitation reduces recidivism, most penal experts agree that correction officials should abandon the idea that prisoners are sick individuals who can be cured with proper treatment. Norman A. Carlson, the federal prisons director, has written: "Corrections remains primarily an art and only partially a science. Consequently, we cannot prescribe with precision the treatment, and it is painfully obvious that we cannot guarantee a cure."[26]

[26] "The Federal Prison System: Forty-five Years of Change," *Federal Probation*, June 1975.

David Fogel, director of the Illinois Law Enforcement Commission, argues in his book *We Are the Living Proof* that release dates should not be contingent upon behavior in prison. He recommends short, fixed sentences and elimination of parole boards. And he stresses that the participation of prisoners in rehabilitation programs be placed on a voluntary basis. Another criminologist who contends that "choice" should be an integral part of prisoner rehabilitation is Norval Morris of the University of Chicago. Morris believes that the "medical model" should be discarded for two reasons: (1) how a criminal behaves while in prison is not indicative of how he will behave if released to the community, and (2) psychological change cannot be coerced. On May 14, 1976, the U.S. Bureau of Prisons is scheduled to dedicate a new correctional institution at Butner, N.C., that will be administered along the lines prescribed by Morris in his book *The Future of Imprisonment.*

Once at Butner, inmates will be allowed to choose which, if any, psychological treatment projects they want to participate in. All prisoners will be required to work, but they will be given the freedom to choose what they do and when they will do it. Training programs will include optical lens grinding, television production and even police science. To eliminate any uncertainty over release dates, Butner inmates will have definite parole dates set in advance. The new federal prison, with its white concrete buildings, has the look of a modern college *(see above).* It is divided into seven single-story living units, each housing 50 inmates. There will be no bars on the windows. In fact, prisoners will have keys to their private rooms.

The U.S. Bureau of Prisons is optimistic about the new approach and hopes it can be adopted elsewhere. At the same time, prison officials realize there is no panacea for solving the nation's prison problem. Caught between the public's call for longer sentencing and the explosive potential of overcrowded prisons, they are still searching for answers.

Selected Bibliography

Books

Clark, Ramsey, *Crime in America,* Simon and Schuster, 1970.

Frankel, Marvin E., *Criminal Sentences,* Hill and Wang, 1972.

Mitford, Jessica, *Kind and Usual Punishment,* Alfred A. Knopf, 1973.

Morris, Norval, *The Future of Imprisonment,* The University of Chicago Press, 1974.

Wicker, Tom, *A Time To Die,* Ballantine Books, 1975.

Wilson, James Q., *Thinking About Crime,* Basic Books, 1975.

Articles

Anderson, George M., "Jails, Lockups and Houses of Detention," *America,* Jan. 10, 1976.

Conrad, John P., "The Need for Prison Reform," *Current History,* August 1971.

"Crime: A Case for More Punishment," *Business Week,* Sept. 15, 1975.

Dershowitz, Alan M., "Criminal Sentencing in the United States," *The Annals* of the American Academy of Political and Social Science, January 1976.

——"Let the Punishment Fit the Crime," *The New York Times Magazine,* Dec. 28, 1975.

Fersch, Ellsworth, "When to Punish, When to Rehabilitate," *American Bar Association Journal,* October 1975.

Flanagan, John J. "Imminent Crisis in Prison Populations," *American Journal of Correction,* November-December 1975.

Glaser, Daniel, "Achieving Better Questions: A Half Century's Progress in Correctional Research," *Federal Probation,* September 1975.

Huff, C. Ronald, "The Prisoners' Union: A Challenge for State Corrections," *State Government,* summer 1975.

Lamott, Kenneth, "Is Prison Obsolete?" *Horizon,* summer 1975.

Serrill, Michael S., "Is Rehabilitation Dead?" *Corrections Magazine,* May-June 1975.

Trial: The National Legal Newsmagazine, March 1975 entire issue.

Studies and Reports

Advisory Task Force to Study Local Jails for Virginia State Crime Commission, "Report," December 15, 1975.

Editorial Research Reports, "Racial Tensions in Prisons," 1971 Vol. II, p. 799; "Rehabilitation of Prisoners," 1965 Vol. II, p. 741.

National Advisory Commission on Criminal Justice Standards and Goals, *Corrections,* Jan. 23, 1973.

Robinson, William H., et al., "Prison Population and Costs," Congressional Research Service, Library of Congress, April 24, 1974.

United States General Accounting Office, "Department of Labor's Past and Future Role in Offender Rehabilitation," Aug. 7, 1975.

CRIMINAL RELEASE SYSTEM

by

John Hamer

June 18
1 9 7 6

Editor's Note: Updated statistics on the number of state and federal prisoners, as discussed on p. 103, are found in the editor's note preceding the report "Reappraisal of Prison Policy."

CRIMINAL RELEASE SYSTEM

I N WASHINGTON, D.C., in early April, an 18-year-old youth was charged with the murder of a 35-year-old man in an apparent hold-up attempt. Two months earlier the suspect had been released without bond after allegedly trying to rob a woman at gunpoint, and over the past three years had been convicted of armed robbery, shoplifting, grand larceny and burglary.

In Los Angeles earlier this year, an 18-year-old was charged with assault and robbery of an 85-year-old woman. The youth, authorities discovered, was already out on parole for the second-degree murder of another elderly woman in the same neighborhood in 1974.

In Baltimore, a criminal with a record of nearly 20 arrests over the last dozen years was arrested for burglary and released on personal recognizance. Within the next six months he was arrested for mail larceny and released on recognizance, arrested on two charges of burglary and released on recognizance, arrested for attempted burglary and released on bond. Finally he pleaded guilty to one burglary after the other charges were dropped.

These cases are only a few examples of what has come to be known across the nation as "revolving door" justice. Individuals with long records of past criminal activity again and again are being rearrested for new crimes committed while they are out on bail or personal recognizance awaiting trial, on probation, on parole, on furlough, or on some other form of release. Repeated instances of such cases have outraged many Americans who are already deeply concerned about the increase in crime over the past several years. "Almost everywhere you go, you hear people complain," stated a recent summary of the problem in *U.S. News & World Report*. "Criminals arrested one day are often back on the street the next day, committing new crimes even before they can be tried for their past crimes. Many arrested as criminals are never brought to trial. When tried, relatively few are convicted. Even when convicted, few are sent to prison."[1]

---

[1] "'Revolving Door' Justice—Why Criminals Go Free," *U.S. News & World Report*, May 10, 1976, p. 36.

Many citizens and public officials are calling for tougher measures to combat crime, demanding that more criminals be locked up and given longer sentences. Almost all persons involved with the criminal justice system—police, judges, prosecutors, defense attorneys, bail agents, probation officials, parole officers, and others—have been feeling the heat as the public and the news media focus on particular abuses and broader problems. Everyone wants to know what has gone wrong and what can be done about it.

All this has stimulated a reexamination of the criminal justice and release systems, but it has produced few answers and no panaceas. Thoughtful analysts have concluded that the blame cannot be placed on any one element of the system, for many are at fault. There is growing agreement that much of what has been tried in good faith in the past simply has not worked, and that new methods and procedures must be developed. Central to the debate is the nagging problem that weakens the entire system of criminal justice and maddens countless citizens—the inability to keep known criminals off the streets.

Scarcity of Statistics for Evaluating the System

"[I]f we accept the premise that the criminal justice system exists primarily for the purpose of preventing, controlling, and reducing crime, we ought first to know how much crime actually occurs," wrote Richard A. McGee, president of the American Justice Institute, in a recent issue of *Trial* magazine. *"Unfortunately, we do not and never have known the complete answer to this question."* [Italics in the original.] The FBI's *Uniform Crime Reports*, the best-known source of information about crime in the United States, are based on police statistics of known crimes and arrests in seven categories—homicide, rape, robbery, aggravated assault, burglary, larceny and auto theft. They form the FBI's "index" of serious crime.

However, recent polls and studies of crime victims have indicated that only about 65 per cent of the robberies, 30 per cent of the burglaries and 25 per cent of the rapes are ever reported to the police. Homicides and car thefts generally are reported, but in the other categories the actual amount of crime may be far greater than official statistics show. "Experts have estimated that there are 13,000,000 crimes committed annually in the United States," wrote Gary F. Glenn, a statistics officer in the New York City Police Department, in a recent issue of *The Police Chief.*[2] But only about half of those crimes are ever reported.

---

[2] "Crime *Does* Pay!" *The Police Chief,* January 1976, p. 53.

Moreover, Glenn continued, fewer than one million adult criminals are incarcerated annually. In 1970, for example, it is estimated that 5.5 million "index" crimes were committed in 4,088 cities throughout the United States. About 3 million of these were reported to the police, resulting in only 1.5 million arrests. Of those arrested, only 114,209 were found guilty. "According to these statistics, only 2 per cent of these criminal offenders were found guilty as charged," Glenn wrote.

To evaluate the American criminal release system, it would help further to have reliable statistics not only on the number of persons arrested, but on what happens to them through various stages of the criminal justice system. But McGee wrote in *Trial* magazine: "To the best of this writer's knowledge, complete information based on follow-up actions or transactions with each offender arrested have not been routinely collected, classified, and published in any state or major subdivision of a state anywhere in this country." Nor are there any comprehensive statistics on criminal repeaters in the United States, although FBI studies have shown that up to 65 per cent of those arrested for federal crimes are rearrested within a few years of their release.[3]

One effort to compile comprehensive follow-up data on arrested offenders was made by the California Department of Justice's Bureau of Criminal Statistics. It developed a computerized system that includes the records of persons arrested for felonies and follows their cases through the criminal justice system. In 1974, the most recent year for which complete figures are available, there were 1,485,000 arrests in California, including 400,000 felonies. From those felony arrests a sample of 95,000 cases from four populous counties—Los Angeles, Orange, San Diego and San Bernadino—was taken and then narrowed to a base of 1,000 to make the figures more comprehensible. The results showed that more than half of those arrested were not convicted, fewer than 15 per cent were convicted of felonies, and only 10 per cent actually served time in jail or prison.[4]

A similar study was conducted for *U.S. News & World Report* in cooperation with the Institute for Law and Social Research in Washington, D.C. It found that two-thirds of the persons arrested for serious crimes in the nation's capital were not con-

---

[3] Barbara Puls, "Recidivism Statistics," Congressional Research Service, Library of Congress, May 1, 1975, p. 22.

[4] "A Description of the Offender-Based Transaction Statistics System, A Preliminary Report, 1974," California Department of Justice, Bureau of Criminal Statistics, December 1975. *See box, p. 444.*

Disposition of 1,000 California Felony Arrests, 1974

575 were not convicted:
   109 were released by the police
   164 were released because the prosecutor filed no complaint
   302 were dismissed, acquitted, remanded to juvenile court, had charges reduced to misdemeanors and not convicted, or dismissed on felony complaints in lower courts

425 were found guilty by plea or trial:
   236 were sentenced in the lower court on misdemeanor complaints
   42 were disposed of in lower courts on felony complaints
   147 were convicted of felonies and sentenced in Superior Court

Of the **147** convicted of felonies:
   74 were placed on probation with some jail time as a condition of sentence, and more than half served 6-12 months in jail
   36 received straight probation without jail time
   19 were sent to state prison with indeterminate sentences
    6 received civil commitments to the state narcotic rehabilitation center
    6 were turned over to the California Youth Authority because they were under age 21
    5 were sentenced to county jail without probation
    1 was committed to a state mental hospital

SOURCE: California Department of Justice; *Trial* magazine, March 1976

victed, and of the one-third who were convicted, only about one-half spent any time in jail or prison. It also found that 60 per cent of those arrested for felonies in Washington had prior criminal records; about 25 per cent were already out on probation, parole or some form of pretrial release. The study further found that from 1971 to 1975, only 7 per cent of those arrested for serious crimes accounted for 24 per cent of all such arrests; some were arrested as many as 10 times during that period.

Of *100* arrests in Washington, D.C., in 1974, the study found that in *24* cases the prosecutor declined to prosecute because of insufficient evidence, lack of witnesses or other reasons. In *40* cases, charges were dropped later by the prosecutor or dismissed by a judge. In *26* cases, the suspects pleaded guilty, often to a lesser charge. Only *10* cases actually went to trial, resulting in *3* acquittals and *7* convictions. Of those criminals convicted, *3* were released after being fined or placed on probation, while only 4 went to jail or prison. Of those incarcerated, the study predicted that two-thirds would be paroled when they first became eligible, usually after serving the minimum sentence. Even before they are paroled, many inmates will be released on temporary furloughs to work, study or visit, the study said. "Add up these figures, and it becomes apparent that on any given day countless numbers of criminals will be walking the streets, free to commit fresh crimes," the magazine concluded.

Chances for Release in a Complex Process

One reason that so many criminal suspects, defendants and convicts go free is that there are so many complicated steps in the criminal justice system, each providing an opportunity for release. Earl J. Silbert, U.S. Attorney for the District of Columbia, recently described the system of criminal justice in the nation's capital as a "non-system," characterized by "total fragmentation and inefficiency" of various agencies.[5] Many other large cities have similar problems. Moreover, different agencies often develop rivalries that work to the detriment of all. "[T]he various organizational entities within the criminal justice system tend to act independently of each other and often at cross purposes," wrote Ronald I. Weiner of American University's Center for the Administration of Justice.[6]

A look at the process of criminal justice shows why so many criminals drop through the cracks. First of all, police make arrests in less than half of the reported cases of serious crime. Police sometimes make bad arrests, violate the suspect's rights, or fail to come up with credible evidence or reliable witnesses. When defendants are arrested, they are fingerprinted and taken to a prosecutor, who "prefers"—files—initial charges. But sometimes complainants change their minds and decide not to press charges, or overburdened prosecutors simply decide to drop cases that might have been won.

If defendants are held, they are brought before a magistrate who (1) explains the charges against them, (2) decides if release is to be granted on bail or recognizance, (3) sets bail, if any, and (4) assigns defense counsel. There follows a preliminary hearing before a judge or a grand jury, followed by an official presentment (or indictment) of charges upon which defendants are arraigned and plead guilty or not guilty. It is estimated that 90

---

[5] Quoted in *The Washington Post*, April 10, 1976.
[6] "The Criminal Justice System at the Breaking Point," *Social Work*, November 1975, p. 437.

per cent of all criminal convictions are based on the defendant's own plea of guilty.[7]

However, many of these guilty pleas are the direct result of a process of negotiation known as plea bargaining—a pre-arraignment deal between the prosecution and the defense in which defendants are offered a lenient sentence if they agree to plead guilty, usually to a lesser charge, thus saving the state the time and expense of a trial.[8] Plea bargaining is a controversial practice that clearly allows many defendants to be released sooner, but it also allows the nation's courts to function without becoming hopelessly clogged. But even those who defend plea bargaining concede that it has serious flaws, and there have been widespread efforts in recent years to correct abuses of the practice while maintaining its benefits.

If defendants plead not guilty, a series of preliminary motions eventually lead to a trial, resulting in either acquittal or conviction. Upon conviction defendants are sentenced to probation, imprisonment or to pay fines, but they may appeal their convictions and sentences. Prosecutors, in contrast, are not permitted to appeal acquittals or light sentences. Defendants generally are released pending appeal if they were not convicted of violent crimes and are not considered dangerous to society.

"There is still another way for a defendant to gain his freedom after he has been apprehended," Gary F. Glenn wrote in *The Police Chief.* "In large cities, the overloaded courts and jails work for him, if he knows how to use them. If his lawyer knows how to constantly use procedural trickery in order to request postponements of a case, the complainant will continuously be brought into court simply to be told that there has been another postponement. Witnesses and complainants will sooner or later become weary of coming into court for adjournments and delays, especially when they lose a day's wages for each appearance. Once the witness or complainant fails to show up, a judge may simply throw the case out. All the odds are in favor of the criminal." In Washington, D.C., the average interval from time of arrest to the end of a trial is 181 days—about six months.

Controversy Over Bail and Pretrial Detention

Whether to confine or release arrested persons prior to trial is an issue that has aroused particularly strident debate in the field of criminal justice in recent years. In making a decision at

---

[7] Donald J. Newman, *Conviction: The Determination of Guilt or Innocence Without Trial* (1966), p. 3.

[8] See "Plea Bargaining," *E.R.R.*, 1974 Vol. I, pp. 427-446.

the initial hearing stage, the magistrate considers whether the defendant is likely to return voluntarily, the hardship or inconvenience that would face the defendant if confined, and—in some cases—the defendant's potential danger to the community. Obviously, this decision is of vital importance to defendants and to the public.

Defendants who are confined cannot live with or support their families, maintain community ties, or help with their own defense by searching for witnesses or evidence. Wrongly accused defendants are subjected to the squalor and hazards of jail, and possibly its criminalizing effects. Jailed defendants who ultimately are convicted may be placed on probation when sentenced—subjecting them to the irony of being jailed when presumed innocent and freed when found guilty. On the other hand, the public relies on the courts for protection when the decision to release or confine is made. If a released defendant fails to reappear for trial, the law is flouted. If a defendant commits new crimes while free, the community is mocked and endangered.

The most commonly used device to obtain a defendant's release pending trial and to guarantee his or her reappearance is posting bail, an old practice *(see p. 96)* whereby the court fixes an amount of money the defendant must put on deposit in order to be released. If the defendant shows up for all required court appearances, the entire amount is usually refunded; if not, forfeiture may result. In determining the amount of bail, the court generally considers the gravity of the offense, the strength of the case against the defendant, and the defendant's prior criminal record. The magistrate also may consider the defendant's background, community ties, financial status and character references.

Today most defendants make use of bail bonds, paying from 5 to 10 per cent of the bail to a commercial establishment which then posts a bond for the full amount with the court. Even so, a primary criticism of the bail system is that it discriminates against defendants on the basis of wealth. A study in New York, where the bail bond fee is 5 per cent, found that:

If bail set at	And defendant thus had to pay	Defendants unable to raise bail
$ 500	$ 25	25%
1,500	75	45
2,500	125	63

In 1967, the President's Commission on Law Enforcement and Administration of Justice (Crime Commission) concluded: "By and large, money bail is an unfair and ineffective device. Its glaring weakness is that it discriminates against poor defendants, thus running directly counter to the law's avowed purpose of treating all defendants equally."[9] Although by law bail is solely intended to insure a defendant's appearance at trial, it is often used by judges to keep criminals off the streets. This practice is of questionable legality and, some argue, of dubious effectiveness. Professional criminals or those involved with organized crime usually have little trouble making bail even though they may be as dangerous as indigent criminals or amateurs.

The Federal Bail Reform Act of 1966[10] stated that to the extent possible, defendants should be released on their own recognizance—also referred to as personal surety, nominal bond or personal recognizance—if the court determines that they are reliable enough to show up for subsequent court appearances. Judges are supposed to gather sufficient information about defendants to determine the risk of releasing them. They are authorized to release defendants to the custody of others, and to restrict their travel, association or abode. Procedures were established for the speedy review of bail decisions. Special provisions for capital cases and bail for convicted persons pending appeal permit judges to consider explicitly the element of danger in deciding whether to release an offender. Even so, information gathering is laborious and decision making is subjective. Experience has shown the public is seldom afforded reliable protection from criminal repeaters.

Problems Involved in Probation and Parole

Two of the most widely criticized elements of the criminal justice system are probation and parole. Probation is a sentence under which convicted offenders are released upon promise of good behavior and agreement to accept supervision and to abide by specific requirements, such as reporting to a probation officer or to the court regularly. Parole, in contrast, is granted after convicted criminals already have served part of their sentences in prison. They are released under certain conditions of conduct, movement and accountability, and remain in the community—under supervision—until their sentences have expired.

---

[9] Cited by the President's Commission on Law Enforcement and Administration of Justice in "The Challenge of Crime in a Free Society," February 1967, p. 131.

[10] See *1966 CQ Almanac*, pp. 572-575.

Probation—the most frequent sentence in the nation today—is generally regarded as having failed to achieve its primary objectives of protecting the community and rehabilitating offenders. "Formal probation for adults is a costly and frequently meaningless function," wrote Irving F. Reichert Jr., executive director of the San Francisco Bar Association, in a recent issue of *Judicature*. "The courts' expectations of adult probation services and supervision are unrealistically broad, and the caseloads borne by probation officers are impossibly heavy."[11]

The President's Crime Commission found that probation officers had so many cases assigned to them that their supervision typically consisted of a 10- to 15-minute interview once or twice a month. The situation today is no better and may be worse in some jurisdictions, according to probation authorities. Furthermore, many probation officers lack the training or resources to deal with the problems confronting their clients. These problems may include a background of poverty, ghetto living conditions, bad family life, inferior education, and peer group pressure to commit crime.

State and local governments are primarily responsible for administering probation programs, although the federal government provides funds and aid through the Law Enforcement Assistance Administration (LEAA), an agency established by the Omnibus Crime Control and Safe Streets Act of 1968.[12] But according to a recent survey by the General Accounting Office of probation in four U.S. counties,[13] the programs are not working effectively. "Probation systems are in crisis," the report stated. "To date, the LEAA's efforts have had little effect on improving probation systems."[14] Of some 1,200 probationers studied, about 55 per cent fled, had their probations revoked, or were convicted of new crimes.

Parole draws criticism for much the same reason that probation does—many parolees return to crime. Of the more than 200,000 men and women in federal and state prisons, about 70 per cent will be eligible for parole during the coming year. If past patterns continue, between 35 and 40 per cent of those eligible will be granted parole. However, many of those released will return to prison within a fairly short time. In 1974, a Citizens'

---

[11] "Why Probation Fails," *Judicature*, January 1976, p. 288.
[12] See *1968 CQ Almanac*, pp. 225-237.
[13] Maricopa County, Ariz.; Multnomah County, Ore.; Philadelphia County, Pa.; and King County, Wash.
[14] "State and County Probation: Systems in Crisis," report to Congress by the Comptroller General of the United States, May 27, 1976, p. i.

Inquiry on Parole and Criminal Justice was conducted in New York, headed by former Attorney General Ramsey Clark and Professor Herman Schwartz of the State University at Buffalo. It found that in a typical five-year period, half of the prisoners on parole commit a crime or violate parole rules. Eighty per cent of these persons are returned to prison.

Evolvement of Release Procedures

T HE PRACTICES of releasing suspected offenders to await a decision on their fate, and of releasing convicted offenders on certain conditions as part of their punishment, both date back to antiquity although they generally were not written into law until the Middle Ages. In 1275 the English Parliament enacted the Statute of Westminster, a bail law that codified common practices and attempted to standardize procedures. It contained a long list of bailable offenders and offenses, which grew longer and more detailed over the years so that the law of bail became quite cumbersome.

Many judges and magistrates evaded the statutes through various devices and kept bailable offenders locked up. In 1679, Parliament enacted a *habeas corpus* law that gave persons who had been detained swift access to other judges for a hearing. To counter the practice of setting extremely high bail to detain offenders, Parliament inserted a provision in the English Bill of Rights of 1689 stating that "excessive bail ought not to be required...." Johnny H. Killian of the Library of Congress wrote: "It was part of a three-pronged protection against pretrial detention. A series of statutes specified the types of offenders who were bailable; the *habeas corpus* statute gave prisoners access to judges who would follow those bail statutes; and the excessive bail guarantee prevented evasion of the statutes by stipulating reasonable bail."[15]

The Virginia Declaration of Rights, adopted in 1776, borrowed the English Bill of Rights' clause against excessive bail and fines. Almost identical language became part of the Constitution when the U.S. Bill of Rights was added. In addition to the constitutional clause, the Judiciary Act of 1789 provided that in federal cases: "[U]pon all arrests in criminal cases, bail shall be admitted, except where the punishment may be death, in which

---

[15] Johnny H. Killian, "Bail and Preventive Detention," a report by the American Law Division, Legislative Reference Service, Library of Congress, April 17, 1969, p. 4.

case it shall not be admitted but by the Supreme or a circuit court, or by a justice of the Supreme Court, or a judge of a district court, who shall exercise their discretion therein...." It is unclear whether Congress intended to guarantee the absolute right to bail for non-capital crimes, but three-fourths of the states today have constitutional provisions guaranteeing that right in state cases.

Probation and Juvenile Courts: Their Origins

Probation was originally designed to aid youthful and first offenders, who previously had been punished alongside adult criminals. In 1841 John Augustus, a Boston bootmaker and temperance advocate, posted bail for a man charged with drunkenness. Augustus helped the man get reestablished and went on to assist hundreds of adults and children accused of various offenses. About the same time in Birmingham, England, magistrates began imposing only token sentences and placing youthful offenders in the custody of their parents or masters for careful supervision. As this practice grew, it developed several common characteristics: suspension of sentence; recognition of good behavior; supervision of delinquents and convicts by benevolent volunteers and charitable organizations.

These practices evolved into a distinct institution in the latter half of the 19th century. In 1878 the Massachusetts legislature authorized the appointment of a paid probation officer to serve the Boston criminal court, and subsequent legislation made probation mandatory in all Massachusetts courts. In England, similar statutes were enacted, beginning in 1879. They culminated in the Probation of Offenders Act of 1907 which established salaried probation officers in all English criminal courts. "The eve of the 20th century may be considered as the turning point in the history of probation," an analyst wrote.[16] Before 1900 only five states had probationary laws; within a few decades nearly every state had them.

The juvenile court movement developed almost simultaneously with probation. In 1899 Minnesota enacted the first law providing for separate "juvenile probation"; Illinois passed a similar measure later the same year. A special court for the treatment of juveniles was soon established in Chicago for offenders through the age of 16. Delinquents were placed under the supervision of court-appointed probation officers, but were allowed to live at home during the probationary periods. "The juvenile court caused a transformation of the probationary

---

[16] N. S. Timasheff, "Probation in Contemporary Law: A Centennial Survey," *New York University Quarterly Law Review*, May 1941, p. 498.

system from a local to a national institution," stated a Library of Congress report. "Probation became an institution recognized not only by legislation effected in the states and territories, but by federal statutes as well."[17]

Introduction of Prisoner Parole and Furlough

The practice of parole also developed in the 19th century. The term comes from the French, *parole d'honneur*, "word of honor," a pledge by prisoners of war, in return for conditional freedom, not to try to escape or to bear arms against their captors. In the United States, a series of laws enacted in New York provided for indefinite sentences and parole with supervision and a return to custody for violation of parole rules. The Elmira (N.Y.) Reformatory, established in 1876, was the first institution to act as the center of an established parole system. By 1900 parole laws were in effect in nearly half of the states, and by 1922 the federal government and all but four states had enacted parole statutes. About 20 states today have full-time parole boards of three or more members, usually appointed by the governor, while other states have part-time or non-paid boards. The U.S. Board of Parole has eight full-time members appointed by the President.

Persons sentenced to federal prisons normally become eligible for parole after completion of one-third of their sentences. Although there are certain guidelines for determining parole eligibility, the granting or denial of parole remains largely within the discretion of the parole boards. The boards generally consider the nature of the crime committed and public attitudes toward the offense. In 27 states, those convicted of the most violent crimes—murder, rape or kidnapping—are banned from parole eligibility by state statutes.

Another method of criminal release that has won a place in the American correctional system in recent years is the furlough. Before a convict is granted parole, he or she may be given a temporary "trial run" in civilian society, usually under the care of a parent, spouse or other guardian. Furloughed prisoners generally must return to their penal institutions at night, on weekends, or after a predetermined number of days or weeks have elapsed. Although there have been some widely publicized abuses of convict furloughs, most jurisdictions insist that the experiment has been successful. In Massachusetts in 1974, 98.4 per cent of the furloughed prisoners returned on time; in Virginia in 1974, of 3,145 convicts granted furlough only 41—or 1.3 per cent—failed to meet the terms of their release.[18]

---

[17] "General Effects and Purposes of Probation and Parole in the United States," Legislative Reference Service, Library of Congress, Dec. 11, 1957, p. 4.

[18] "Furlough Convicts…Menace to Society or a Good Idea?" *U.S. News & World Report*, March 24, 1975, p. 65.

Proposals for Changing the System

AMERICA seems to be in the midst of a profound reappraisal of public attitudes toward crime and criminals, although the outcome is not yet clear. There is considerable agreement across the political spectrum on the need for careful revision of the criminal justice and release systems, but deep divisions remain as to the best way of making effective changes. Only a few years ago, there was a widespread and bitter debate across the nation between those (mostly liberals) who argued that the only way to reduce crime was to attack its "root causes"—poverty, racial discrimination, unemployment and other deprivations—and those (mostly conservatives) who insisted that the only way was to "get tough" with criminals—more police, more prisons, longer sentences and revival of the death penalty. Today both approaches are considered unrealistic for dealing with the problem at hand. Criminologists are trying to determine what does work sufficiently to make some difference.

James Q. Wilson of Harvard University, in his widely praised book *Thinking About Crime* (1975), contends that "society has not done as well as it could have in controlling crime because of erroneous but persistent views about the nature of man and the capacities of his institutions."[19] He points out that a 20 per cent reduction in U.S. robbery still would leave us with the highest robbery rate of almost any western nation, but would prevent about 60,000 robberies a year. "Yet a 20 per cent reduction is unlikely if we concentrate our efforts on dealing with the causes of crime or even if we concentrate on improving police efficiency," Wilson states. But such a reduction is possible by "incapacitating a larger fraction of the convicted serious robbers." Wilson argues that since most serious crime is committed by repeaters, priority should be given to separating repeat offenders from society through certain and prompt incarceration.

He describes an unpublished 1973 study by Shlomo and Reuel Shinnar of the City College of New York which concluded that if every person convicted of a serious offense were imprisoned for three years, the rate of serious crime would be only one-third what it is today. The reduction would be solely the result of incapacitation of known criminals, and might be even greater if the additional effects of deterrence and rehabilitation were con-

---

[19] *Thinking About Crime*, pp. 198-199.

sidered. These estimates are based on "uncertain data and involve assumptions that can be challenged," Wilson concedes. "But even assuming they are overly optimistic by a factor of two, a sizable reduction in crime would still ensue."

Wilson urges that the nation adopt a new sense of realism in dealing with crime, admitting that some things can be changed and some things cannot. It cannot alter the number of juveniles who first experiment with crime, he concludes, nor is it likely to lower the recidivism rate. And there is still uncertainty whether the police can apprehend significantly more criminals. But, he adds:

> We can certainly reduce the arbitrary and socially irrational exercise of prosecutorial discretion over whom to charge and whom to release, and we can most definitely stop pretending that judges know, any better than the rest of us, how to provide "individualized justice."

> We can confine a larger proportion of the serious and repeat offenders and fewer of the common drunks and truant children. We know that confining criminals prevents them from harming society, and we have grounds for suspecting that some would-be criminals can be deterred by the confinement of others.[20]

Disfavor With Indeterminate Sentencing, Parole

The concept of fixed sentencing, as opposed to indeterminate sentencing, is winning support. Indeterminate sentencing has fallen out of favor with many leading criminologists who say that it results in longer sentences than most judges would give, gives administrative authorities undue control over prisoners' lives, permits disparities in sentencing, and is psychologically damaging to prisoners who never know when they will be released and who are forced to play games with the system.

The real power to determine the length of convicted criminals' sentences rests with parole boards—the U.S. Board of Parole for federal prisoners or one of the state parole boards for those in state and local institutions. With the virtually nationwide acceptance of indeterminate sentences in this century, the parole boards—along with prosecutors and prison officials—make up, in effect, an administrative system for fixing sentences that has taken considerable power away from the courts. Parole boards are semi-autonomous agencies that operate within the federal and state justice departments; members are appointed by the executive branches and are seldom subject to public account-

---

[20] *Ibid.*, p. 208.

ability. Alvin J. Bronstein, director of the American Civil Liberties Union's national prison project, wrote:

> Ordinarily, a person sentenced to a fixed term of years becomes eligible for parole only after serving one-third of the term.... If the sentence is indeterminate, however, the prisoner theoretically is eligible for parole immediately.... In practice, then, the parole board, and not the judge, decides how long and under what conditions a prisoner will serve time.[21]

Parole boards generally have absolute discretion in granting or denying parole, with virtually no due process provisions governing their proceedings. Maurice Sigler, a former chairman of the U.S. Board of Parole, candidly expressed the burden of the job when he said: "We have this terrible power.... We sit up here playing God."[22] Parole boards commonly contend that opening up their deliberations to prisoners or to the public—in other words, granting due process—would interfere with their efforts to rehabilitate prisoners. However, this argument carries little weight today in the face of increasing evidence that rehabilitation is a myth, and that the central aim of American prisons during the last few decades—to rehabilitate prisoners—has been a dismal failure.[23]

"The era of the indeterminate sentence—of the administrative model of sentencing—is quickly drawing to a close," Alan Dershowitz, a professor of law at Harvard University, wrote recently. "Reaction is beginning to set in."[24] Similarly, Judge Marvin E. Frankel said in his book *Criminal Sentences: Law Without Order* (1973) that "indeterminate sentencing, as thus far employed and justified, has produced more cruelty and injustice than the benefits its supporters envisage." Frankel advocates a change "in favor of a definite sentence, known and justified on the day of sentencing (and probably much shorter than our sentences tend to run)."

Calls for 'Flat-Time' or Mandatory Sentences

In a message to Congress on crime in June 1975, President Ford proposed mandatory sentences for certain violent and serious crimes. The following November, Sen. Edward M. Kennedy (D Mass.) introduced legislation to impose a mandatory two-year minimum sentence for some violent street crimes and to create sentencing guidelines through a federal commission on sentencing.[25] And in February 1976, Attorney

---

[21] "Rules for Playing God," *The Civil Liberties Review*, summer 1974, pp. 117-118.
[22] Quoted by Bronstein, p. 118.
[23] See "Reappraisal of Prison Policy," *E.R.R.*, 1976 Vol. I, p. 185.
[24] "Criminal Sentencing in the United States: An Historical and Conceptual Overview," *The Annals* of the American Academy of Political and Social Science, January 1976, p. 130.
[25] See "Making Time Fit the Crime," *Trial*, March 1976, pp. 14-15.

General Edward H. Levi proposed that the federal parole system be abolished, the sentencing power of federal judges be reduced, and a permanent federal commission be created to set sentencing guidelines.

But support for fixed sentencing is by no means universal. "In the last analysis...it is extremely unlikely that either 'flat-time' or 'mandatory' sentencing will emerge as an acceptable general solution to the sentencing dilemma," Dershowitz wrote. "Flat-time sentencing is simply too extreme a remedy; by eliminating all flexibility and requiring judges to impose the identical sentence on every single defendant convicted under the same statute, flat-time sentencing threatens to create a system so automatic that it will produce major injustices of its own."[26] He maintained that it is impossible to come up with a single just sentence for all armed robbers or for all murderers, and that some degree of flexibility must remain. Mandatory minimum sentencing is not a complete solution either, Dershowitz argued, "since it deals only with discretion at the minimum end of the statutory spectrum and not with discretion at the maximum end."

Dershowitz favors a system of "presumptive sentencing" under which the legislature would set the minimum and maximum sentences for given crimes and also would decide what term a typical first offender should receive. Sentences would be increased by a fixed factor of, say, 25 per cent for each prior conviction on a defendant's record. The trial judge could raise or lower the sentence for mitigating or aggravating circumstances, also specified by the legislature. Any sentence that departed from the prescribed range would require appeals court review. The nature of parole boards also would be changed drastically—since they no longer would determine the length of indeterminate sentences, they could concentrate on referring inmates to special agencies for readjustment aid.

The vast majority of sentences for a given degree of crime would cluster about the legislatively prescribed presumptive sentence, Dershowitz believes. He also expects that under presumptive sentencing a far greater number of serious criminals would be imprisoned but that the median duration of their imprisonment would be reduced. "In the end," he concedes, "neither this nor any other solution to the sentencing dilemma will prove to be a panacea. Discretion and disparity

---

[26] "Let the Punishment Fit the Crime," *The New York Times Magazine*, Dec. 28, 1975, pp. 26-27.

will not be eliminated: Policemen will still decide whom to arrest; prosecutors will still engage in plea-bargaining and Presidents and governors will still pardon and commute. But a major source of discontent and unfairness will be regulated."

Dangers of Overcrowding Prisons and Courts

Another criticism of fixed sentences is that they would make the jails and prisons even more overcrowded than they are already. The combined population of federal and state prisons neared 250,000 early in 1976, an 11 per cent increase over the previous year. Edith E. Flynn, associate professor of criminal justice at Northeastern University, cited estimates that about $25-billion is needed to replace outmoded prisons and to construct additional institutions to alleviate the present level of overcrowding. "Given the state of the economy, and given the fact that neither Congress, state legislatures, nor cities and municipalities will appropriate the necessary funds that would make any significant dent in this construction backlog, the call for mandatory minimum sentences is nothing short of irresponsible," Flynn wrote.[27]

Also suffering from severe overcrowding are the court dockets. Many offenders are given light sentences in return for saving the system the trouble and cost of a trial. If judges are asked to impose sentences befitting the seriousness of the crime, they must have the time and capacity to handle all cases with careful deliberation. "If we were willing to make enormous increases in the budgets for our court systems, including prosecutors and public-defender officers, the pressure on prosecutors and judges for artificially low sentences would ease and mandatory minimum sentencing would have little significance," said James Vorenberg, a professor of law at Harvard University.[28] Police resources are large in comparison with those of prosecutors, courts and prisons, which is one reason that arrests far outnumber convictions.

Even so, many observers believe the courts could do a better job of protecting society if they concentrated on dangerous crimes and somehow were spared such burdensome tasks as handling routine traffic offenses. Another great need is for an information system that would enable law-enforcement officials to keep track of criminal repeaters and accused offenders. In many cities, according to William Hamilton, president of the Washington Institute for Law and Social Research, "record-

---

[27] "Turning Judges Into Robots?" *Trial*, March 1976, p. 20.
[28] Writing in *The New York Times*, Dec. 22, 1975.

District of Columbia Crime Bill

In 1970, Congress passed and President Nixon signed into law the District of Columbia Court Reform and Criminal Procedure Act, a massive anti-crime program for the nation's capital that contained far-reaching, sometimes experimental provisions for dealing with crime and criminals. Among the most controversial elements of the bill was its pretrial, or preventive, detention section. Previously, persons charged with non-capital federal offenses could be released on bail unless they were not likely to appear for trial, but judges were not authorized to consider the danger a defendant on bail could pose to the community.

The D.C. crime bill authorized pretrial detention of up to 60 days for persons charged with certain dangerous crimes when the court found no combination of release conditions that would assure the community's safety. The same detention was authorized for persons charged with certain crimes of violence who were drug addicts, who had been convicted of violent crimes within the previous 10 years, or who allegedly had committed the crime while free on bail, probation or parole.

Recently, however, there have been numerous cases of criminals committing new crimes while out on pretrial release, and the 1970 law has been criticized as ineffective. According to Bruce Beaudin, director of the District of Columbia Bail Agency, the law is not being used the way it was intended. Judges contend that prosecutors must make a specific motion to initiate a preventive detention hearing, but some prosecutors are reluctant to do so because the hearing procedures are burdensome and require prosecutors to lay out much of their case in advance. Judges have been setting high bail for dangerous defendants, but bail is often reduced by other judges on motion by the defense. This year after a series of violent crimes committed by defendants out on release, District of Columbia Superior Court judges voluntarily changed their procedures to ensure that more dangerous offenders would be held on pretrial detention.

keeping is so poor officials literally don't know what they're doing."[29] Richard A. McGee wrote in *Trial* magazine: "Every state needs a crime accounting system which records every single transaction within the total criminal justice system. It should be operated by an independent agency which also should be subject to periodic outside audit."

One city that has had some success in keeping habitual criminals off the streets is New Orleans. With the help of a grant from the Law Enforcement Assistance Administration's "career criminal program," the city police identified 18,000 persons with a record of five felony arrests or two felony convictions. If

---

[29] Quoted in *U.S. News & World Report*, May 10, 1976, p. 40.

rearrested, they were subjected to energetic prosecution. "There's a hard-core group of career criminals who are responsible for most serious crime, and I believe we can get to them," District Attorney Harry F. Connick has said. "If there was a way to rehabilitate them, I'd say, 'Fine, do it.' But I don't know of any, and until there is one that's effective, you've just got to separate those people from society."[30]

"Wicked people exist. Nothing avails except to set them apart from innocent people."

James Q. Wilson
Thinking About Crime (1975)

If the repeat offenders are consistently allowed to go free, and continually commit more crimes, there is a growing danger that public outrage will manifest itself in vigilantism or other harsh measures. Judge Harold H. Greene of the District of Columbia Superior Court has warned: "Faced with a choice between civil liberties accompanied by widespread disorder, on the one hand, and order even at the price of liberty, on the other, they [the public] have almost always chosen order. Thus, there is real danger that if something is not done soon to remedy the crime situation, popular anger and frustration will find outlets in ways that none of us will like or appreciate."[31] Much of the American public today believes that the criminal release system favors offenders over victims. But the public almost certainly will take steps to secure its safety sooner or later, one way or another.

---

[30] Quoted by Michael Putney, *The National Observer*, May 22, 1976.

[31] Quoted by Laurin A. Wollan Jr., "Coping With Crime in Tomorrow's Society," *The Futurist*, June 1976, p. 127.

Selected Bibliography

Books

Frankel, Marvin E., *Criminal Sentences: Law Without Order*, Hill and Wang, 1973.
Ohlin, Lloyd E. (ed.), *Prisoners in America*, Prentice-Hall, 1973.
Von Hirsch, Andrew, *Doing Justice: The Choice of Punishment*, Hill and Wang, 1976.
Wilson, James Q., *Thinking About Crime*, Basic Books, 1975.

Articles

Bronstein, Alvin J., "Rules for Playing God," *The Civil Liberties Review*, summer 1974.
Dershowitz, Alan, "Let the Punishment Fit the Crime," *The New York Times Magazine*, Dec. 28, 1975.
Flynn, Edith E., "Turning Judges Into Robots?" *Trial*, March 1976.
Glenn, Gary F., "Crime *Does* Pay!" *The Police Chief*, January 1976.
Kress, Jack M.. "Progress and Prosecution," *The Annals* of the American Academy of Political and Social Science, January 1976.
McGee, Richard A., "Taking Factual Aim at the Crime Myths," *Trial*, March 1976.
Reichert, Irving F. Jr., "Why Probation Fails," *Judicature*, January 1976.
" 'Revolving Door' Justice—Why Criminals Go Free," *U.S. News & World Report*, May 10, 1976.
Weiner, Ronald I., "The Criminal Justice System at the Breaking Point," *Social Work*, November 1975.
Wollan, Laurin A. Jr., "Coping With Crime in Tomorrow's Society," *The Futurist*, June 1976.

Studies and Reports

Committee for Economic Development, "Reducing Crime and Assuring Justice," June 1972.
Doyle, Charles, "Bail in the United States," Legislative Reference Service, Library of Congress, July 23, 1969.
Editorial Research Reports, "Reappraisal of Prison Policy," 1976 Vol. I, p. 185; "Plea Bargaining," 1974 Vol. I, p. 427; "Police Innovation," 1974 Vol. I, p. 283; "Reform of the Courts," 1970 Vol. I, p. 403.
General Accounting Office, "State and County Probation: Systems in Crisis," May 27, 1976.
Killian, Johnny H., "Bail—Preventive Detention," Legislative Reference Service, Library of Congress, Sept. 4, 1969.
National Advisory Commission on Criminal Justice Standards and Goals, final report (seven volumes), 1973.
President's Commission on Law Enforcement and Administration of Justice, "The Challenge of Crime in a Free Society," February 1967.

Politics and the Federal Courts

by

Mary Costello

**June 24
1 9 7 7**

Editor's Note: As of July 7, 1978, House and Senate conferees had only one major problem left to resolve on a bill that would add 152 new judges to the federal court system. Conferees had yet to agree on whether the fifth circuit court of appeals, a southern court serving six states and the Canal Zone, should be split in two. Resolution of this dispute will determine the fate of the bill and whether President Carter will be handed the largest single block of judicial patronage in the nation's history. The House passed the judgeships bill on Feb. 7, 1978, while the Senate approved its version on May 24, 1977.

To the Senate's satisfaction, conferees agreed to accept a watered-down version of a House merit selection provision, which critics charge is likely to have no significant effect on Senate patronage selection of judges. Interest in merit selection of U.S. attorneys and judges was rekindled in January 1978, when President Carter fired David W. Marston, a Republican U.S. attorney in Philadelphia.

POLITICS AND THE FEDERAL COURTS

P RESIDENT CARTER has promised to choose the judges
he wants appointed to the federal courts on the basis of
"strict merit," not partisan politics. It is easier said than done,
as Carter discovered when he encountered strong Senate opposition to the establishment of commissions to evaluate
nominations to the courts of appeal and district courts. He did
manage, in an executive order signed Feb. 14, to set up panels to
supply him with the names of the "best qualified" persons for
the circuit courts of appeals. The order, however, did not apply
to the far more numerous district court appointments.

Carter's pledge is unlikely to dampen the controversies over
judicial philosophy that have surrounded the federal courts
since they were established almost 200 years ago. Such controversies are inevitable in view of the power U.S. judges wield.
Federal judges interpret the Constitution and the statutes, but
the fact that they are appointed to the bench only if they win the
approval of both the President and the Senate ensures that
these jobs will be subjected to partisan and ideological considerations.

It is too early to determine the kind of men and women the
President will appoint to the federal courts, but it is probable
that he will choose a large number. There are about two dozen
vacancies to be filled and there is a consensus that many more
federal judges are needed. This need was also apparent during
the Nixon-Ford presidency but the Democratic-controlled
Congress was unwilling to act upon numerous proposals to
create new federal judgeships. Now, with a Democrat as
President, the House is expected to approve a bill which the
Senate passed May 24 to create 113 new district and 35 new circuit court judgeships. While there are no vacancies on the
Supreme Court, five of the nine justices are 68 or older.[1]

Carter will thus have an opportunity to affect what critics
deplore and supporters applaud as the Nixon-Ford legacy.
Between 1969 and 1976, the two Republican Presidents chose
five of the nine Supreme Court justices on the bench today, 57 of
the 97 judges on the U.S. courts of appeals, and 221 of the 400

---

[1] Chief Justice Warren E. Burger, 69; William J. Brennan Jr., 71; Thurgood Marshall, 68;
Harry A. Blackmun, 68; and Lewis F. Powell Jr., 69. The other justices are Potter Stewart,
62; Byron R. White, 60; William H. Rehnquist, 52; and John Paul Stevens, 57.

federal district court judges. Most of these appointees were Republican loyalists who shared Nixon and Ford's belief in judicial restraint, opposed the activism and stress on individual rights that had characterized the Supreme Court under the late Chief Justice Earl Warren, and leaned toward legal interpretations that favored law-enforcement agencies rather than accused criminals.

In his critical study of the federal judiciary, author Joseph C. Goulden described the "archtypical" Nixon appointee as a person (1) under 50 years of age, (2) certifiably "hard-line" on law-and-order issues, (3) not overly intellectual, (4) with an active dislike for "counter-culture" people, and (5) having a politically valuable tie with a group with which the administration wished to be friends.[2] These judges, by and large, satisfied the people who had accused the federal judiciary of going beyond its legitimate authority to interpret the laws and thus usurping the power of Congress and state legislatures.

Supporters of so-called activism on the federal bench contend that the courts have not overstepped their constitutional mandate. The executive and legislative branches failed to respond to charges of unconstitutional or unfair practices, they insist, leaving the courts no choice but to intervene. This view was summed up by U.S. District Court Judge Frank M. Johnson, who has ordered Alabama officials to make specified changes in the state's prison and mental health systems. "I didn't ask for any of these cases," Johnson said. "In an ideal society, these judgments and decisions should be made by those to whom we have entrusted these responsibilities. But when government institutions fail to make these judgments and decisions in a manner which comports with the Constitution, the federal courts have a duty to remedy the violation."[3]

Strict Constructionism: High Court Record

Harvard sociologist Nathan Glazer argues that such justifications for judicial activism "will not hold water." Writing in *The Public Interest,* a magazine identified with intellectual conservatism, he said: "The legislature and executive have far more resources than the courts to determine how best to act. If they don't, it is because no one knows how to, or there is not enough money to cover everything, or because the people simply don't want it. These strike me as valid considerations in a democracy, but they are not considered valid considerations when issues of social policy come up as court cases for judgment."[4]

---

[2] Joseph C. Goulden, *The Benchwarmers* (1974), p. 72.
[3] Quoted by Martin Tolchin in *The New York Times,* April 24, 1977.
[4] Nathan Glazer, "Towards an Imperial Judiciary?" *The Public Interest,* fall 1975, p. 118.

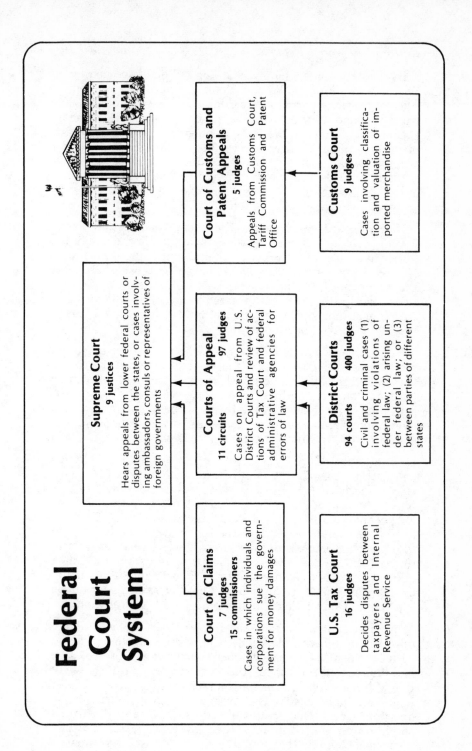

Federal Court System

Supreme Court
9 justices

Hears appeals from lower federal courts or disputes between the states, or cases involving ambassadors, consuls or representatives of foreign governments

Court of Claims
7 judges
15 commissioners

Cases in which individuals and corporations sue the government for money damages

Courts of Appeal
11 circuits   97 judges

Cases on appeal from U.S. District Courts and review of actions of Tax Court and federal administrative agencies for errors of law

District Courts
94 courts   400 judges

Civil and criminal cases (1) involving violations of federal law; (2) arising under the federal law; or (3) between parties of different states

U.S. Tax Court
16 judges

Decides disputes between taxpayers and Internal Revenue Service

Court of Customs and Patent Appeals
5 judges

Appeals from Customs Court, Tariff Commission and Patent Office

Customs Court
9 judges

Cases involving classification and valuation of imported merchandise

111

By the late 1960s, there was strong public opposition to the liberal activism of the Warren Court. Criticism focused on the court's decisions on racial discrimination, school prayer, pornography and particularly the rights of accused criminals. Richard M. Nixon, in his 1968 presidential election campaign, pledged to appoint judges who would interpret the Constitution strictly, would not "coddle" criminals, smut peddlers or political radicals and would not sacrifice the rights of the majority of law-abiding citizens for a small and undeserving minority—things which he inferred the Warren Court had done.

Nixon's first appointment to the court, Chief Justice Warren E. Burger, was welcomed by those favoring a less active or less libertarian judiciary. Burger's appointment, coming soon after Nixon took office in 1969, was followed by those of Harry A. Blackmun in 1970, and Lewis F. Powell Jr. and William H. Rehnquist in 1972, who all appeared to meet Nixon's strict constructionist, law-and-order criteria. So did John Paul Stevens, President Ford's selection in 1975.

The Burger Court is often described as more restrained and more conservative than its predecessor. But terms like conservatism and restraint to describe the court are often misleading. Nathan Glazer and others have questioned the Burger Court's restraint; some believe that in terms of the impact on the daily lives of people, more activist decisions have been handed down since 1969 than during Warren's tenure (from 1954 to mid-1969).

Despite its alleged conservatism, particularly in criminal cases, the Burger Court in 1972 extended the Warren Court's *Gideon* decision *(see opposite page),* which required states to provide a lawyer for indigent defendants in criminal cases. Earlier this year, the Burger Court ruled that states must make law libraries and trained legal personnel available to prisoners to protect their access to the courts. The court has also refused to overturn the controversial 1966 *Miranda* decision which requires the police to advise suspects of their rights. And on June 6, state laws requiring mandatory death sentences for anyone convicted of murdering a police officer were held invalid.

In non-criminal matters, the Burger Court has also handed down some "liberal" decisions. Carter, in a campaign debate with President Ford last October, said that the present court had "fairly well confirmed" the Warren Court's rulings in civil rights. It has extended the ban on racially segregated schools to include private academies, overturned most restrictions on abortion, ruled that states could not prevent illegitimate children from inheriting from their fathers, upheld many suits by women claiming they were the victims of sex discrimination, and refused to condone lower court efforts to restrict the press in

Leading Warren Court Cases

Brown v. Board of Education, 347 U.S. 483 (1954). Racial segregation in public schools is unconstitutional.

Cole v. Young, 351 U.S. 536 (1956). Restricted the dismissal of government employees considered security risks.

Jencks v. United States, 353 U.S. 657 (1957). Defendant in a federal trial must be furnished FBI records that will be used by the government in prosecuting him.

Mallory v. United States, 354 U.S. 449 (1957). Confessions by suspects who are subjected to unnecessary delays before being brought before a judge for arraignment cannot be admitted in court.

Roth v. United States; Alberts v. California, 354 U.S. 476 (1957). Obscenity must be determined on the bases of (1) whether to the average person, (2) applying contemporary community standards, (3) the dominant theme of the material, (4) taken as a whole, (5) appeals to prurient interests.

Yates v. United States, 354 U.S. 298 (1957). Advocacy to overthrow the government is illegal only as an incitement to action, not as an abstract doctrine.

Gomillion v. Lightfoot, 364 U.S. 339 (1960). Drawing of political districts along racial lines is unconstitutional.

Baker v. Carr, 369 U.S. 186 (1962). Federal courts have the right to review questions of legislative apportionment.

Engles v. Vitale, 370 U.S. 421 (1962). Use of compulsory prayer in public schools is unconstitutional.

Fay v. Noia, 372 U.S. 391 (1963). Relaxed requirements for allowing state prisoners to seek *habeas corpus* relief in federal courts.

Gideon v. Wainwright, 372 U.S. 335 (1963). States must supply indigent defendants with counsel in criminal trials.

New York Times v. Sullivan, 376 U.S. 254 (1964). Comments about public officials are libelous only if false statements are made with actual malice.

Reynolds v. Sims, 377 U.S. 533 (1964). Legislative apportionment must meet "one-man, one-vote" rule.

Griswold v. Connecticut, 381 U.S. 479 (1965). State laws forbidding the use of contraceptives by married couples violate their constitutional right to privacy.

Harper v. Board of Elections, 383 U.S. 663 (1966). States cannot require citizens to pay poll taxes in order to vote.

Miranda v. Arizona, 384 U.S. 436 (1966). Police must advise suspects that anything they say may be used against them, that they have a right to remain silent and are entitled to have a lawyer present during questioning.

United States v. Wade, 354 U.S. 436 (1967). Defendants are entitled to the assistance of counsel during pretrial lineups before identifying witnesses.

Witherspoon v. Illinois, 391 U.S. 510 (1968). State practices of excluding from juries in capital punishment cases persons who opposed the death penalty are invalid.

the coverage of criminal trials. In the Pentagon Papers case in 1971, it refused to uphold the government's claim to secrecy.[5]

The philosophy of the Burger Court is perhaps best summed up as a conviction that the already overburdened federal courts are not the appropriate forum for solving problems better handled by Congress, state and local governments, and state courts. There is some evidence to indicate that the majority of Americans share this view.[6] The Society of American Law Teachers does not. In a report issued last October, the organization suggested that the most valuable contribution of the Warren Court may have been "its efforts to make the federal courts more available and responsive to the claims of those wronged by governmental and powerful private misconduct."[7]

Chief Justice Burger "deplored" this development, the Society of American Law Teachers continued, and under his leadership "the Supreme Court is making it harder and harder to get a federal court to vindicate a broad range of federal constitutional and legal rights. In some cases, prior decisions have been overruled, either explicitly or silently; in other contexts, restrictive implications in prior cases have been taken up and expanded; in still other situations, new approaches developed by the lower courts have been repudiated."

Uproar Over Activism of Lower Court Judges

By limiting access to federal courts, the Supreme Court presumably will be able to reduce not only the number of decisions these tribunals have handed down but the kinds of decisions that in recent years have drawn some of the most criticism—on such controversial issues as school busing, consumer fraud, state and local government administration, zoning ordinances and employment practices. This limitation, in turn, may reduce the number of cases that are submitted to the Supreme Court on appeal. Another influence on the lower federal courts, although more subtle, stems from a "strict constructionist" Supreme Court. In a 1973 study of the Burger Court, James F. Simon said that the lower federal courts "will have to take notice of the new court's posture and act accordingly."[8]

The effect of Nixon and Ford appointees to federal district and appeals courts also has been observed. Carol H. Falk,

---

[5] See "Secrecy in Government," *E.R.R.*, 1971 Vol. II, pp. 627-650.

[6] See, for example, "A Report Card on the Supreme Court," *U.S. News & World Report*, March 7, 1977.

[7] Society of American Law Teachers, "Supreme Court Denial of Citizen Access to Federal Courts to Challenge Unconstitutional or Other Unlawful Actions: The Record of the Burger Court," October 1976, pp. 1-2.

[8] James F. Simon, *In His Image: The Supreme Court in Richard Nixon's America* (1973), p. 294.

writing in the *Wall Street Journal,* March 2, 1977, noted that the Fifth Circuit Court of Appeals, serving six Deep South states *(see p. 121),* "made a series of major desegregation decisions of crucial benefit to the civil rights movement" during the 1950s and 1960s. But as a result of six Nixon-Ford appointees to the 15-member bench, "civil rights plaintiffs have been set back in a variety of cases involving school desegregation, voting rights and jury discrimination."

Despite the large number of Nixon-Ford appointees, supporters of "judicial restraint" are unhappy with the performance of many federal courts. Much of their ire has focused on such decisions by district court judges as Arthur Garrity's orders for large-scale school busing in Boston, Frank M. Johnson's takeover of state prisons and mental hospitals in Alabama, and Virgil Pittman's ruling that the city government in Mobile, Ala., must elect its members by voting districts rather than citywide in order to reflect the black share of the population.

Another criticism of the federal judiciary, which Carter has addressed, is as old as the republic. It involves the way in which appointees are selected and the quality of the men and women who are chosen. The selection of federal judges is essentially a partisan affair, usually a reward for party loyalty and service. Custom dictates that the President obtain the Senate's concurrence in all appointments to the federal judiciary, although the Constitution specifies this requirement only for Supreme Court nominations. Unlike the publicity and scrutiny given Supreme Court nominees, men and women are confirmed or not confirmed for lower court judgeships almost in secret. The main reason is the traditional practice of "senatorial courtesy." If either senator from the state where the vacancy occurs is of the President's party, this practice gives him virtual power of appointment.

The senator sends his choice or choices to the Department of Justice for a check on the candidate's personal and professional background. It sends the information to an American Bar Association committee for review. The ABA returns a report on the candidate's fitness for office to the department, which forwards it to the Senate Judiciary Committee. Then, as described by Nina Totenberg of National Public Radio: "A blue slip with the nominee's name on it is sent to both senators from the state. If either senator, regardless of party, fails to return the blue slip, the nomination is, for all practical purposes, dead. This is called 'senatorial courtesy.' In fact it is absolutely blackball."[9] Once the blue slips are returned, Senate approval is all but certain. But on rare occasion fellow senators do balk at a

---

[9] Nina Totenberg, "Will Judges Be Chosen Rationally?" *Judicature,* August-September 1976, pp. 94, 99. *Judicature* is published by the American Judicature Society.

colleague's choice for the federal bench. Such an occurrence took place in 1965 when Sen. Edward M. Kennedy's candidate for a judgeship in Massachusetts, Francis X. Morrissey, was strongly opposed and had his name withdrawn from consideration.

"Any attempt to diversify the background of federal judges or to improve their quality might become a futile exercise as long as political patronage continues to skew selections," James Goodman of the Committee for Public Justice wrote recently.[10] But as Senate opposition to President Carter's merit selection panels indicated, many senators are unwilling to give up their power over appointments. Critics of the system contend that there has not been more opposition to relinquishing control over circuit court appointments because circuits cover a number of states and individual senators have less power over who is chosen.

What is surprising in a process as political as the selection of federal judges is not that there are mediocre, unqualified or partisan judges but that so many are competent, honest and effective. Probably the favorite example of how well the system works, for all its flaws, was the Watergate trial conducted by Judge John J. Sirica of the U.S. District Court in Washington, D.C. Sirica, a Republican appointed to the federal judiciary by President Eisenhower, was important not only for his perseverance in the case, Joseph C. Goulden wrote, but as a symbol of "the independence of the federal judiciary...."

Question of Judicial Workload and Salaries

Efforts at improving the quality of federal judges is just one of the problems facing the U.S. court system. A more immediate problem is the number of cases which federal judges must decide. Since he became Chief Justice, Burger has complained about the "intolerable" workload of federal judges and has pleaded for the approval of more judgeships. A glance at the growing number of cases brought to the federal courts, in contrast to the relatively static number of judges available to hear them, suggests that the federal courts may indeed face a crisis. The number of cases filed in three representative years, as recorded by the Administrative Office of the United States Courts and the Supreme Court was:

Year	District Courts	Circuit Appeals Courts	Supreme Court
1956	93,000	3,600	2,052
1969	112,000	10,000	4,202
1976	172,000	18,000	4,761

[10] James Goodman, "The Politics of Picking Federal Judges," *Juris Doctor,* June 1977, p. 26.

Arguments that the number of cases accepted in U.S. courts should be reduced or the number of judges increased have been challenged. Just before his retirement in 1975, Justice William O. Douglas wrote the following dissent in *Warth v. Seldin* (1975), a case that restricted minority residents in challenging suburban zoning practices: "I would lower technical barriers and let the courts serve that ancient need [of dispensing justice]. They can in time be curbed by legislative or constitutional restraints if an emergency arises. We are today far from facing an emergency. For in all frankness, no justice of this Court need work more than four days a week to carry his burden."

The Alexander M. Bickel of Yale Law School argued that Douglas was a very untypical judge and that his uniqueness must be taken into account when considering his views on the judicial workload. In 1973, Douglas had been on the court for over 34 years, Bickel wrote, and "decision for him is quite apparently a series of high-speed, high-volume events." But Douglas's insistence that federal judges could and should be hearing more cases is valid only "if the task of decision is more an individual administrative or executive event than a collective scholarly and deliberative process, if...the court can 'process' cases after the fashion of a high-speed, high-volume enterprise, if all that counts is 'the bottom line,' and if a day spent in deep constitutional contemplation is a day partly wasted."[11]

In addition to too much work, many federal judges have complained of low salaries and meager raises in the face of inflation. Some judges who have left the bench in recent years have said that low pay, together with heavy workloads, had caused them to resign. In an address to the American Bar Association in Seattle on Feb. 13, 1977, Burger noted that "since March 1969, when judicial salries have increased only 5 per cent, the cost of living rose more than 60 per cent." During the same time, he said, the number of cases disposed of by federal judges rose 36 per cent. A group of federal judges filed suit in February 1976 claiming that because of inflation their salaries had,in effect, been reduced unlawfully. Their argument was rejected by the U.S. Court of Claims on May 19, 1977.[12] By that time, Congress had approved a raise for district court judges to $54,500, for circuit court judges to $57,500, for Supreme Court associate justices to $72,000 and for the Chief Justice to $75,000.

---

[11] "The Caseload of the Supreme Court," a study published by the American Enterprise Institute for Public Policy Research, November 1973, pp. 26-28.

[12] The suit, joined in by 140 judges, charged that the inflation-caused salary reduction violated Article III, Section 1, which holds that judges' "compensation...shall not be diminished during their continuance in office." The Court of Claims ruled that "the Constitution affords no protection from such an indirect, non-discriminatory lowering of judicial compensation."

Changes in Role of Federal Courts

T HE CONSTITUTION isolates federal judges from the political process by providing that they "shall hold their offices during good behavior" (Article III, Section 1), and it ensures that they will be part of that process by stipulating that the President "shall nominate and, with the advice and consent of the Senate, shall appoint...judges of the Supreme Court" (Article II, Section 2). The Constitution also gives Congress the power to establish "such inferior courts as are necessary" (Article III, Section 1). Although there are no guidelines on how "inferior" court judges should be appointed, they were from the start also named by the President and confirmed by the Senate.

A federal court system was authorized by the Judiciary Act of 1789. It provided for a Supreme Court of six members and for 13 district courts, one in each state. The districts were divided into three circuits and a circuit court was created for each. Since the act made no provisions for circuit court judges, each circuit court was presided over by two Supreme Court justices and the judge of the district where the court was held. The system had at least two defects: (1) in an era when travel was slow and arduous, Supreme Court justices obliged to "ride circuit" often resigned rather than subject themselves to these biannual duties; (2) justices who had originally heard the case on circuit were often obliged to hear it again on appeal to the Supreme Court. It was not until 1891 that separate Circuit Courts of Appeals were established.

The influence of prevailing political, economic and social mores on the federal courts was apparent in the three major eras that have characterized the courts since the late 18th century. In the first phase, from 1789 until the Civil War, the courts and particularly the Supreme Court were preoccupied with the nation-state relationship. During the second period, from the end of the Civil War until about 1937, the main focus was on the balance between business and government. After 1937, the courts shifted from being the backers of property and privilege to the defenders of social and economic policy and, increasingly, of individual rights.

In the early years of the republic, the Supreme Court was neither powerful nor influential. The first Chief Justice, John Jay, resigned after six years to become governor of New York, a post he had actively campaigned for while on the court. Two others—John Rutledge and Oliver Ellsworth—followed in quick succession until John Marshall came to the court in 1801 and remained for 34 years as Chief Justice. It was Marshall who made the judiciary a co-equal branch of government.

This claim was established first in the celebrated case of *Marbury v. Madison* in 1803. The case involved a pedestrian matter but the Marshall-led court adroitly rendered a decision setting forth the doctrine of judicial review—the right to declare an act of Congress unconstitutional.[13] This doctrine was responsible for the fact that American judges were "invested with immense political power," Alexis de Tocqueville wrote in 1835. The reason for this power "lies in the simple fact that the Americans have acknowledged the right of judges to found their decisions on the Constitution rather than on the laws. In other words, they have permitted them not to apply such laws as may appear to them to be unconstitutional."[14] While the Supreme Court found many state laws unconstitutional during Marshall's tenure, it was not until the eve of the Civil War that the court again held an act of Congress to be in violation of the Constitution.

That decision came in the Dred Scott case.[15] Scott, a slave, had been taken by his former master into territory that had been declared free by Congress in the Missouri Compromise. Chief Justice Roger B. Taney declared for the majority that Scott was still a slave and the Missouri Compromise was unconstitutional since Congress had no authority to limit slavery. The North was outraged by the ruling, which hardened the national temper that led to the Civil War.

Traditional Emphasis on Property Rights

This right to property, so prominent in Taney's ruling, was to become the court's dominant issue until well into the next century. Robert G. McCloskey sums up the period from 1865 to 1937: "The major interest of the Supreme Court as a molder of governmental policy became the relationship between the government and business; and the major value of the court was the protection of the business community against government.... The fear that the states would wound or destroy the nation was replaced by the fear that government, state or national, would unduly hinder business in its mission to make America wealthy and wise."[16]

The American Bar Association, founded in 1878 by wealthy lawyers representing corporate interests, wielded considerable influence in the selection of Supreme Court and lower federal court judges. Joel B. Grossman wrote in his book *Lawyers and*

---

[13] The case—5 U.S. (1 Cranch) 137—concerned the claim of William Marbury, who had been commissioned a justice of the peace in the District of Columbia by President Adams just before he left office. Marbury sued James Madison, Secretary of State in President Jefferson's new administration, to deliver the commission, claiming that Madison's refusal violated the Judiciary Act of 1789. The Marshall-led court ruled that the act itself was unconstitutional. Under the guise of giving a legal victory to his political enemies, the Jeffersonians, Marshall set forth the court's authority to void an act of Congress.

[14] Alexis de Tocqueville, *Democracy in America* (1948 edition), p. 100.

[15] *Scott v. Sanford*, 60 U.S. 393 (1857).

[16] Robert G. McCloskey, *The American Supreme Court* (1960), pp. 104-105.

Judges: The ABA and the Politics of Judicial Selection (1965) that bar association leaders "saw the judiciary as the last bastion of defense against encroachments on the entrepreneurial prerogative and intensified their efforts to assure the recruitment of judges who shared their own views of society." These efforts, Grossman continued, "were clear and frank attempts to gain a measure of control over the decision-making process."

Solicitude for property rights was particularly pronounced during the tenure of Chief Justice William Howard Taft in 1921-30. To ward off what it regarded as government intrusion in the free enterprise system, the Taft Court struck down an unusually large number of state laws and 22 acts of Congress, including minimum wage laws, and curbs on child labor and on the use of injunctions in labor disputes. Taft summed up his judicial philosophy in a book published a year after he became Chief Justice. "In the last analysis, personal liberty includes the right of property.... Our primary conception of a free man is one who can enjoy what he earns."[17]

President Hoover's appointment of Charles Evans Hughes in 1930 to succeed Taft seemed to herald a less conservative era on the Supreme Court. But the Hughes Court became involved in a bitter clash with Congress and the Roosevelt administration over New Deal legislation it was declaring unconstitutional. Roosevelt responded by asking Congress early in 1937 to let him appoint an additional federal judge for every judge who had been on the bench for 10 years and did not retire within six months after reaching 70 years of age.

This "court-packing" plan would have permitted Roosevelt to appoint six justices immediately to the Supreme Court, presumably ensuring a majority sympathetic to the New Deal. Congress refused to approve the proposal, but the President's campaign brought about a change of heart on the court. Within a few months after the plan was submitted, the Hughes Court ruled that a minimum wage law similar to the one it had declared unconstitutional was valid, and it upheld the constitutionality of the 1935 National Labor Relations Act which gave workers the right to bargain collectively. Of the court's change in direction, it was said that "a switch in time saved nine."

During the years the federal courts were preoccupied with economic *laissez-faire,* there were two other noteworthy developments in the judiciary. One was congressional approval of The Court of Appeals Act of 1891 which divided the country into nine circuits and in each set up a court of appeals consisting

---

[17] William H. Taft, *Liberty Under Law: An Interpretation of the Principles of Our Constitutional Government* (1922), p. 25.

U.S. Circuit Courts of Appeals

District of Columbia Judicial Circuit. Clerk's office, Washington, D.C.

First. Maine, New Hampshire, Massachusetts, Rhode Island and Puerto Rico; clerk's office, Boston.

Second. Vermont, Connecticut and New York; clerk's office, New York City.

Third. New Jersey, Pennsylvania, Delaware and the Virgin Islands; clerk's office, Philadelphia.

Fourth. Maryland, North Carolina, South Carolina, Virginia, West Virginia; clerk's office, Richmond, Va.

Fifth. Alabama, Florida, Georgia, Louisiana, Mississippi, Texas and the Canal Zone; clerk's office, New Orleans.

Sixth. Ohio, Michigan, Kentucky, Tennessee; clerk's office, Cincinnati, Ohio.

Seventh. Indiana, Illinois, Wisconsin; clerk's office, Chicago.

Eighth. Arkansas, Iowa, Missouri, Minnesota, Nebraska, North Dakota, South Dakota; clerk's office, St. Louis.

Ninth. Alaska, Arizona, California, Montana, Nevada, Oregon, Idaho, Washington, Hawaii and Guam; clerk's office, San Francisco.

Tenth. Colorado, Wyoming, Utah, Kansas, Oklahoma, New Mexico; clerk's office, Denver.

of three judges. The second was ratification of the Fourteenth Amendment in 1868. This post-Civil War amendment, which was to become the basis for many of the controversial federal court decisions in the 1950s and 1960s, stated, in part: "No State shall make or enforce any law which shall abridge the privileges or immunities of citizens of the United States; nor shall any State deprive any person of life, liberty or property without due process of law; nor deny to any person within its jurisdiction the equal protection of the laws."

Focus on Due Process and Equal Protection

Reliance on the due process clause of the Fourteenth Amendment was the basis for *Powell v. Alabama* (1932), which Anthony Lewis of *The New York Times* later described as "one of the few incontestably great cases in the Supreme Court's history." This was the so-called "Scottsboro Case," involving an Alabama state court conviction of several blacks for rape and the question of whether the defendants had the effective assistance of counsel. Supreme Court Justice George Sutherland—"one of the four 'conservatives' so hateful to New Deal liberals"—wrote the majority opinion which held that the defendants had been denied "reasonable time and opportunity to secure counsel." This was the first time the Supreme Court had reversed a state criminal conviction because of unfair procedures at trial. Noting that the case was to serve as a precedent for the most controversial of the Warren Court's rulings a quarter of a century later, Lewis concluded: "Judge Sutherland could hardly have imagined the scope of the constitutional revolution that was to follow *Powell v. Alabama.*"[18]

There were several reasons for the post-1937 change in the federal courts from defense of property to sympathy for government regulation and individual rights. Roosevelt's attempt to "pack" the courts was probably not the most important of them. Sheldon Goldman contends that the depression-born "political, social and economic environments ultimately were the source of demands on the Hughes Court to sustain the constitutionality of New Deal legislation."[19] FDR's influence on the federal courts also came from the large number of appointments he made during his 12 years in office. From 1933 until 1945, Roosevelt placed nine men on the Supreme Court and 194 on the lower federal courts. But it was not until the mid-1950s that the Supreme Court and somewhat later that the lower courts emerged as upholders of individual rights under the equal protection and due process clauses of the Fifth and Fourteenth Amendments.

The Supreme Court under Hughes's successor, Harlan Fiske Stone (1941-46), was a tribunal in which "civil liberties questions were moving into an increasingly significant position on the judicial agenda." Stone's successor, Frederick Moore Vinson (1946-53), led a court which was "on the whole much less hospitable to civil liberties claims, distinctly more inclined to approach problems in this field in a spirit of 'judicial modesty.' " Despite its tendency toward restraint, the Vinson Court produced some "remarkable breakthroughs," including the steel seizure case.[20]

It was the Supreme Court under Chief Justice Warren (1953-69) which based many of its civil rights rulings on the premise that the Fourteenth Amendment made the protection of laws and other constitutional amendments applicable to the states. The first of the landmark decisions that were to characterize the Warren Court came on May 17, 1954. Speaking for a unanimous court, Warren declared that racial segregation in public schools was inherently discriminatory and therefore in violation of the equal protection clause. This *Brown* decision and later ones relying on the equal protection and due process clauses increased the workload of the federal courts and brought them, particularly the Supreme Court, under attack. President Eisenhower is said to have called his appointment of Warren to

---

[18] Anthony Lewis, *Gideon's Triumph* (1965), pp. 105, 209.

[19] Sheldon Goldman, *The Federal Courts as a Political System* (1976), p. 10.

[20] Robert G. McCloskey, *The Modern Supreme Court* (1972), pp. 49, 57, 126. In *Youngstown Sheet and Tube Co. v. Sawyer*, 343 U.S. 579 (1952), the court ruled that President Truman's order for the seizure of most of the country's steel mills without congressional authorization was unconstitutional.

the court "the worst damnfool mistake I ever made." Criticism of the Warren Court grew more intense in the years following the *Brown* decision. Sen. Sam J. Ervin (D N.C.), a constitutional scholar, accused the liberal majority[21] of trying "to revise the Constitution while professing to interpret it...."[22]

Reaction to Concern Over Individual Rights

Attacks on the Warren Court often took more concrete form. As early as 1955, Congress began considering legislation to curb the court's power to strike down state laws, deprive it of authority to review several types of cases and reverse some of its decisions by enacting new laws. During the 1950s and increasingly during the 1960s, there were calls for Warren's impeachment. Justice William O. Douglas was the subject of two impeachment efforts in Congress.

The first occurred in 1953 after he had temporarily stayed the execution of Julius and Ethel Rosenberg, who had been convicted of passing U.S. atomic secrets to Russia in World War II. The second, sparked by frustration among supporters of the nomination of G. Harold Carswell to the court in 1970, was led by House Republican leader Gerald R. Ford. In a House speech on April 15, 1970, a week after Carswell's rejection, Ford called for Douglas's impeachment on five charges. Ford said that Douglas had:

> **1.** Dissented in a 1966 obscenity decision against Ralph Ginzburg, publisher of *Eros* magazine.
> **2.** Suggested in his book *Points of Rebellion* that civic violence could be justified.
> **3.** Published an article in the April 1970 issue of *Evergreen Review* which contained nude photographs.
> **4.** Been associated with the Albert Parvin Foundation while on the court.
> **5.** Been a consultant for the Center for the Study of Democratic Institutions, a "leftish" organization, at a time when the center was the recipient of Parvin Foundation funds.

A special House Judiciary subcommittee created to investiate the charges found, Dec. 3, 1970, that there were no grounds for impeachment.[23]

Two years earlier, Congress had blocked President Johnson's attempt to elevate Abe Fortas to Chief Justice and move Homer Thornberry of Texas into Fortas's vacated seat. Both were personal friends of the President. Charging "cronyism" and, in Fortas's case, improper receipt of funds from a foundation,

---

[21] Warren, Brennan, Douglas, Marshall, Abe Fortas, Arthur Goldberg and sometimes Hugo L. Black.

[22] "Role of the Supreme Court: Policymaker or Adjudicator?" a debate between Ervin and Ramsey Clark, sponsored by the American Enterprise Institute for Public Policy Research in Washington, D.C. (1972), p. 10.

[23] See Congressional Quarterly's *The Supreme Court: Justice and the Law* (1973), p. 25.

Republicans in Congress united with conservative Democrats to force the lame-duck Johnson administration to withdraw Fortas's nomination. The withdrawal also doomed Thornberry's nomination.[24] Warren had announced his intention of resigning on June 26, 1968, but as a consequence of Johnson's rebuff by Congress, remained on until well into the following year when Nixon's nominee, Burger, won Senate confirmation and took his seat.

Burger reflected Nixon's and perhaps the nation's view of the proper role of federal judges. "That courts encounter some problems for which they can supply no solution is not invariably an occasion for regret or concern; this is an essential limitation in a system of divided power," Burger had written as a judge on the U.S. Court of Appeals for the District of Columbia. In an address to the Ohio Judicial Conference in 1968, while still an appellate judge, Burger charged:

> The Supreme Court has been revising the code of criminal procedures and evidence 'piecemeal' on a case-to-case basis, on inadequate records and incomplete factual data rather than by the orderly process of statutory rule-making.... I suggest to you that a large measure of responsibility for some of the bitterness in American life today over the administration of criminal justice can fairly be laid to the method which the Supreme Court has elected to use.

To a greater or lesser degree, the other four Nixon-Ford appointees to the Supreme Court shared Burger's views on law and order, judicial restraint and the impropriety of seeking redress for all problems in the federal courts. On the whole, the Burger Court has been less sympathetic to the rights of criminals, those protesting racial bias, and individuals and groups seeking access to the federal courts. But Nathan Glazer, an advocate of judicial restraint, and Professor Abram Chayes of Harvard Law School, a defender of judicial activism, have noted that the Burger Court has been as active—although not necessarily in the same ways—as the Warren Court. Nathan Lewin of Georgetown Law School described this activism: "Just as the Warren Court decisions often went beyond the facts of a particular case to announce sweeping new legal or constitutional doctrine, the flowering of the Burger Court has resulted in a readiness to issue broad pronouncements that exceed what is needed to decide a particular case."[25]

---

[24] For background, see "Challenging of Supreme Court," *E.R.R.*, 1968 Vol. II, pp. 741-760.

[25] Nathan Lewin, "Avoiding the Supreme Court," *The New York Times Magazine*, Oct. 17, 1976, p. 93. See also Abram Chayes, "The Role of the Judge in Public Law Litigation," *Harvard Law Review*, May 1976.

Ways to Cope With Court Overload

J UDICIAL ACTIVISM of the Warren Court opened federal courts more fully to persons seeking redress for alleged constitutional violations. But that fact alone does not begin to explain today's heavy dockets. Abram Chayes has described a change in the type of case coming to federal courts and adding to the courts' workload. Cases seeking simple "compensation for past wrongs" and confining their impact to the immediate parties, he said, have given way to cases which may affect many people not directly involved in the suit. Class-action lawsuits are examples of these.[26] The great increase in the number of national and state laws and regulations also has placed more questions before the courts.

More than that, there is the American propensity to turn to the courts, particularly the federal courts, for solutions to problems that were traditionally settled in the legislatures or elsewhere—or not at all. The result of all of these factors has been a large increase in the number and complexity of cases brought to federal courts. With this increase has come a host of proposals for reducing the burden on federal judges.

One proposal is to shift certain cases from the federal to the state courts. There are four times as many state and local judges as federal judges—about 23,000 compared to 500. Chief Justice Burger has been a strong supporter of using state courts to relieve the federal caseload. Under his leadership, the Supreme Court has restricted access to the federal courts with "procedural roadblocks," including stricter requirements for standing and justiciability, greater weight to comity and federalism and reduced consideration for *habeas corpus* relief, Andre R. Jaglom wrote recently in a Harvard legal journal. He continued:

> This restriction has resulted in a fundamental shift in the responsibility for protecting individual rights in the federal system from the federal judiciary to the states. This shift can be regarded in some respects as a return to the roles of the federal and state governments as they existed prior to the Civil War.... Until the spate of jurisdictional legislation at the time of the Civil War, it was well established 'that private litigants must look to the state tribunals in the first instance for the vindication of federal claims.'[27]

Cases involving residents of different states are frequently cited as the type of case better handled in state than in federal

---

[26] See "Class-Action Lawsuits," *E.R.R.*, 1973 Vol. I, pp. 1-20, and "Casualty Insurance: Troubled Industry," *E.R.R.*, 1977 Vol. I, pp. 101-120.

[27] Andre R. Jaglom, "Protecting Fundamental Rights in the State Courts: Fitting a State Peg to a Federal Hole," *Harvard Civil Rights-Civil Liberties Law Review*, winter 1977, pp. 63-64.

court. These "diversity" suits, which usually involve car accident or insurance claims, can be instituted in federal court, even if there is no federal question, as long as $10,000 or more is at stake. More than 30,000 diversity cases are filed in federal court each year. Chief Justice Burger told the American Bar Association convention in Seattle on Feb. 13, 1977: "I would strongly urge that the Congress totally eliminate diversity...of citizenship cases from the federal courts." He said this would "have no effect on access to a federal court on federal questions." The Justice Department is preparing a bill that would end the right of a plaintiff in a typical diversity case to bring suit in the federal courts of his own state against an out-of-state defendant.

The transfer of cases to state courts presents a number of problems. Alabama state courts recently ran out of funds, forcing the postponement of hundreds of trials until the state provided the needed money. Many state court judges, like their federal counterparts, have much more work than they can handle. The long delays in bringing cases to trial have been a concern for years.[28] Far more serious in the view of civil libertarians, consumer groups and environmentalists is the kind of relief they can expect in most state courts. Laughton McDonald of the American Civil Liberties Union finds the record disturbing:

> State courts [McDonald said] have tolerated every conceivable form of racial discrimination, whether in education, ownership of property, housing, the administration of justice, public accommodations or voting. Times have changed, but they have changed principally in the federal courts and the resistance to change from state judiciaries has been bitter and unyielding. History has shown that it is the federal courts that provide an effective forum for protecting constitutional rights, and that when the doors of the federal courthouse are shut, the Constitution is ignored.[29]

Selective Enlargement of the Court System

The transfer of some cases to state courts might ease but would not solve the congestion in U.S. courts. According to the Administrative Office of the United States Courts, 160,000 cases were pending in the district courts on June 30, 1976, an average of about 400 for each of the 398 judges. *Business Week* reported recently: "Professor John Barton of Stanford Law School has estimated that if the growth rate of federal appeals remains constant, by the year 2010 there will be one million appeals decided each year requiring 5,000 judges. With appeals running at 10 per cent of the total cases initiated, that would mean that the courts

---

[28] See "Reform of the Courts," *E.R.R.*, 1970 Vol. I, pp. 403-422.
[29] Laughton McDonald, "Has the Supreme Court Abandoned the Constitution?" *Saturday Review*, May 28, 1977, p. 11.

would be hit with 10 million cases annually. Long before then, of course, the system would have collapsed."[30]

Those opposed to limiting access to the federal courts argue that there are better ways of saving the system from collapse. Their proposals are for appointing more and better-qualified judges, creating new tribunals, and improving court administration and planning. Congress is close to completing action on the creation of some 150 new judgeships. The Carter administration also has asked Congress to give the 164 full-time and 323 part-time magistrates broader duties in civil and criminal cases.

Under terms of legislation enacted in 1968, magistrates are lawyers appointed by district court judges for eight years (full-time) or four years (part-time) to conduct preliminary hearings and consider petitions. The Carter administration's proposal would let magistrates decide almost any district court case in which the parties involved agreed to be tried by them. Attorney General Bell has estimated that they might relieve judges of up to 16,000 cases a year and reduce the delays in coming to trial. In civil cases, according to the Administrative Office of the United States Courts, the average time from issue to trial in district courts in 1976 was 11 months, the same as in four of the five previous years. Comparable figures were not available for criminal cases. However, the median time for the disposal of both civil and criminal cases was shorter because of plea bargaining and other out-of-court settlements.[31] Shown below is median time in months from filing to disposal in U.S. district courts.

	1976	1975	1974	1973	1972	1971
Criminal	3.1	3.6	3.8	3.9	3.4	3.0
Civil	9	9	9	10	9	9

Other suggested ways of lessening the burden on the federal courts is to make greater use of arbitration, further develop the concept of no-fault liability,[32] and add more non-judicial personnel to gather and organize information for judges on the complex issues that face them. A Department of Justice Committee on Revision of the Federal Judicial System strongly recommended the creation of new administrative tribunals. "The cases that should be transferred to the new tribunals are those that involve repetitive factual disputes and rarely give rise to important legal questions." These include claims under the Social Security Act, the Federal Employers Liability Act, the Consumer Product Safety Act and the Truth-in-Lending Act. The committee estimated that such tribunals could relieve

---

[30] "The Chilling Impact of Litigation," *Business Week*, June 6, 1977, p. 58.
[31] See "Plea Bargaining," *E.R.R.*, 1974 Vol. I, pp. 429-446.
[32] See "Automobile Insurance Reform," *E.R.R.*, 1971 Vol. I, pp. 25-44.

the federal courts of "more than 20,000 cases, perhaps more than 30,000 cases" a year.[33]

At the urging of Chief Justice Burger and others, Congress in 1973 created the Commission on Revision of the Federal Court Appellate System, headed by Sen. Roman L. Hruska (R Neb.). In its report two years later, the commission recommended that the Ninth Circuit, stretching from the Mexican border to the Arctic Circle, and the Fifth Circuit, embracing six southern states, be subdivided. Burger told the 1977 ABA convention that the number of appeals in the Fifth Circuit had increased by 650 per cent since 1962 while the number of judges had gone up by only 40 per cent. Appeals in the Ninth Circuit had grown by more than 500 per cent in that time. Burger recommended that the two circuits be subdivided into three divisions each, not two as the Hruska Commission had suggested. The bill the Senate passed May 24 to increase the federal judgeships would create a new circuit by splitting Louisiana and Texas from the Fifth Circuit to form a new Eleventh Circuit. The bill did not attempt to break up the Ninth Circuit. Two-thirds of its caseload is in California and there was strong objection to splitting the state between two circuits.

Another proposal by the Hruska Commission was far more controversial. It was that a seven-member National Court of Appeals be established above the circuit courts and directly below the Supreme Court, creating a new link in the appeals chain. In one form or another, this idea had been around for decades and was intended to accomplish one or more of the following goals: (1) reduce the Supreme Court's backlog of cases; (2) resolve conflicting rulings by the various appellate courts; (3) reduce the temptation to file multiple appeals in the hope of receiving a favorable decision in one of the circuit courts; (4) clarify state court interpretations of federal laws; and (5) screen requests for review of cases that now go directly to the Supreme Court.

The Advisory Council for Appellate Justice and the ABA both endorsed the idea but the Department of Justice Committee opposed it. A National Court of Appeals, the committee said, "almost surely would increase the already heavy burden on the Supreme Court" since the Supreme Court would have to spend additional time to determine whether cases should be reviewed initially by it or the new court and would have to scrutinize each National Appeals Court decision "very carefully" to ensure that "an issue had not been finally resolved or even dicta pronounced in a manner contrary to its own views." A second objection was

---

[33] Department of Justice Committee on Revision of the Federal Judicial System, "The Needs of the Federal Courts," January 1977. The committee was appointed by President Ford under the chairmanship of Robert H. Bork, then the Solicitor General.

that there would be four separate stages of federal adjudication rather than three.

Search for Non-Judicial Solutions to Disputes

By far the best way to relieve the strain on the courts is to persuade people to take many of their grievances elsewhere. But Americans have always turned to the courts to solve problems. Almost a century and a half ago, the French visitor Alexis de Tocqueville observed that "scarcely any political question arises in the United States that is not resolved, sooner or later, into a judicial question." Donald L. Horowitz is convinced that "the tendency to commit the resolution of social-policy issues to the courts is not likely to be arrested in the near future."[34] The House Judiciary Subcommittee on Courts, Civil Liberties and the Administration of Justice opened hearings on this question on June 20.

Burger insists that the courts are not meant to make or administer law and that these tasks should, as the Constitution specifies, be left to the legislative and executive branches. This view was summed up in 1964 by Justice John M. Harlan in his dissent in the famous "one-man, one-vote" case, *Reynolds v. Sims.* The Constitution, Harlan said, "is not a panacea for every blot on the public welfare, nor should this Court, ordained as a judicial body, be thought of as a general haven for reform movements." The Constitution, he added, "is an instrument of government, fundamental to which is the premise that in a diffusion of governmental authority lies the greatest promise that this nation will realize liberty for all its citizens."

There is, however, a Catch 22 in the "return to federalism" proposals. It is estimated that some 150,000 new laws are enacted and a countless number of rules and regulations promulgated in the United States each year at all levels of government. Legislators and administrators have shown little eagerness for dealing with the issues, some of them constitutional and many of them controversial, arising from these laws and regulations. Burger has requested that every bill affecting the federal courts be accompanied by a "judicial impact statement." If such a statement indicated that passage of a bill would increase the burden on the courts, the bill should either be reconsidered or more judges should be appointed to cope with the expected extra work. Steps to relieve the federal court burden are likely to be forthcoming only when that burden becomes intolerable. Many believe that point is close at hand. But whatever steps are taken, the federal courts will continue to be the focus of political controversy.

[34] Donald L. Horowitz, "Are the Courts Going Too Far?" *Commentary,* January 1977, p. 40. Horowitz, a lawyer, is the author of a new book, *The Jurocracy: Government Lawyers, Agency Programs and Judicial Decisions.*

Selected Bibliography

Books

Chase, Harold W., *Federal Judges: The Appointing Process,* University of Minnesota Press, 1972.

Dunne, Gerald T., *Hugo Black and the Judicial Revolution,* Simon & Schuster, 1977.

Goldman, Sheldon and Thomas P. Jahnige, *The Federal Courts as a Political System,* Harper & Row (second edition), 1976.

Goulden, Joseph C., *The Benchwarmers: The Private World of the Powerful Federal Judges,* Weybright and Talley, 1974.

Lewis, Anthony, *Gideon's Triumph,* Random House, 1964.

McCloskey, Robert G., *The Modern Supreme Court,* Harvard University Press, 1972.

Simon, James F., *In His Image: The Supreme Court in Richard Nixon's America,* David McKay, 1973.

The Supreme Court: Justice and the Law, Congressional Quarterly Inc., 1973.

Articles

American Bar Association Journal, selected issues.

Chayes, Abram, "The Role of the Judge in Public Law Litigation," *Harvard Law Review,* May 1976.

Gillers, Stephen, "Unequal Access to the Courts," *The Nation,* Jan. 29, 1977.

Glazer, Nathan, "Towards an Imperial Judiciary?" *Public Interest,* fall 1975.

Goodman, James, "The Politics of Picking Federal Judges," *Juris Doctor,* June 1977.

Jaglom, Andre R., "Protecting Fundamental Rights in State Courts: Fitting a State Peg to a Federal Hole," *Harvard Civil Rights-Civil Liberties Law Review,* winter 1977.

Judicature, selected issues.

Lamb, Charles M., "Exploring the Conservatism of Federal Appeals Court Judges," *Indiana Law Journal,* winter 1976.

McDonald, Laughlin, "Has the Supreme Court Abandoned the Constitution?" *Saturday Review,* May 28, 1977.

Steamer, Robert J., "Judicial Accountability," *The Human Rights Review,* fall 1976.

Reports and Studies

Administrative Office of the United States Courts, selected reports and studies.

American Law Institute, "Study of the Division of Jurisdiction Between State and Federal Courts," 1969.

Bickel, Alexander M. "The Caseload of the Supreme Court," American Enterprise Institute for Public Policy Research, November 1973.

Committee on the Judiciary, House of Representatives, "The United States Courts: Their Jurisdiction and Work," 1975.

Department of Justice Committee on Revision of the Federal Judicial System, "The Needs of the Federal Courts," January 1977.

Editorial Research Reports, "Challenging the Supreme Court," 1968 Vol. II, p. 741.

Society of American Law Teachers, "Supreme Court Denial of Citizen Access to Federal Courts to Challenge Unconstitutional or Other Unlawful Actions: The Record of the Burger Court," October 1976.

Access to Legal Services

by

Sandra Stencel

**July 22
1977**

ACCESS TO LEGAL SERVICES

A CCORDING TO the basic laws of economics, excess supply usually results in lower prices and greater accessibility to a product. Conversely, high prices along with growing difficulty in obtaining the product should indicate an inadequate supply. But the law of supply and demand does not always function smoothly, as the current state of legal services in the United States demonstrates.

In the past 10 years, law has become the country's fastest growing profession. There are now approximately 445,000 lawyers in the United States. The nation has one lawyer for every 484 persons—a higher ratio than in any other country except Israel. Despite the number of attorneys, there appears to be a significant demand for legal services that has not been met. The problem, according to a *Trial* magazine editor, Barbara A. Stein, revolves around two factors: (1) the public's ignorance of how to find an attorney as well as the kind of services lawyers provide, and (2) an apparent inability of the legal profession to deliver services at prices that are reasonable.[1]

A recent survey by the American Bar Association and the American Bar Foundation underscored the magnitude of the problem. Only about one-third (35.8 per cent) of the adults who were surveyed had ever consulted a lawyer, and only about a quarter (27.9 per cent) had actually retained a lawyer. One reason so many people appear to avoid lawyers is the perceived cost of their services. Over 60 per cent of the respondents to the survey agreed to the statement: "Most lawyers charge more for their services than they are worth."

In addition, more than a quarter of the respondents said that "lawyers needlessly complicate clients' problems." The survey indicated that many people do not know where to turn for legal advice or how to determine a lawyer's competence. Nearly half of the people questioned said that if they needed to choose a lawyer they would ask friends, relatives or neighbors to recommend one. The telephone book was the next most frequently mentioned source.[2]

---

[1] Barbara A. Stein, "Legal Economics," *Trial,* June 1976, p. 12. *Trial* is published by The Association of Trial Lawyers of America.

[2] Survey results published in *alternatives: legal services & the public,* Vol. 3, No. 1, January 1976. *alternatives* is a bimonthly newsletter of the ABA Consortium on Legal Services and the Public. Research for the survey was conducted by the ABA's Special Committee to Survey Legal Needs in collaboration with the American Bar Foundation.

In the past, discussions of access to legal services generally centered on the problems of people too poor to pay any legal fees at all—people who constitute about 20 per cent of the population. Although much more needs to be done before a truly effective or comprehensive legal services program is available to persons in the lowest economic brackets, legal aid programs financed by the government and private sources have begun to meet the legal needs of the poor. At the other extreme, people in the upper 10 per cent of the economic spectrum have sufficient funds to take care of even very high legal costs.

Caught in the middle are perhaps 140 million Americans who do not qualify for free legal aid and who cannot afford standard legal fees which now average $40 to $50 an hour in urban areas. The legal needs of the middle class "have been greatly overlooked," said a Philadelphia lawyer, Robert T. Richards.[3] In recent years the legal profession has begun to rectify this oversight. Programs designed to improve the availability of legal services to people of moderate means have sprung up across the nation.

Introduction of Pre-Paid Legal Insurance

One answer to the problem of providing low-cost legal services is pre-paid legal insurance. Under such plans, which are similar to Blue Cross and other health insurance programs, individuals or someone acting on their behalf contribute regularly to a fund for legal services that the individuals may need or use in the future. By spreading the cost of services over a large number of people over a period of time, the expense to the individual client is kept relatively low. Pre-paid plans are "probably the best way for the majority of Americans to be able to assure themselves of legal assistance when they need it," according to James Fellers, a former president of the American Bar Association.[4]

In addition to providing reasonably priced legal services, pre-paid plans encourage members to practice "preventive law"—to seek legal advice before they get into trouble, not just afterward. The ABA survey indicated that in only three situations—(1) the making of wills, (2) serious difficulty with a former spouse about alimony and child support, and (3) difficulties with custody of children[5]—did the majority of Americans consult with lawyers. When faced with other legal problems—such as the acquisition of property, personal injuries, landlord-tenant disputes, serious problems with a creditor, or denial of constitutional rights—most people either consulted a non-legal resource, handled the problem themselves, or did nothing about it.

---

[3] Quoted in *The New York Times*, May 2, 1977.

[4] Quoted in "Pre-paid Legal Services," a pamphlet published by the Resource Center for Consumers of Legal Services.

[5] Inexplicably, divorce itself was not among the situations listed.

Lawyer Surplus

Current problems with the delivery of legal services exist side by side with a growing surplus of lawyers. Since 1968, enrollment in the nation's law schools has doubled to approximately 125,000 students. Women have accounted for much of this increase. Today about 23 per cent of all law students in the United States are women, up from 8.5 per cent in 1971.

Nearly 30,000 students graduate from law school each year, but according to the latest figures from the Bureau of Labor Statistics, there are only about 21,000 jobs awaiting them in the legal profession. Nearly one-third of all law school graduates must seek jobs in other fields. By 1985, the Bureau of Labor Statistics estimates, there may be as many as 100,000 surplus lawyers.

Some of the graduates who do find jobs are prospering as never before. Starting salaries at top New York law firms average $25,-000 a year. Outside of New York, starting salaries at top firms run about $5,000 less. The median income for lawyers in private practice is slightly under $30,000—considerably less than the median income of the nation's doctors, which is above $50,000.

According to the ABA there are now about 150 full-scale prepaid legal insurance plans operating in the United States, covering approximately two million people. Lillian Deitch and David Weinstein estimate that such plans may cover 10 million to 20 million subscribers by 1985.[6] Prepaid plans vary widely according to how they are run, how much they cost, who operates them and what benefits they provide. Most plans now operating in the United States are sponsored by labor unions and are funded through collective bargaining agreements or from union dues. Other plans are administered by state and local bar associations, credit unions, insurance companies and other private businesses. One of the newest providers is Blue Cross, the nation's biggest health insurer. Its western Pennsylvania unit started writing legal insurance policies in May, selling to individuals as well as groups—a major innovation, according to Sandy DeMent, executive director of the Resource Center for Consumers of Legal Services.[7]

The cost of pre-paid legal insurance ranges from $25 to $300 a year, typically falling between $40 and $90. Benefits vary greatly, from fairly modest amounts of advice, office work and litigation services to coverage of almost every legal need that might arise. Some plans even provide for "major legal" expenses

---

[6] Lillian Deitch and David Weinstein, *Prepaid Legal Services: Socioeconomic Impacts* (1976), p. 6. Deitch is an economist and Secretary of the Futures Group. Weinstein is an independent consultant in matters concerning the administration of justice and protection of personal property.
[7] The Resource Center for Consumers of Legal Services is a tax-exempt, nonprofit organization that was established in 1975 in Washington, D.C., to analyze, produce and promote the most effective techniques for developing legal services plans.

just as health plans cover "major medical" problems. Most plans, however, do not provide coverage when lawsuits are initiated by the insured, an exclusion designed to discourage trigger-happy litigants.

Pre-paid legal insurance dates only from the early 1970s, and it has spread considerably in the last four years. A 1973 amendment to the Taft-Hartley Act allowed legal services to be a subject for collective bargaining. At its 1973 convention, the AFL-CIO recommended that pre-paid plans be incorporated into the collective bargaining programs of all affiliated national and international unions. The pre-paid movement achieved an important breakthrough in February 1975, when the ABA, after intense debate, adopted rules for the establishment, operation and promotion of pre-paid plans. Such plans also received a boost from last year's tax reform law, which put legal insurance on a par with health insurance, granting tax exemptions both for employers' premium payments and for the dollar value of services provided under insurance coverage.

Critics of legal insurance say such programs could lead to higher, not lower, legal costs. They cite the tendency of health care costs to rise under health insurance programs such as Blue Cross and Blue Shield. If legal insurance becomes widespread, the critics say, lawyers will feel free to raise prices, as doctors have done, confident that the insurance companies will pay whatever they charge.

Legal Clinics for Middle-Income Americans

Another alternative to traditional methods of providing legal services is the legal clinic. Patterned after low-cost medical clinics, legal clinics provide basic legal services for substantially lower prices than those charged by most lawyers. Most clinics also let clients pay in installments or with credit cards. Legal clinics are able to keep prices down by handling a high volume of cases and by making use of "paralegals" *(see box, p. 138)*, standardized forms and procedures, and other money-saving efficiencies.

Persons who oppose legal clinics argue that they provide unfair competition that will drive out individual lawyers and small law practices. Clinic advocates say that competition is healthy for any business. They add that clinics do not take potential clients away from existing lawyers, but instead draw people who otherwise would not seek legal advice. Legal clinics were never intended as a panacea for every legal problem, Denver lawyer Karen Metzger wrote in *Trial* magazine. Rather, they were viewed as a means of handling routine matters such as uncontested divorces, individual bankruptcies, consumer problems, traffic questions, landlord-tenant disputes, wills, and real estate transactions.[8] Generally, legal clinics are not prepared to pursue big cases pushed by consumer, environmental or other public interest groups—most of these are handled by "public interest" law firms financed through foundation grants.[9]

The country's first legal clinic was set up in Los Angeles in 1972 by two young lawyers, Stephen Z. Meyers and Leonard D. Jacoby. Today, Meyers and Jacoby have four offices in the Los Angeles area which serve about 350 clients a month. Despite their success only about 10 other legal clinics are known to be operating around the country. The slow growth of legal clinics, according to Meyers and Jacoby, is due to the opposition of the organized bar, which, they say, feels "economically threatened by such a successful attempt at delivering high-quality, low-cost legal services."[10] On the other hand, the ABA itself is sponsoring an experimental legal clinic in Philadelphia. Fees at the eight-month-old clinic range from $10 for the initial visit to $350 for an uncontested divorce.

Supreme Court's Decision on Advertising

The number of legal clinics in the United States is expected to increase significantly now that the Supreme Court has lifted restrictions on advertising legal fees and services. The court ruled June 27 that state laws and bar association rules against advertising by lawyers violated the First Amendment right to free speech. Supporters of legal clinics had long maintained that the clinics needed to advertise to attract enough business to offer low rates.

The ruling reversed a decision by the Arizona Supreme Court. The Arizona court last year upheld the public censure of two young attorneys, John Bates and Van O'Steen, who had placed an ad in a Phoenix newspaper, the *Arizona Republic,* to publicize their legal clinic. The censure was rooted in an advertising ban originated by the ABA in 1908 and subsequently adopted in all of the states, either by statute or court-imposed regulation. Defenders of the ban said it helped protect consumers from unscrupulous lawyers, discouraged needless lawsuits, and preserved the dignity and standards of the legal profession.

But the Supreme Court rejected these arguments. Justice Harry A. Blackmun, writing for the majority, said: "It is at least somewhat incongruous for the opponents of advertising to extol

---

[8] Karen Metzger, "Legal Clinics: Getting into the Routine," *Trial,* June 1976, p. 32.

[9] Public interest law generally is defined as legal representation for persons and groups that have been unrepresented or underrepresented. *(See p. 565.)*

[10] Quoted in "Legal Clinics: Lawyers in Storefronts," *Consumer Reports,* May 1977, p. 287.

Use of Paralegals

Some traditional law firms, as well as legal clinics and public interest law firms, have turned to non-lawyers —paralegals—to help them with their work. Lay persons have been involved in the practice of law since colonial times, when no special training was required to assume the role of attorney or judge. But according to Constance D. Capistrant, executive director of the National Alliance of Paralegal and Consumer Interests, it was not until the 1960s that paralegals were employed extensively to perform "lawyer tasks."

Today paralegals perform a wide variety of tasks. They may interview clients and witnesses; prepare case histories and do legal research; assist in preparing depositions, motions and pleadings; preparing wills and materials for divorce, custody and adoption proceedings, real estate transfer closings and incorporation filings.

Training of paralegals is almost as varied as the types of work they do. Some paralegals are trained on the job—some through experience as legal secretaries. Others hold degrees in paralegal studies from two- or four-year colleges. Still others are trained in special paralegal institutes, some of whose programs accept persons with only a high school diploma.

---

the virtues and altruism of the legal profession at one point, and, at another, to assert that its members will seize the opportunity to mislead and distort." Blackmun went on to say: "Bankers and engineers advertise, and yet these professions are not regarded as undignified. In fact, it has been suggested that the failure of lawyers to advertise creates public disillusionment with the profession. The absence of advertising may be seen to reflect the profession's failure to reach out and serve the community."

In a dissenting opinion, Justice Lewis F. Powell[11] said he was "apprehensive" that the decision "will be viewed by tens of thousands of lawyers as an invitation to engage in competitive advertising on an escalating basis." Powell did not oppose all advertising by attorneys, but decried price advertising: "It has long been thought that price advertising of legal services inevitably will be misleading because such services are individualized...and because the lay consumer of legal services usually does not know in advance the precise nature and scope of the services he requires.... The type of advertisement before us will inescapably mislead many who respond to it. In the end it will promote distrust of lawyers and disrespect for our own system of justice."

---

[11] Others dissenting were Chief Justice Warren E. Burger, Justices Potter Stewart and William H. Rehnquist. Joining Justice Blackmun in the majority opinion were Justices William J. Brennan Jr., Byron R. White, Thurgood Marshall and John Paul Stevens.

The majority opinion made clear that the decision was a narrow one concerning the newspaper advertising of routine services and fees, and that there remained a large area in which such attorney advertising could be curtailed or regulated. "There may be reasonable restrictions on the time, place and manner of advertising," Blackmun wrote. Advertising that was false, deceptive or misleading was subject to restraint, as well as advertising focusing on the claimed quality of service or involving in-person soliciting of clients. The decision left unclear whether television and radio ads would be acceptable.

It is too early to assess the impact of the Supreme Court ruling. Most observers say that it will principally benefit young attorneys just starting out in the business, smaller firms and legal clinics. For the moment, most big law firms appear to be adopting a wait-and-see attitude. There is much disagreement as to how legal costs will be affected by advertising. In the majority opinion, Blackmun wrote: "It is entirely possible that advertising will serve to reduce...the cost of legal services to the consumers." But others contend that the added expense of advertising will be shifted to clients, thus diluting whatever consumer savings might result from increased competition.

There also has been some concern expressed that the expense of advertising will bear hardest on the new members of the profession rather than on established law firms. James G. Reardon, president of the Massachusetts Academy of Trial Lawyers, said last year: "[Advertising] would be most unfair to those least able to afford it—the young practitioner just launching his career who has no allowance in his budget for an expensive campaign. Those firms whose volume of cases makes it possible for them to absorb such cost would have no need to hype an already successful office."[12]

Public Interest Law Movement

NEBRASKA LAWYER Roscoe Pound, who later would become America's foremost legal educator, delivered an address entitled "The Causes of Popular Dissatisfaction with the Administration of Justice" to the House of Delegates of the American Bar Association at its 1906 meeting in St. Paul, Minn. Pound told his fellow jurists: "The law does not respond quickly to new conditions. It does not change until ill effects are felt; often not until they are felt acutely." Those familiar with the

---

[12] Quoted by Barbara A. Stein, "Is Professional Advertising Unprofessional?" *Trial*, June 1976, p. 37.

history of public interest law have little reason to question Pound's words. A study undertaken in the 1970s by F. Raymond Marks for the American Bar Foundation concluded that the organized bar was "slow to recognize the consequences of the inequality of access to legal representation." Marks wrote:

> Although early views of a lawyer's responsibility to represent all who sought representation did include reference to the unpopular cause or client, they failed to include any recognition of a duty to represent those who lacked the lawyer's price.[13]

To a great extent, the legal profession was simply reflecting the attitudes of the broader community where, before the beginning of the 20th century, little formal attention was directed to the needs of the poor.

The access of the poor to legal services was further restricted by the emergence of a minimum fee concept which prevented lawyers from basing their charges on the client's ability to pay. Paradoxically, however, the adoption of minimum fee schedules forced the legal profession to face up to the problems of the poor. "If attention had not been paid to those who could not afford minimum fees," Marks wrote, "the bar would have been open to community charges and to self-admission that law and justice were for the rich and not the poor."

This new concern led to the establishment of legal aid societies to assist those who could not pay for legal advice. Legal aid services were available in New York City as early as 1876, and by 1916 there were 41 legal aid organizations in the United States, according to Emery Brownell.[14] The following year, the first national conference of state and local bar associations adopted a resolution urging the associations to help in forming and administering "Legal Aid societies for...the worthy poor." In 1922, the American Bar Association recommended that every state and local bar association appoint "a Standing Committee on Legal Aid Work."

One reason for the organized bar's growing interest in legal aid work was the publication in 1924 of Reginald Heber Smith's classic work, *Justice and the Poor*. Smith wrote that legal aid societies were "relieving the bar of a heavy burden by performing for the bar its legal and ethical obligation to see that no one shall suffer injustices through inability, because of poverty, to obtain needed legal advice and assistance." For Smith, legal aid work was a professional duty and not a charitable option. Most lawyers, however, did not share Smith's outlook. To them, Marks observed, "legal aid work was something that was out-

---

[13] F. Raymond Marks, *The Lawyer, The Public, and Professional Responsibility* (1972), pp. 15-16.

[14] Emery Brownell, *Legal Aid in the United States* (1951), p. 11.

side of professional pursuits—in fact, as organized, it was done by others, by staff lawyers considered marginal by the bar generally...." He added: "This is not to say that individual lawyers did not contribute money to legal aid, or, as a matter of charity, render assistance to 'deserving poor' on a no-fee or a reduced fee basis; they did. It is simply to say that the bar as a whole did not assume this responsibility."[15]

Court-Required Counsel; Poverty Programs

One aspect of poverty law did command growing attention—the problem of the indigent criminal defendant. One explanation for this, according to Marks, is that since relatively few lawyers made their living as defense attorneys, "the notion of professional responsibility to include free legal counsel in that area would bring little threat to the economic self-interest of the bar as a whole." But even more significant "was the awareness that the Sixth Amendment of the Constitution provides that a person accused of a crime shall be entitled to the assistance of counsel." Gradually the courts adopted the position that when defendants could not afford a lawyer, the courts would appoint one to represent him without charge.

In 1932, the Supreme Court extended the right to counsel to indigent defendants in state cases involving the death penalty.[16] This right was applied in 1938 to all federal felony cases and in 1963 to indigents in all felony cases.[17] The Supreme Court in 1966 established the suspect's right to counsel during police questioning, and in 1967 it ruled that juvenile courts must provide youths with counsel, even though these court proceedings are considered civil rather than criminal.[18]

Legal aid came into its own in the mid-1960s during the civil rights movement. *Fortune* magazine writer Peter Vanderwicken traced the legal activism of the 1960s to the summer of 1964 when some 400 law students and young lawyers went to Mississippi to defend civil rights workers who were registering blacks to vote. "They discovered there," Vanderwicken wrote, "that the blacks' problems were compounded by their inability to get legal advice and protection."[19]

President Johnson made access to legal services an important part of his war on poverty. When the Office of Economic Opportunity was established in 1965, it included legal services in the Community Action Program. The inadequacies of privately funded legal aid programs had been described the previous year

---

[15] Marks, *op. cit.*, pp. 18-19.
[16] *Powell v. Alabama*, 287 U.S. 45 (1932).
[17] *Johnson v. Zerbst*, 304 U.S. 458 (1938) and *Gideon v. Wainwright*, 372 U.S. 335 (1963). For a discussion of events leading to the *Gideon* decision, see *Gideon's Trumpet* (1964) by Anthony Lewis.
[18] *Miranda v. Arizona*, 384 U.S. 436 (1966) and *In re Gault*, 387 U.S. 1 (1967).
[19] Peter Vanderwicken, "The Angry Young Lawyers," *Fortune*, September 1971, p. 77.

by the president of the National Legal Aid and Defender Association. In the organization's 1964 annual report, he said: "Too often troubled people find that legal aid does not really exist in their communities or that it is fenced off from them by too stringent eligibility rules, anachronistic policy on the type of cases handled, lack of publicity, insufficient staff personnel or unconscionable delay in services."

Within a year of OEO's establishment, its budget for legal services ($20-million) was nearly double that of the legal aid societies affiliated with the National Legal Aid and Defender Association ($11.7-million). During fiscal year 1967, the anti-poverty agency boosted the funds allocated to legal services projects by $5-million. By the end of 1967, according to Sar A. Levitan, the legal services program was funding 250 projects, providing legal assistance in 48 states, employing nearly 2,000 lawyers in 800 neighborhood law offices, and devoting 49 other projects to research, training and technical assistance. OEO lawyers helped poor people fight creditors and landlords in court, obtain divorces and declare bankruptcy.[20] The 1968 *Report of the National Advisory Commission on Civil Disorders* commended the legal services program for making "a good beginning in providing legal assistance to the poor."[21]

The legal services program became mired in controversy in succeeding years. Conservative critics charged that its interests were social activism rather than helping poor people. The Nixon administration, opposed to much of Johnson's anti-poverty program, sought to dismantle the Office of Economic Opportunity and its legal services program. Supporters of legal services for the poor sought to preserve the program by placing it in an independent, quasi-private corporation. Nixon, in 1971, vetoed one bill to create a legal services corporation and threatened to veto another the following year, thereby effectively killing the measure.[22] A Senate filibuster blocked a similar bill in 1973. Legal services legislation in 1974 became embroiled in Watergate pressures, but was passed and signed by Nixon a few days before his resignation.

The Legal Services Corporation Act established an 11-member board to govern the corporation, with the members appointed by the President and subject to Senate confirmation. The law restricted the activities of legal services lawyers in several ways. For example, they were prohibited from handling cases involving such controversial matters as school

---

[20] Sar A. Levitan, *The Great Society's Poor Law: A New Approach to Poverty* (1969), p. 179.

[21] The commission was set up by President Johnson on July 27, 1967, after riots erupted in Newark, Detroit and several other cities. The commission was instructed to find the underlying causes of the riots and to recommend courses of action.

[22] See Congressional Quarterly, *Congress and the Nation*, Vol. III, p. 608.

desegregation, abortion and draft evasion. The act also contained a provision intended to eliminate "back-up centers"—outside "poverty law" research centers doing work for legal services programs.

Bills to lift some of these restrictions were approved in May 1977 by the House Judiciary Committee and the Senate Human Resources Committee but have not received floor action.[23] The president of the Legal Services Corporation, Thomas Ehrlich, testified in favor of removing all restrictions on legal services attorneys, a position supported by the American Bar Association. "Poor people should not be prevented from vindicating their rights through lawful means simply because a given issue may be politically unpopular," Ehrlich told the Senate Subcommittee on Employment, Poverty and Migrant Labor on April 25.

Ralph Nader and the Citizen Law Movement

While legal services lawyers concentrated on individual cases and client needs, other public interest lawyers litigated issues affecting broad segments of the public, such as consumer and environmental protection. Nearly 100 public interest law centers now operate in the United States, according to a recent study conducted by the Council for Public Interest Law.[24] Mitchell Rogovin, co-chairman of the council, wrote recently in the *American Bar Association Journal:*

> These centers were established in response to the problem that policy formulation in our society is too often a one-sided affair, a process in which only the voices of the economically or politically powerful are heard.... Ordinary citizens, because they are poorly organized and without financing, are unable to purchase the legal representation necessary to make their interests known, too.... Public interest law centers, by giving voice to citizen views in public policy deliberations, have made great strides in correcting this imbalance and assuring that government works for everyone, not just the rich and powerful.[25]

Ralph Nader is probably the country's best-known public interest lawyer. His career in consumer advocacy drew national attention with the publication of his book *Unsafe at any Speed* in November 1965 and General Motors' mishandled attempt to investigate his private life.[26] Although Nader attacked the entire U.S. automobile industry for emphasizing profits and styl-

---

[23] See *CQ Weekly Report,* June 4, 1977, p. 1104.

[24] Council for Public Interest Law, *Balancing the Scales of Justice: Financing Public Interest Law in America* (1976). The Council for Public Interest Law was set up in January 1975 under the sponsorship of the American Bar Association and the Edna McConnell Clark Foundation, the Ford Foundation and the Rockefeller Brothers Fund.

[25] Mitchell Rogovin, "Public Interest Law: The Next Horizon," *American Bar Association Journal,* March 1977, p. 336.

[26] The GM-sponsored investigation by private detectives drew a public apology from the corporation's president, James M. Roche, at televised hearings before the Senate Subcommittee on Executive Reorganization, March 22, 1966. Roche acknowledged that the investigation entailed some "harassment" of Nader.

ing rather than safety, he concentrated his fire on the Chevrolet Corvair. Chevrolet's subsequent decision to stop making the car and Congress's passage of the National Traffic and Motor Vehicle Safety Act of 1966 were both attributable to the book's influence.

Having won his initial victory on auto safety, Nader turned his attention to other areas where he felt the public interest was threatened. These included health hazards in mining, safety standards for natural-gas pipelines, the lot of American Indians, and indiscriminate use of X-rays in dental examinations. In the past decade Nader has greatly expanded the scope of his activities on behalf of consumers. To this end he has set up a number of organizations staffed largely by idealistic young people who receive small salaries and work exceptionally long hours—as does Nader himself.

The parent Nader organization is the Center for the Study of Responsive Law, based in Washington, D.C. Other important Nader groups are the Public Interest Research Group and the Corporate Accountability Research Group. Under the umbrella of a group called Public Citizen Inc., Nader sponsors seven public interest groups: Congress Watch, Critical Mass (an environmental group), Health Research Group, Freedom of Information Act Clearinghouse, Litigation Group, Tax Reform Research Group and the Public Citizen Visitors Center.

One of the earliest public interest law firms in the nation is not connected with the Nader organization. It is the Washington-based Center for Law and Social Policy, which engages in consumer affairs, environmental issues, health care, foreign affairs, women's rights, occupational safety and health, mine safety and media access. The Mental Health Law Project, an offshoot of the center, is devoted entirely to protecting the rights of mental patients. Some public interest groups, such as the Natural Resources Defense Council and the Sierra Club Legal Defense Fund are devoted to environmental issues.

Although the practice of public interest law is centered in Washington, such firms are now operating across the nation. Public Advocates, a San Francisco firm, is involved in education, employment, women's rights and the environment. The Women's Law Fund in Cleveland specializes in sex discrimination issues. Others are found elsewhere.

Problem of Funding Public Interest Firms

Over the years, public interest law has had a continuing problem: the lack of adequate and stable sources of funding. The principal source of funding has been foundation grants. But some persons fear this source may soon dry up. This fear was in-

Legal Conduct and Competence

Responding to a growing number of malpractice suits against lawyers, the American legal community has mounted a campaign to rid the profession of dishonest and incompetent members. In the past four years, there has been a 172 per cent increase in disciplinary actions taken against lawyers by professional legal groups. More than $8-million a year now is being spent on lawyer discipline—most of it by the legal profession itself.

Not everyone is satisfied with lawyers' efforts to police themselves. A recent report commissioned by Public Citizen, a Ralph Nader group, concluded that lawyers' self-regulation attempts had failed to provide adequate disciplining either of lawyers or judges. Although clients filed more than 37,000 complaints against lawyers in 1976, only 1,757 lawyers were disciplined, according to the American Bar Association.

In recent years the public has begun to take a more active role in judging legal competency. Herbert S. Denenberg, a former Pennsylvania insurance commissioner, has written "The Shoppers' Guide to Lawyers," a pamphlet now included in the *Shoppers' Guide Book*. The ABA advises the public not to hesitate to discuss fees with a lawyer. A good lawyer, the association said, should be able to provide a reasonably exact estimate of the costs for his services.

---

creased by the economic recession of 1973-74, which reduced the assets of most private foundations, inducing them to cut back on their grants. The Ford Foundation, for example, announced a 20 per cent across-the-board decrease in its support for public interest law.[27] Foundation funding presents other problems as well. Along with the money comes an Internal Revenue Service prohibition on lobbying by tax-exempt organizations.

The funding problems of public interest law firms were aggravated by a 1975 Supreme Court decision, *Alyeska Pipeline Service Co. v. Wilderness Society*,[28] which brought a halt to the widespread practice of awarding attorney's fees to the winning side in public interest cases. Striking down an award of attorney's fees to environmental groups which had challenged construction of the Alaska oil pipeline, the Supreme Court held that federal judges could not make such awards unless Congress expressly authorized them to do so.[29]

The congressional response to the *Alyeska* decision was the Civil Rights Attorney's Fees Awards Act of 1976. This act authorized fee awards, in the discretion of the courts, to victorious parties in cases brought under federal civil rights laws;

---

[27] See Carlyle W. Hall Jr., "In the Public Interest," *The Center Magazine*, January-February 1977, p. 31.

[28] 421 U.S. 240 (1975).

[29] A number of environmental and civil rights statutes provide for fee awards and were not affected by the *Alyeska* decision.

fee awards already available under other laws were left intact. Although most public interest advocates applauded the new law, Howard Lesnick, a law professor at the University of Pennsylvania, expressed concern that the foundations might seize on it to justify a further decrease in their support of public interest law firms.[30]

One funding proposal is to increase the contributions of the organized bar—perhaps through a system of voluntary checkoffs from annual bar association dues. A checkoff system for the benefit of legal aid has been in effect for many years in Chicago, and recently the Arizona State Bar established a dues checkoff for public interest firms in that state. The Council for Public Interest Law has proposed creation of a National Fund for Public Interest Law, to help finance public interest law efforts nationwide, especially in localities where resources are not readily available. The council has proposed that the ABA develop a voluntary dues checkoff system for this national fund, a plan supported by Supreme Court Justice Thurgood Marshall, among others.[31]

Another proposal is to let the government provide citizen advocates. They are already provided in a number of state attorneys general offices, and New Jersey is now operating a public advocate office as a separate state agency. "Placing the representation of the public in the hands of the state gives the public interest lawyer a secure base he or she has never enjoyed before," wrote Barbara Stein.[32] However, such plans pose problems. "Because public interest law centers are so heavily involved in the monitoring of government," argued Mitchell Rogovin of the Council for Public Interest Law, "it is crucial that their major support continue to come from nongovernmental sources."

Resolution of 'Minor Disputes'

PERSONS CONCERNED with improving the quality and broadening the scope of citizen access to legal help have found themselves in the middle of a complex debate over the role of the courts in resolving the conflicts and problems of American society. Among those who argue that the resolution of so-called "minor disputes" should be removed as much as

---

[30] Howard Lesnick, "What Next for Public Interest Law," *Judicature,* May 1977, p. 467.
[31] See Thurgood Marshall, "Financing Public Interest Law Practice: The Role of the Organized Bar," *American Bar Association Journal,* December 1975, p. 1488.
[32] Barbara A. Stein, "Public Interest Law: A Balancing Act," *Trial,* February 1976, p. 14. See also Arthur Penn, "Advocate from Within," *Trial,* February 1976, p. 20.

possible from the traditional legal framework is Chief Justice Warren E. Burger. "The notion that most people want black-robed judges, well-dressed lawyers and fine-paneled courtrooms as the setting to resolve their disputes is not correct," Burger said in a speech May 27. "People with problems, people with pains, want relief, and they want it as quickly and inexpensively as possible." If we do not devise substitutes for the courtroom processes, Burger continued, "we may well be on our way to a society overrun by hordes of lawyers hungry as locusts...."[33]

Burger has long spoken in favor of reducing federal court workloads. Under Burger's direction, the Supreme Court in recent years has handed down a number of decisions that have limited the types of cases that the federal courts may hear.[34] This has been done in some cases simply by stating that federal courts must use great discretion in intervening in state court proceedings. It has been done in other cases either by a stricter interpretation of the standards that a person must meet to get into court or by procedural obstacles to class action suits.

In his campaign to reduce the court's workload and to develop alternatives to litigation, Burger has recently been joined by a powerful ally—Attorney General Griffin B. Bell, a former federal appellate court judge. Bell generally endorses Burger's position that the court system is overcrowded, and he has said that one of his main priorities as Attorney General will be to provide better access to justice without putting an additional strain on the resources of the courts. To help achieve this goal, Bell has set up a new Office for Improvements in the Administration of Justice, headed by a former University of Virginia Law professor, Daniel J. Meador.

Proposed Substitutes for the Judicial Process

The Department of Justice announced recently that it was sponsoring an experimental program to give the public a speedy and inexpensive way to resolve minor disputes through neighborhood justice centers that would serve as alternatives to the courts. Bell said that three experimental centers, all funded with federal money but under local control, would be in operation by the fall. The centers would attempt, through mediation, to settle the sort of disputes—domestic spats, claims by customers against merchants, arguments between landlord and tenants—that clog the dockets of the lower courts in American cities.

---

[33] Burger made his remarks at a conference on the resolution of minor disputes sponsored by the American Bar Association at Columbia University in New York. The conference was a follow-up of an April 1976 conference convened by the Chief Justice in St. Paul, Minn., to commemorate the 70th anniversary of Roscoe Pound's address on "The Causes of Popular Dissatisfaction with the Administration of Justice."

[34] See "Politics and the Federal Courts," *E.R.R.*, 1977 Vol. I, pp. 473-496. See also *CQ Weekly Report*, June 18, 1977, pp. 1229-1234.

Other alternatives to litigation currently being explored include wider use of arbitration, mediation and conciliation; decriminalization of victimless crimes; expansion of the no-fault concept; and promoting the use of ombudsmen and newspaper and radio "action lines." Provisions requiring compulsory arbitration already are in effect in Pennsylvania, Ohio and New York, and in some cases apply to virtually all lawsuits involving claims for damages up to $10,000. Disputes between parties that have a continuing relationship, such as those between landlord and tenants, employer and employees, and certain disagreements over sales of consumer goods, are particularly suitable for resolution by arbitration, according to Junius L. Allison, a professor of law at Vanderbilt University.[35]

There has been much discussion recently of expanding the small claims court system. An ABA task force concluded that "revitalization and expanded use of small claims courts offers substantial promise of assuring the delivery of justice to all citizens in a manner which is both speedy and efficient."[36] Experiments with small claims courts in the United States began about 1913, after Roscoe Pound suggested there was a need to "make adequate provision for petty litigation." In 1924, Reginald Heber Smith, the legal aid pioneer, called for an alternative forum in which the poor litigant could seek relief in matters involving difficulties with landlords, creditors and employers. Early experiments with small claims courts in Oregon, Kansas and Cleveland, Ohio, were based on these suggestions.

The main advantage to the small claims courts, often hailed as "the people's court" or "consumer's forum," is that plaintiffs can file their cases for a small fee, usually about $6, and usually do not have an attorney. The cases are often settled in less than two months. However, even with the relaxed rules, people representing themselves often do not do well in small claims cases. A Virginia judge said recently that most citizens who represent themselves are at a disadvantage because they do not present adequate evidence and testimony. "People just haven't been to law school and they're facing someone who has and they usually end up losing," said Robert M. Hurst, chief judge of the Fairfax County General District Court.[37]

Opposition to Limiting Access to the Courts

The commitment by Burger and Bell to develop alternatives to litigation has provoked much opposition from consumer and

[35] Junius L. Allison, "Problems in the Delivery of Legal Services," *American Bar Association Journal*, April 1977, p. 519.

[36] American Bar Association, "Report of Pound Conference Follow-Up Task Force," August 1976, p. 12. The task force was headed by Griffin B. Bell, currently the Attorney General.

[37] Quoted in *The Washington Post*, May 15, 1977.

environmental groups, representatives of the poor and public interest lawyers. They argue that the federal courts ought to remain the principal instruments for resolving many of the disputes under discussion. They also fear that Burger's view of access to the federal courts is in reality an attempt to undermine their cases. Shutting down procedural access to the courts is seen by these individuals and groups as a veiled attack on the substantive rights and remedies that they wish to pursue in the federal courts.

"Obviously, certain matters can and should be resolved in forums that are cheaper, quicker, and more informal than the courts," wrote Charles R. Halpern, executive director of the Center for Public Interest Law. "But the effort to identify these matters and to create these forums should not blind us to the importance of opening the courts to a range of significant cases that are too frequently kept out by doctrinal restrictions and high litigation costs."[38]

Sandy DeMent of the National Resource Center for Consumers of Legal Services questioned Burger's selection of minor disputes as the best cases to be funneled into alternative forums. Why not pick on antitrust cases, contract cases or other large issues, she asked? DeMent told Editorial Research Reports that she is not opposed to developing alternatives to litigation, but she said that it was imperative that their use be kept voluntary. She expressed the fear that people would be coerced into using them, and thus effectively denied their day in court.

Public interest lawyers are particularly concerned about the recent Supreme Court decisions that have limited citizen access to the federal courts. Halpern wrote: "The Supreme Court's decisions on standing, class actions, and awards of attorney's fees reflect a trend toward making legal recourse less accessible to ordinary citizens. Such decisions are likely to increase popular dissatisfaction with the administration of justice. It is essential to reverse that trend."

Numerous bills have been introduced in Congress to overturn many of the restrictive Supreme Court decisions and increase citizen access to the courts. Although the bills differ widely in their focus, the one feature common to all is that they run counter to the Supreme Court's effort to reduce the caseload of the federal courts. President Carter placed himself on record April 6 in his consumers' message as favoring "access to justice" legislation. The issues are complex and the debate is certain to continue for some time to come.

---

[38] Charles R. Halpern, "Should Courts Redress Citizen Grievances?" *Judicature*, November 1976, p. 163.

Selected Bibliography

Books

Buckhorn, Robert F., *Nader: The People's Lawyer,* Prentice-Hall, 1972.
Deitch, Lillian and David Weinstein, *Prepaid Legal Services,* Lexington Books, 1976.
Downie, Leonard Jr., *Justice Denied,* Praeger, 1971.
Levitan, Sar A., *The Great Society's Poor Law: A New Approach to Poverty,* Johns Hopkins Press, 1969.
Marks, F. Raymond, *The Lawyer, The Public, and Professional Responsibility,* American Bar Foundation, 1972.
McCarry, Charles, *Citizen Nader,* Saturday Review Press, 1972.

Articles

Allison, Junius L., "Problems in the Delivery of Legal Services," *American Bar Association Journal,* April 1977.
Carter, Luther J., "Public Interest Lawyers: Carter Brings Them Into the Establishment," *Science,* May 27, 1977.
Hager, Barry M., "Access to Justice," *Congressional Quarterly Weekly Report,* June 18, 1977.
Hall, Carlyle W. Jr., "In the Public Interest," *The Center Magazine,* January-February 1977.
Halpern, Charles R., "Should Courts Redress Citizen Grievances?" *Judicature,* November 1976.
"How to Choose a Lawyer (and what to do then)," *Consumer Reports,* May 1977.
"Lower Fees, Better Service—Changes Coming in Law Practice," *U.S. News & World Report,* Sept. 22, 1975.
Rogovin, Mitchell, "Public Interest Law: The Next Horizon," *American Bar Association Journal,* March 1977.
St. Antoine, Theodore J., "Growth Patterns in Legal Services," *AFL-CIO American Federationist,* March 1976.
"The Chilling Impact of Litigation," *Business Week,* June 6, 1977.
"To Advertise or Not to Advertise," *American Bar Association Journal,* March 1977.
Trial magazine, selected issues.

Reports and Studies

American Bar Association, "A Primer of Prepaid Legal Services," April 1976.
——"Report of the Pound Conference Follow-Up Task Force," August 1976.
——"Report on the National Conference on the Causes of Popular Dissatisfaction with the Administration of Justice," April 1976.
"Causes of Popular Dissatisfaction with the Administration of Justice," Hearings Before the Senate Committee on Constitutional Rights, May 19, 1976.
Editorial Research Reports, "Legal Profession in Transition," 1972 Vol. II, p. 581; "Politics and the Federal Courts," 1977 Vol. I, p. 473.
"Reducing the Costs of Legal Services: Possible Approaches by the Federal Government," A Report prepared for the Senate Subcommittee on Representation of Citizens Interests, Oct. 8, 1974.

CHANGING U.S. DRUG POLICY

by

Richard C. Schroeder

Jan. 23
1976

Editor's Note: The Carter administration has come out in favor of decriminalization of marijuana use. President Carter told Congress Aug. 2, 1977, that federal criminal penalties for possession of an ounce or less of marijuana should be dropped, but that federal enforcement efforts against drug traffickers should be intensified. Carter emphasized that his proposal would not affect state drug laws. Since the original publication of this report, five more states have removed criminal penalties for possession of small amounts of marijuana — Minnesota, New York, North Carolina, Mississippi and Nebraska.

The Criminal Code Reform Act of 1978, which was approved by the Senate Jan. 30, 1978, called for reducing penalties for possession of small amounts of marijuana. Possession of less than 150 grams of marijuana was classified as a misdemeanor; possession of less than 30 grams (about one ounce) was classified as an infraction under which no imprisonment could be ordered. For a discussion of House action, see p. 2.

In his August 1977 drug abuse message to Congress, President Carter emphasized the need for international cooperation to control the production and transport of dangerous drugs into the United States. He also said that federal research and enforcement activities would be expanded beyond the current emphasis on heroin to include barbiturates, amphetamines, alcohol and tobacco.

CHANGING DRUG POLICY

T HE FEDERAL government is preparing another assault on drug abuse. In a post-Christmas statement issued at his Vail, Colo., vacation retreat, President Ford endorsed a Domestic Council study calling for new efforts to stem the rising tide of heroin addiction and the abuse of other hard drugs. The President said he would send Congress a message outlining his anti-drug proposals in the next few months.

Whether this new offensive will reach the proportions of President Nixon's celebrated 1971 "war" on drugs is not yet clear. Nixon characterized heroin addiction as "Public Enemy No. 1" and declared "if we cannot destroy the drug menace in the United States, then it will surely destroy us." In the wake of his declaration, the federal government set up a host of new anti-drug agencies for treatment and prevention, and for law enforcement. Federal spending on drug programs doubled in a single year.[1]

Ford's statement, though more moderate in tone than Nixon's, nevertheless had a similar ring of urgency. The President said: "Drug abuse is a tragic national problem which saps our nation's vitality. It is also a major contributor to our growing crime rate. All of us must redouble our efforts to combat this problem." The Ford administration's priorities, however, appear to differ sharply from those of its predecessor. The Nixon "war" was all-encompassing, hitting at users and sellers of "soft" drugs, such as marijuana, as well as traffickers in narcotics. The Domestic Council study,[2] on which President Ford will base his recommendations to Congress, makes careful distinctions between different kinds of drugs according to their potential harm to individuals and society.

The most startling of the findings in this White Paper of the Domestic Council Task Force was that of all the commonly abused drugs, marijuana holds the least potential for harm to the individual and society. As a result, the Council recommended that priority in federal anti-drug efforts be given to reduction of the demand and supply of more dangerous drugs:

---

[1] See "World Drug Traffic," *E.R.R.*, 1972 Vol. II, p. 927.

[2] *White Paper on Drug Abuse: A Report to the President,* Domestic Council Drug Abuse Task Force, September 1975.

heroin, barbiturates and amphetamines—particularly amphetamines that are injected intravenously. It also urged that attention be paid to compulsive users of drugs of any kind.

Recommendations From U.S. Domestic Council

The Council did not suggest that all federal programs zero in on heroin, barbiturates and amphetamines, nor did it endorse the decriminalization of marijuana, a step recommended by the National Commission on Marijuana and Drug Abuse in 1972.[3] Instead, it argued that "where resource constraints force a choice, those drugs with the potential for causing the highest social cost should be given priority." In another departure from previous policy, the Council study called for a better balance between law enforcement programs, on the one hand, and prevention and treatment efforts on the other. Under the Nixon administration, law enforcement gradually assumed an expanding priority, while treatment and prevention remained relatively static.[4]

Federal law enforcement, the Domestic Council emphasized, should focus on major trafficking organizations and individuals instead of concentrating on street-level arrests of pushers and users, the practice of the Drug Enforcement Administration (DEA) in recent years.[5] The Council proposed fuller use of federal conspiracy laws to bring charges against the "kingpins": "Since the leaders of trafficking organizations normally insulate themselves from overt illegal acts by delegating these acts to subordinates, conspiracy cases often are the only effective means for law to reach them." The study also endorsed a proposal previously made by President Ford for mandatory minimum sentences for persons convicted of trafficking in hard drugs and for stricter penalties for those who engage in the drug trade while on bail or parole.

At the international level, the Council study singled out Mexico for attention as the major new source of heroin reaching the U.S. market. It proposed the creation of an inter-agency committee, composed of representatives of the DEA, State and Justice Departments, to coordinate extradition and expulsion proceedings against narcotics violators. It also recommended procedures for tighter control of prescription drugs, including closer monitoring of the prescription practices of physicians.

The major fiscal implications in the study concern drug-abuse education and vocational rehabilitation, two of the weakest links in the chain of anti-drug efforts at all levels, federal, state and

---

[3] See "Marijuana and the Law," *E.R.R.*, 1975 Vol. I, p. 123.
[4] See Sibyl Cline's "The Federal Drug Abuse Budget for Fiscal Year 1975" in *Governmental Response to Drugs: Fiscal and Organizational* (1975), p. 2.
[5] See *Congressional Quarterly Weekly Report*, July 5, 1975, p. 1427.

local. Anti-drug films and printed material have been attacked repeatedly as "counterproductive" because of their use of scare tactics and their indiscriminate condemnation of all drugs as dangerous.[6] Similarly, the scarcity and weakness of vocational rehabilitation programs have been characterized by an expert as the "Achilles heel of addiction policy."[7] The Domestic Council called for increased funding for both areas.

Mixed Response to the Council Recommendations

Drug experts have voiced cautious approval of the Domestic Council study, and especially of its low-key, pragmatic approach to drug-abuse prevention. A key theme of the study was expressed in the following passage:

> We must be realistic about what can be achieved and what the appropriate federal role is in the war against drugs. We should stop raising unrealistic expectations of total elimination of drug abuse from our society.... Regrettably, we probably will always have a drug problem of some proportion. Therefore we must be prepared to continue our efforts indefinitely, in order to contain the problem at a minimal level, and in order to minimize the adverse social costs of drug abuse.

Dr. Thomas E. Bryant, president of the Drug Abuse Council, a private organization of drug-policy research, said in an interview: "In tone, the White Paper [of the Domestic Council] is, by far, the best any administration has come out with." But Bryant said he regretted that the study lacked specifics. "It emphasizes prevention, which is good, but it doesn't spell out what that means," he said. For that reason, he added, the study "is not useful as a plan for implementation."

Peter Bourne, former assistant director of the White House Special Action Office for Drug Abuse Prevention (SAODAP), said he believed the study committed the administration for the first time to policies which had only been implied in the past. In an interview, he mentioned a commitment to balance treatment and law enforcement efforts, and a commitment to sort out the varying social costs of different drugs. For example, the report downgraded cocaine as a dangerous drug. "Contrast this," he said, "with the way the DEA tried to stimulate hysteria about cocaine a few years ago."

Bourne was disappointed, however, that the authors of the study did not endorse the idea of removing criminal penalties for the use of marijuana. Moreover, he said, "They should have dealt with the need for more treatment facilities—there are

---

[6] See, for example, Patricia M. Wald and Annette Abrams, "Drug Education," in *Dealing With Drug Abuse, A Report to the Ford Foundation: The Drug Abuse Survey Project* (1972), pp. 123-172.
[7] Graham S. Finney, *Drugs: Administering Catastrophe* (1975), p. 88.

waiting lists for treatment slots all around the country. They should have examined the need for treatment of non-opiate abusers, and they should have reexamined the issue of heroin maintenance for heroin addicts."

To some critics, the recommendation for placing less emphasis on marijuana law enforcement amounts to "selective law enforcement" that may breed even more disrespect for the law than enforcement of existing laws, bad as they may be.[8] The recommendation has also been called a "smokescreen," since the vast majority of marijuana arrests are made at the local level under state and municipal laws. A hands-off policy on the part of the federal government would not significantly reduce the number of arrests for possession or use of marijuana, which came to 445,600 in 1974, the last full year for which the Federal Bureau of Investigation has compiled crime statistics. There was also uneasiness about making extensive use of conspiracy statutes. It is an axiom of the legal profession that conspiracy is charged when there is insufficient evidence to obtain convictions more directly related to the offense.

Increase in Supply of Heroin and Other Drugs

Despite the objection, many federal officials are willing to use conspiracy law and virtually any other tool available to check the flow of hard drugs in the illicit market. The Domestic Council's White Paper is a virtual admission that, despite years of effort and the expenditure of about $3 billion, America's drug problems are worse than they were before President Nixon issued his "war" call in June 1971.

Current estimates of the nation's heroin addicts range as high as 750,000. The White Paper candidly stated: "There are several hundred thousand daily chronic users of heroin not currently in treatment. These chronic users represent only a small percentage of those who have ever used heroin." The study further noted that there was a decline in the availability of heroin in a number of big cities during the peak of the Nixon "war" in 1972 and 1973, but that all indicators are now rising to record levels.[9]

President Ford has expressed alarm over the situation on a number of occasions. In commissioning the Domestic Council study in May 1975, he reported to Congress that "recent evidence suggests an increase in the availability and use of dangerous drugs in spite of the creation of special federal agencies and massive federal funding during the past six years." Later, on Oct. 20, the President said: "The prevalence and incidence of

---

[8] See, for example, editorials in *The Christian Science Monitor,* Dec. 30, 1975, and *The Washington Post,* Jan. 2, 1976.

[9] For background on the heroin situation in the United States over the past decade, see "Heroin Addiction," *E.R.R.,* 1970 Vol. I, p. 385, and "World Drug Traffic," *E.R.R.,* 1972 Vol. II, p. 927.

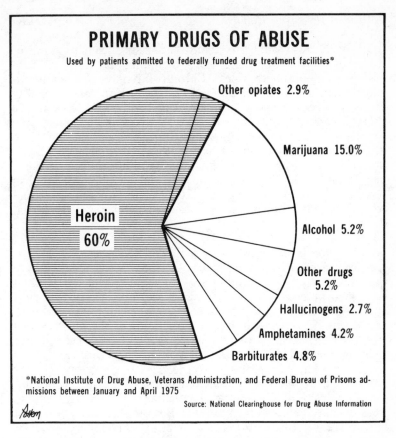

PRIMARY DRUGS OF ABUSE

Used by patients admitted to federally funded drug treatment facilities*

Other opiates 2.9%

Marijuana 15.0%

Heroin 60%

Alcohol 5.2%

Other drugs 5.2%

Hallucinogens 2.7%

Amphetamines 4.2%

Barbiturates 4.8%

*National Institute of Drug Abuse, Veterans Administration, and Federal Bureau of Prisons admissions between January and April 1975

Source: National Clearinghouse for Drug Abuse Information

drug abuse remains high. Cities which only two years ago were reporting a decline in heroin use are now reporting an increase and the demand for treatment continues to rise." He echoed the same theme in endorsing the Domestic Council's recommendations on Dec. 26.

New York is a bellwether city for American addiction. By any standard of measurement, it has the largest addict population of any city in the nation, and it is the primary target for drug traffickers. *The New York Times* reported Dec. 8 that "New York is experiencing its worst illegal narcotics trafficking problems in five years.... Narcotics investigators believe that not since the late 1960s have such large supplies of heroin and cocaine been smuggled into the city by drug dealers." Since late in 1974, similar reports have been coming in from other cities and areas of the country. District of Columbia officials have found a rise in the incidence of serum hepatitis[10] and deaths from overdoses of drugs. Chicago earlier had reported a 100 per cent increase in overdose deaths.

[10] The disease is caused by the use of unsterilized hypodermic needles.

There is also concern about the rising consumption of dangerous but non-narcotic drugs, including barbiturates, tranquilizers and amphetamines. "Chronic, intensive, medically unsupervised use of amphetamines and barbiturates probably ranks with heroin use as a major social problem," the Domestic Council report said. "It is clear that their use has increased rapidly in the United States during the last decade. Two different trends have led to this growth: **1.** These drugs are being prescribed more frequently and used more often in the general population.... **2.** Nonmedical use of prescription drugs has become widespread among youth (especially students), a trend which roughly duplicates the recent history of wholly illegal drugs."

Drug experts interviewed by Editorial Research Reports expressed reservations over part of that assessment. Many thought that amphetamine abuse may have leveled off. "You don't hear much about speed freaks these days," said Dr. Bryant of the Drug Abuse Council, although he warned that injection of amphetamines must still be considered one of the most vicious and destructive forms of drug abuse. As to barbiturates, Peter Bourne, formerly of SAODAP, estimated that the supply has remained relatively stable over the past few years. "What is new," Bourne said, "is that barbiturates have become institutionalized and accepted, particularly among the young. They seem to be taken for granted." Bourne said that since most barbiturates in the black market are diverted from legal sources, he thought the problem could be controlled by stricter regulations governing the medical uses of such pills. Noting that England had begun a parogram gradually to eliminate the prescription of barbiturates by physicians, he said the same steps could be taken in this country.

Shifting Patterns of International Drug Traffic

The big change in recent years concerning the supply of drugs is the extent to which Mexico has become the principal source of illicit narcotics, cocaine, marijuana and, to a lesser degree, "uppers and downers" entering the United States. In 1971, when the big push against drugs began, federal narcotics officials said that roughly 15 per cent of America's heroin came from Mexico; some 80 per cent was thought to originate in Turkey and 5 per cent in the "Golden Triangle" region of Southeast Asia.[11] Now, according to the DEA, Mexico is responsible for 75 to 80 per cent of the heroin reaching the United States. Mexico is also the prin-

---

[11] Estimates are necessarily fluctuating and imprecise. In 1971, an official of the Bureau of Narcotics and Dangerous Drugs (since merged into the DEA) said his guess was that Mexico supplied 25 per cent of the U.S. market. Recent studies have indicated that probably no more than 50 per cent came from all Middle East countries, including Turkey.

cipal transshipment point for cocaine coming in from South America.

The country's sudden rise to prominence as a primary source of illicit drugs has put new strains on U.S.-Mexican relations. The Domestic Council recommended that special attention be paid to Mexico's role in the illicit drug traffic, and President Ford said on Dec. 26: "Because of my particular concern about the problem of Mexican heroin, I am directing Secretary of State [Henry A.] Kissinger to express to the Mexican government my personal concern that we explore opportunities for improved control." Stung by U.S. criticism of laxity in combatting the narcotics trade, the Mexican government has undertaken a program of the aerial spraying of herbicides on illicit opium poppy fields in the mountainous northwest region of the country.

Turkey, formerly the major supplier of heroin to the United States, faded from the market in 1972. In that year, the Turkish government, under heavy pressure from the United States, imposed a ban on the growing of opium poppies. At the same time, a cooperative effort by U.S. and French narcotics agents broke up the "French Connection," a group of dope traffickers, mainly Corsicans, operating in and near Marseille in southern France. The Corsicans imported opium and morphine base from Turkey and other Middle East outlets, processed it into heroin in makeshift labs in the Marseille area, and smuggled it into the United States by a variety of routes through Latin America, the Caribbean, Canada and directly into U.S. ports of entry.[12]

The disruption of the Turkish-French network led American dealers to seek other supply sources—in Asia's "Golden Triangle" region, where the borders of Burma, Thailand, Laos and China meet; and in Latin America, principally in Mexico. Although U.S. heroin users experienced temporary shortages in 1972 and 1973, the new supply sources quickly took up the slack and by mid-1974 the market was booming once again.

Official estimates notwithstanding, no one can say with any precision what the current sources of heroin really are. It takes no more than 20 square miles of cultivated land to produce sufficient opium to supply the entire U.S. heroin market for a year—and the opium poppy grows on all continents. The DEA bases its current estimates of Mexican production on the peculiar reddish-brown color and the vinegary taste that characterizes heroin moving out of that country. But the color and taste derive from the refining process that transforms morphine into heroin, not from any unique properties of Mexican poppies.

---

[12] See *The Heroin Trail* (1974), by the staff and editors of *Newsday*.

DEA officials privately concede that Colombia, Costa Rica and Ecuador, and possibly other Latin American countries, appear to be growing opium. Moreover, they have no reliable figures on how much Southeast Asian heroin may be reaching the United States through Mexico and Canada. Even the current talk of Spanish-American and black-American syndicates replacing the old Corsican and Mafia operations may be somewhat off the mark. Given the high unit value of heroin,[13] there may be many more individual entrepreneurs than is commonly supposed.

Prevalence of Usage in America

FOR SOME TIME, Americans have been inclined to equate "the drug problem" with heroin addiction. The Domestic Council's study observed: "The name itself evokes fear in most of us, and many consider heroin to be the drug problem. Most of the federal effort in the drug abuse field has been directed at it."

Heroin is derived from opium, the dried sap of the ipium poppy *(papaver somniferum)*. The opium poppy grows in a wide band of temperate uplands stretching from the Anatolian Plateau in Turkey to the Golden Triangle in Southeast Asia. The poppy also thrives in parts of Europe, Africa and the western hemisphere. As the base for a wide variety of legal, pain-killing drugs, there is a worldwide licit demand for opium of up to 1,775 tons a year. The illicit demand is nearly as high, totaling more than 1,500 tons a year.[14]

Heroin is a powerfully addicting drug, although by no means the most powerful of the opiates. One compound, oripavine, derived from a strain of poppy called *papaver bracteatum*, is said to be "several thousand times more addicting than heroin."[15] Heroin can be smoked or eaten; it may also be sniffed—inhaled—like cocaine. Virtually all users of the drug eventually graduate to injecting the substance, first by "skin-popping," inserting a hypodermic needle just below the surface of the skin, and finally by "mainling," injecting the drug directly into a vein.

---

[13] The 10 kilos (22 pounds) of opium needed to produce one kilo of heroin costs approximately $1,000 at the source—the peasant farmer. Its street value is currently estimated at more than half a million dollars.

[14] General Accounting Office (GAO), *Report to Congress*, "If the United States is to Develop an Effective International Narcotics Control Program, Much More Must be Done," Document No. ID-75-77, July 29, 1975, p. 23.

[15] Leonard B. Greentree, M.D., "No Opium for Pain—A Threatening Medical Crisis," *New England Journal of Medicine*, Dec. 26, 1974, p. 1412.

Initially, users of heroin employ the drug to experience a sudden, euphoric high, or "rush," which passes over into a gentle, dreamy state in which anxiety and tension are relieved and a feeling of well-being is produced. Veteran heroin users, however, rapidly develop a tolerance to increasing amounts of the drug. An addict commonly needs his "fix" not so much to achieve a high but to ward off the pains and nausea of withdrawal, which can be considerable.

Despite the widespread use of heroin in the United States, little is known of its long-term effects on the human system. Research offers conflicting findings as to its effects on potency, fertility and childbirth. Constipation is a common complaint of addicts, since the drug is an anti-diarrhetic. Other illnesses associated with the drug—malnutrition, anemia and serum hepatitis—are generally attributable to the life-style of the addict, rather than to the drug itself. Dr. Vincent P. Dole, an expert on drug addiction, has asserted that "cigarette smoking is unquestionably more damaging to the human body than heroin."[16]

This is not to suggest that heroin is not dangerous. Because of its addictive capacity, the cure rate for heroin users is very low. A large number of "ex-addicts" have merely traded their heroin habit for dependence on other drugs—alcohol, barbiturates or methadone, or combinations of several drugs. Because heroin is illegal, and costly, addiction changes one's life, in most cases permanently. An addict's waking hours are spent almost exclusively in search of the drug, or for money to pay for it. Moreover, an addict runs a high risk of death, since the combination of heroin in the system with barbiturates or alcohol is often fatal. Many so-called heroin "overdose" deaths are attributable to such combinations.

Search for the 'Right' Treatment; Methadone Use

The United States has been searching for the "right" drug-abuse treatment since it experienced a surge of morphine and opiate addition after the Civil War. An early "cure" for morphine addiction was heroin, synthesized in 1898 and used for several years to relieve morphine withdrawal symptoms before medical authorities discovered that it was even more addicting than the drug it was being used to cure. In the late 1800s, however, physicians generally treated drug addiction by gradually reducing the amount of the drug given to the patient. How well gradual withdrawal worked is not known; there was very little follow-up of patients declared "cured" and almost no exploration of the psychological factors underlying drug dependency.

---

[16] Quoted by Edward M. Brecher, *Licit and Illicit Drugs* (1972), p. 25.

The search for cures intensified in the 20th century as the public became increasingly alarmed about drug addiction. In the 1920s, several cities opened narcotic treatment centers, most of which "cured" patients by supplying the drugs to which they were addicted. All were closed within a few years. In the late 1950s and the early 1960s, a number of "therapeutic communities" began operations. They used techniques evolved by Alcoholics Anonymous, principally total withdrawal from drug use and group therapy.

The latest treatment advance is chemotherapy, the use of chemical substances to permit addicts to function as socially useful individuals. In general, the substances administered either replace the drug of addition with less desirable effects or block the effect of the drug. The most widely known and used substance is methadone.[17] Methadone maintenance was pioneered by two New York City physicians, Drs. Vincent Dole and Marie Nyswander, beginning in 1964. Methadone replaces heroin in the addict's system.

Preventing withdrawal pains without producing a "high" state, methadone maintenance combined with psychological counseling and vocational assistance is one of the most successful treatment programs yet devised. Even so, its record is uneven and it is far from providing a complete cure for drug addiction. The Domestic Council's White Paper recommended increased use of LAAM (L-alpha acetyl methadol), a longer-acting form of methadone, in federal treatment programs. Methadone must be taken daily to prevent symptoms while LAAM is effective up to 48 hours.

Popular Stimulants: Amphetamines and Cocaine

While the Domestic Council named heroin as a "principal drug of abuse," it also pointed the finger at a number of other "dangerous drugs" which exact a high personal and social toll from the nation. Perhaps the most serious of these are the amphetamines, or "speed," especially when they are injected. One authority states flatly: "The intravenous injection of large doses of amphetamines...is among the most disastrous forms of drug use yet devised."[18]

Amphetamines are stimulants. Medically, they are used to treat narcolepsy, a rare disease whose victims constantly fall asleep. As appetite suppressants, they have been used—with indifferent results—to treat obesity. Although they are stimulants, amphetamines have been used to treat hyperkinetic children. The drug appears to improve concentration and perfor-

---

[17] See Peter G. Bourne, *Methadone: Benefits and Shortcomings*, Drug Abuse Council, October 1975.

[18] Brecher, *op. cit.*, p. 281.

mance. Quasi-medically, amphetamines are taken by housewives, truck drivers, athletes and students to "jack themselves up" for long periods of time.

The American "speed" epidemic emerged in the 1960s. At that time, users discovered that the effects of the drug could be greatly intensified by mainlining it, rather than popping pills. They also found that combining amphetamines with barbiturates magnified the effects still further. Speed freaks devised the "run," the practice of injecting successive doses over a period of days. During such a run, the user may become paranoid and experience hallucinations. One commonly reported sensation is of bugs crawling all about the body, on and under the skin. Under the influence, a speed user is probably the most irrational and potentially the most dangerous of all drug abusers. He is acutely sensitive to real or imagined insults or threats and capable of extreme violence to protect or avenge himself.

Drug experts say that abuse of "speed" seems to have leveled off and may even be declining, perhaps because users have become gradually aware of its potential for physical and psychic damage. At the same time, a number of non-amphetamine stimulants appears to be growing in popularity. Among these are phenmetrazine (Preludin), methylphenidate (Ritalin) and diethylproprion (Tenuate).

In addition to such synthetic drugs, the country is experiencing an increase in the use of cocaine, also a stimulant, but considered more benign, at least by drug users, than the amphetamines. The Domestic Council called cocaine "the new 'in' drug," and cited a study indicating that more than 10 per cent of the nation's college students had tried it, almost half of them within the past 12 months. Cocaine is a white powder, obtained from the leave of the coca bush, a plant indigenous to the Andean region of South America, where natives have chewed coca leaves for centuries to ward off the pangs of hunger and cold. Virtually all the cocaine found in the United States originates in South America. Seizures of the drug by federal agents and Customs officials have increased 700 per cent since 1969.

The Domestic Council study rated cocaine as potentially less harmful than heroin, barbiturates and amphetamines. Physical dependence on the drug is slight, but psychological dependence may be strong. At present, drug authorities feel that cocaine is not likely to become widely popular because of its high cost. A pound may bring up to $35,000 on the street.

Some drug abusers seek stimulation; others look for relief from tension; a large number want some combination of the two.

The Domestic Council Task Force estimated that as many as 300,000 Americans over the age of 14 may have serious problems resulting from the abuse of barbiturates, non-barbiturate sedatives and tranquilizers.

Society's Depressants: Barbiturates and Tranquilizers

The bulk of America's illicit supply of barbiturates and tranquilizers comes from diversion from legal channels. Up to one-half of the 10 million barbiturate doses manufactured in this country each year may find their way into the black market.[19] Medically, barbiturates are used to induce sleep, relieve anxiety and tension, reduce high blood pressure, and to treat convulsions, epileptic seizures and mental disorders. Pharmacologically, the barbiturates act much like alcohol. They are depressants and can cause drunkenness, with the attendant symptoms of slurred speech, blurred vision, and loss of coordination. Also like alcohol, they can produce long-term damage to body tissues, particularly the liver, although the danger of brain damage is less from barbiturates than from alcohol. And, like alcohol, barbiturates are strongly addictive.

A number of non-barbiturate sedatives also have turned up in the illicit drug market, diverted from legitimate medical channels. Some are as addictive as the barbiturates. The chemical gluthemide is sold commercially as Doriden, and is known on the street as "goofers." Methaqualone, marketed as Quaalude, Sopor, Parest and Optimil, was sold free of federal controls for several years, until its addictive strength became apparent. It is now included in Schedule II of the Controlled Substances Act[20] as a dangerous drug.[21]

A related but separate category of downers are the tranquilizers, which are among the most popular and widely prescribed drugs in America. They include meprobamate (Equinil or Miltown), chlordiazepoxide (Librium) and diazepam (Valium). Valium, manufactured by Hoffman-LaRoche, a Swiss-based pharmaceutical firm that operates Roche Laboratories in New Jersey, is the largest-selling drug on the commercial market, with a total volume of nearly three billion pills a year. Librium, also made by Roche, is in fourth place with sales of one billion. The drugs, formerly exempt from federal controls, were placed under Schedule IV of the Controlled Substances Act in July 1975. Because of their widespread availability and the potential for massive diversion, some drug experts ex-

---

[19] Richard C. Schroeder, *The Politics of Drugs* (1975), p. 154.

[20] The 1970 act classified most drugs used in the United States into five schedules, or categories, according to their medical uses and their potential for abuse. The classifications range from Schedule I: "High potential for abuse; no currently accepted medical use" to Schedule V: "Low potential for abuse...; limited physical or psychological dependence."

[21] See Mathea Falco, *Methaqualone: A Study of Drug Control*, Drug Abuse Council, April 1975.

press concern that tranquilizers may become the next fad of the drug culture.

Psychedelics and Other Forms of Drug Abuse

The psychedelics, or hallucinogens, are a broad category of drugs that act on the central nervous system to alter perception and induce dream-like states of trance. Among the best known are LSD (lysergic acid diethylamide), a derivative of ergot, a natural grain fungus; mescaline, which comes from the peyote cactus plant; and psilocybin, a product of several species of mushrooms. Synthetic hallucinogens include DMT (dimethyl tryptamine); PCP (phencyclidine); STP, also known as DOM (dimethoxymethylamphetamine); and MDA (methylene dioxy-amphetamine). THC (tetrahydrocannabinol), the active ingredient in marijuana, is sometimes classified as a hallucinogen.

Each compound has certain unique effects that appeal to its users. In general, they have the power to alter perception, consciousness and sense of time. Most of them produce a phenomenon known as "synesthesia," a mingling of the senses, in which sounds may be "seen" and sights "heard." Hallucinogens do not produce dependence in those who use them, but medical literature is replete with accounts of severe psychic damage following "bad trips."

Government policy toward psychedelics has been ambiguous for many years. The Controlled Substances Act of 1970 places LSD and other hallucinogens in Schedule I, which is reserved for the most dangerous substances "since they have no accepted medical use in this country."[22] That categorization was made nearly two decades after the Department of Health, Education and Welfare, the CIA, the Army, Navy and Air Force and other government agencies had embarked on experimentation with the drugs. The Domestic Council, in its White Paper, ranked hallucinogens below heroin, amphetamines and barbiturates as personal and social hazards. For the Domestic Council, at least, hallucinogens are not priority drugs in the federal enforcement effort. Whether that classification presages a change in federal policy is not yet clear.

While the Domestic Council study downgraded marijuana as a priority drug, it almost completely ignored two of the most popular drugs in America: alcohol[23] and nicotine. The White Paper stated:

> Alcohol and nicotine are legally obtainable and socially acceptable drugs; with a few exceptions, the drugs considered in this report are not.

---

[22] National Commission on Marihuana and Drug Abuse, *Drug Use in America: Problem in Perspective*, Appendix, Vol. III, Technical Papers of the Second Report of the Commission, March 1973, p. 200.

[23] See "Resurgence of Alcohol," *E.R.R.*, 1973 Vol. II, pp. 989-1005.

Drug experts point out that the federal government has traditionally argued for the prohibition of certain drugs—marijuana, for example—on the grounds of danger to personal health and social well-being. The Task Force acknowledged that "alcohol and nicotine are bonafide substances of abuse whose use often create significant adverse social costs and consequences." The argument implicit in the White Paper is that alcohol and nicotine, regardless of health hazards, are not drugs at all, because the public does not regard them as drugs. If it prevails, such a line of reasoning could have a profound impact on future discussions of drug policy in this country.

Public Policy Questions Ahead

PRESIDENT FORD has characterized the Domestic Council's White Paper as "realistic." In accepting the Council's report, the President said: "Not all drug abuse is equally destructive, and we should give priority in our treatment and enforcement efforts to those drugs which pose the greater risk, as well as to compulsive users of any kind." Drug experts see the President's attitude as a step forward from the shrill oratory that accompanied the Nixon administration's "war" on drugs.

The most immediate effect of the report is likely to be enhancement of the respectability of marijuana. The White Paper stated flatly: "Marihuana[24] has joined alcohol and tobacco as one of the more widely used drugs in the United States." Some people are uneasy about the strategy of "selective law enforcement," but relaxation of federal efforts to curtail marijuana use may pave the way for decriminalization of marijuana at the state and local levels, where most arrests for simple possession occur.

Six states have already removed criminal penalties for possession of small amounts of marijuana for personal use. Oregon led the way in 1973 when it reclassified possession of up to one ounce as a civil violation subject to a penalty of up to a $100 fine. Alaska, Colorado, California, Maine and Ohio have enacted similar decriminalization laws.[25] Keith Stroup, director of the National Organization for the Reform of Marijuana Laws, has said that Hawaii, Minnesota, Michigan, New Jersey, New York,

---

[24] As the word is routinely spelled in official federal publications.

[25] Maine's law becomes effective in March 1976; California's took effect in January; laws in Alaska, Colorado and Ohio came into force in 1975.

Pennsylvania, Washington and Wisconsin are likely to follow suit during 1976.

A softening of federal controls on some drugs poses new problems, both domestically and internationally. The official attitude is that use of the drugs categorized as "lower priority" is still to be discouraged. But easing of law enforcement may be taken as a signal that such drugs—psychedelics and cocaine, as well as marijuana—are not really as harmful as they were made out to be. Sometime before the Domestic Council issued its report, Dr. Jerome Jaffe, former head of the White House Special Action Office for Drug Abuse Prevention, observed: "It is likely that no matter how the government tries to frame its actions, a move away from criminal penalties will be interpreted by many as a sign that marijuana is safe and approved for use."

Internationally, there is sure to be perplexity on the part of governments which, under heavy prodding from the United States, have mounted campaigns to interdict supplies of such substances as marijuana and cocaine. The governments of Mexico and Colombia, in particular, are likely to ask why they should continue to put time and money into anti-drug efforts if the United States has relaxed controls at home.

Balance Between Treatment and Law Enforcement

Drug experts will be watching President Ford's coming message to Congress on drugs. One question will be what kind of balance the President strikes between treatment and prevention of drug abuse on one side, and the enforcement of drug laws on the other. In recent years, law enforcement efforts have received steadily increasing portions of the federal budget while treatment and prevention facilities have been unable to keep pace with rising demand. The White Paper's observation that "several hundred thousand daily chronic users of heroin" are not currently in treatment programs is indicative of the unmet needs in this area. If President Ford adheres to the intent of the White Paper, he will seek additional funds for drug abuse education and vocational rehabilitation in particular.

Implicit in this question is the knotty issue of overall coordination of federal drug programs. When the White House Special Action Office on Drug Abuse Prevention (SAODAP) was created in 1971, it was given vast powers to oversee federal prevention and treatment efforts. President Nixon told its first director, Dr. Jerome Jaffe, he should "knock heads together" to get federal programs moving. But, as the 1972 presidential campaign approached, the Nixon administration's interest in treatment and prevention waned. SAODAP's headquarters were moved from the Executive Office Building near the White

House, to Rockville, Md., 20 miles away. Jaffe, cut off from access to the President, resigned in June 1973. SAODAP was phased out of existence two years later. With it, the power to coordinate the far-flung federal treatment and prevention establishment disappeared.[26]

A second important issue is how quickly and effectively the Drug Enforcement Administration (DEA) can be reformed to carry out the new law enforcement approach outlined in the White Paper. The DEA has undergone heavy criticism virtually since it was created in 1973, through a merger of the Office of Drug Abuse Law Enforcement, the Bureau of Narcotics and Dangerous Drugs, the Office of National Narcotics Intelligence, and part of the Customs Service. Specifically, there have been charges of illegal wiretapping, bribery, diversion of funds and other allegedly corrupt activities by DEA agents.

The Senate Government Operations Permanent Investigations Subcommittee, under Sen. Henry Jackson (D Wash.), conducted hearings in June 1975 on the activities of the DEA. Among the items under investigation was a complaint that DEA agents had concentrated on making small, street-level arrests in order to bolster their records and had virtually ignored prosecution of large-scale drug traffickers. Subcommittee staff investigators said that consequently, in the two years since the DEA had been formed, smuggling of all types of narcotics and street sales of dangerous drugs had increased.[27] According to the subcommittee, the government had spent about $3 billion on drug law enforcement and had little to show for it. Soon before the hearings opened, DEA Director John E. Bartels resigned his post at the request of Justice Department officials. As of late January 1976, the agency was still headed by an acting director, Henry S. Dogin.[28]

Another troublesome matter has been a jurisdictional feud carried on between the DEA and the Customs Service. The feud is long-standing, inherited from decade-old rivalries between the old Federal Bureau of Narcotics and Bureau of Customs.[29] The principal argument is over who should have the power to conduct foreign narcotics intelligence operations. The Domestic Council's White Paper recommended that the jurisdictional dispute be settled by Dec. 31, 1975. On Dec. 16, the DEA and

---

[26] See "The Abuse of Drug Abuse" by Mathea Falco and John Pekannen in *The Washington Post*, Sept. 8, 1974.

[27] See *Congressional Quarterly Weekly Report*, July 5, 1975, p. 1427.

[28] For background on Bartel's dismissal, see "Keystone Narcs," *The New Republic*, Nov. 25, 1975, pp. 5-7, and Ron Rosenbaum, "The Decline and Fall of Nixon's Drug Czar," *New Times*, Sept. 5, 1975, pp. 6-29.

[29] The FBN was the predecessor agency of the Bureau of Narcotics and Dangerous Drugs, which in 1973 was merged into the DEA. The Bureau of Customs was redesignated the Customs Service in 1973 and most of its functions remained in the Treasury Department.

Customs Service signed a "memorandum of understanding" which, in effect, assigns the intelligence function to Customs but directs it to share information with the DEA.

Cyclical Patterns in Drug Addiction in America

"The problem of widespread drug addiction is a recurrent and cyclical one."[30] The United States has had serious problems of drug abuse for the greater part of a century, and it may expect to continue to have them for many years to come. Opiate addiction was widespread during the 19th century, when opiates were freely available as ingredients in patent medicines and prescriptions. The chief victims of the drug were not poor youths in the slums but middle-class housewives who turned to opium preparations for relief from their pains, real and imagined. Dr. David Musto of Yale University estimated that there may have been as many as 400,000 addicts in this country at the turn of the century[31]—equivalent to two million today.

Successive administrations have mounted repeated drives against the drug menace. Each new federal effort has raised the level of public alarm about drugs and has embued the substances with near-mystical powers in the minds of many citizens. The mythology surrounding the subject and the terror instilled in the public have made the task of dealing rationally with the multiple drug problems all the more difficult.

Most federal anti-drug efforts have been founded primarily on increased law enforcement, in the mistaken belief that it is possible to reduce or even eliminate the supply of illicit drugs permanently. Recent experience, however, has shown that it is virtually impossible to stamp out the growth of opium poppies all over the world if, indeed, that could be done without seriously impairing the medical profession's ability to relieve pain. It is probably even more futile to hope to interrupt trafficking in barbiturates or amphetamines, because of the huge volume of these drugs in the legal market and also because of the ease with which amateur chemists can synthesize such compounds.

The Domestic Council has suggested a continuing effort to reduce the supply of illicit drugs and an expanded program to reduce the demand, through increased treatment facilities, better drug abuse education and vocational rehabilitation. Drug experts see this as an overdue admission that demand, not supply, lies at the heart of America's drug problems. In the past, they say, too much attention has been paid to the cops-and-robbers game and too little to providing alternatives to dangerous drugs.

[30] John Helmer and Thomas Vietorisz, *Drug Use, The Labor Market and Class Conflict,* Drug Abuse Council, May 1974, p. 38.

[31] David Musto, *The American Disease: Origins of Narcotic Control* (1973), p. 5 and fn.

Bibliography

Books

Bourne, Peter G. (ed.), *Addiction*, Academic Press, 1974.

Brecher, Edward M., et al., *Licit and Illicit Drugs*, Consumers Union, 1972.

Finlator, John, *The Drugged Nation*, Simon & Schuster, 1973.

Musto, David, *The American Disease: Origins of Narcotic Control*, Yale University Press, 1973.

Newsday staff and editors, *The Heroin Trail*, New American Library, Signet Editions, 1974.

Schroeder, Richard C. *The Politics of Drugs*, Congressional Quarterly, 1975.

Wald, Patricia N., et al., *Dealing with Drug Abuse: A Report to the Ford Foundation*, Praeger Publishers, 1972.

Articles

Bourne, Peter G., "Polydrug Abuse—Considerations in a National Strategy," *American Journal of Drug and Alcohol Abuse*, 1974.

Greentree, Leonard B., "No Opium for Pain—A Threatening Medical Crisis," *New England Journal of Medicine*, Dec. 26, 1974.

The Journal, Addiction Research Foundation, Toronto, Canada, selected issues.

"Keystone Narcs," *The New Republic*, Nov. 25, 1975.

National Drug Reporter, National Coordinating Council on Drug Education, selected issues.

Rosenbaum, Ron, "The Decline and Fall of Nixon's Drug Czar," *New Times*. Sept. 5, 1975.

United Nations Bulletin on Narcotics, selected issues.

Reports and Studies

Cline, Sibyl, *Turkish Opium in Perspective*, Drug Abuse Council, December 1974.

—"Federal Drug Abuse Budget for Fiscal Year 1975," in *Governmental Response to Drugs: Fiscal and Organizational*, Drug Abuse Council, 1975.

Drug Abuse Council, *Heroin Maintenance: The Issues*, second printing, July 1975.

Domestic Council, Drug Abuse Task Force, *White Paper on Drug Abuse: A Report to the President*, September 1975.

Drug Enforcement Agency, *Fact Sheets*, 1973.

Editorial Research Reports, "Heroin Addiction," 1970 Vol. I, p. 385; "World Drug Traffic," 1972 Vol. II, p. 927; "Marijuana and the Law," 1975 Vol. I, p. 123.

Falco, Mathea, *Methaqualone: A Study of Drug Control*, Drug Abuse Council, April 1975.

Finney, Graham S., *Drugs: Administering Catastrophe*, Drug Abuse Council, 1975.

General Accounting Office, report to Congress, July 29, 1975.

Helmer, John, and Thomas Vietorisz, *Drug Use, the Labor Market and Class Conflict*, Drug Abuse Council, March 1974.

Hunt, Leon G., *Recent Spread of Heroin in the United States: Unanswered Questions*, Drug Abuse Council, July 1974.

National Commission on Marihuana and Drug Abuse, *Marihuana: A Signal of Misunderstanding*, First Report, 1972.

—*Drug Use in America: Problem in Perspective*, Second Report, 1973.

VIOLENCE IN THE SCHOOLS

by

Suzanne de Lesseps

**Aug. 13
1 9 7 6**

Editor's Note: The Ford Foundation, on July 9, 1978, released a year-long study on juvenile violence in the United States. Titled *Violent Delinquents: A Report to the Ford Foundation from the Vera Institute of Justice,* the study found that violent crimes by juveniles, particularly robbery and assault, are increasing, although they still represent a small proportion of the illegal activities of the young.

VIOLENCE IN THE SCHOOLS

T HE PUBLIC image of innocent schoolchildren carrying apples to the teacher has given way to that of gangs of juveniles brandishing switchblades in the halls. School violence has become such a serious national problem, according to a study done for the Justice Department's Law Enforcement Assistance Administration, that it should be fought from the federal level.[1] In the words of the School Public Relations Association: "It is a problem that is elusive; a costly problem that involves fear of physical harm and emotional public demands for safer schools, and worst of all, a problem that so far defies solution."

Last year, according to the National Education Association, American schoolchildren committed 100 murders, 12,000 armed robberies, 9,000 rapes and 204,000 aggravated assaults against teachers and other students. The annual cost of vandalism to schools is almost $600-million—an amount equal to that spent on textbooks in 1972—according to the Senate Judiciary Subcommittee to Investigate Delinquency. In June 1975, the subcommittee heard teachers and administrators from around the country detail incidents of vandalism and violence in their schools.

A teacher from Atlanta said an eighth-grade boy had blackened her eye. Others told of gang warfare, stabbings, thefts, assaults, destruction of school facilities, and in one case, the killing of elementary school pets. "The past few years have seen violence and vandalism become an almost daily occurrence on school grounds," Amy Hittner, a San Francisco teacher, testified. "...I have seen females beaten and severely scratched by other females, males beaten, stabbed, shot and one murdered in the school. Rarely is a fight between persons of the opposite sex."

Statistics on school crime vary and are sketchy and approximate. Many teachers and administrators have been reluctant to report acts of vandalism and violence for fear they would appear to be doing a poor job. School surveys have been taken, however, and one conducted by the Senate subcommittee has

---

[1] "Planning Assistance Programs to Reduce School Violence and Disruption," study done by Research for Better Schools, Inc., January 1976.

gained attention. The subcommittee's survey of 757 schools across the country reported the following increase in school violence at those schools between 1970 and 1973:

Homicides	Up 18.5%	Assaults on teachers	Up 77.4%
Rapes and attempted		Burglaries of school	
rapes	40.1	buildings	11.8
Robberies	36.7	Drug and alcohol offenses	
Assaults on students	85.3	on school property	37.5

In a preliminary report issued last year, the subcommittee noted that student violence and vandalism occurred more often in large urban secondary schools than elsewhere. But the subcommittee's study also found that the problem touched younger students and smaller communities as well. "It should be emphasized...that this is not a problem found exclusively in large cities or solely involving older students," the report stated.[2] According to a study done by the National School Public Relations Association, 55 per cent of major disruptions occurred in cities with populations exceeding one million, in contrast to 26 per cent in cities under 100,000.

Spillover of Yough-Gang Violence Into Schools

Youth gangs are blamed for much of the school violence in large urban areas. According to a recent study by Walter B. Miller of the Harvard Center for Criminal Justice, "it is probable that violence perpetrated by members of youth gangs in major cities is at present more lethal than at any time in history."[3] Miller also found that youth gangs are terrorizing larger numbers of people and are much harder to control than the gangs of the 1950s and 1960s. In his year-long investigation, the Harvard professor concentrated on the six cities he believed to have the most critical youth-gang problems—New York, Chicago, Los Angeles, Philadelphia, Detroit and San Francisco. His work was financed by the Law Enforcement Assistance Administration and was described as the first comprehensive national study of youth gangs.

Miller found evidence that youth-gang violence has infiltrated the public schools—an area that used to be considered neutral territory. He reported that gangs have attacked not only rival gang members in the schools but also teachers and students who are not gang members. Typically, a gang claims "ownership" of a classroom, gym, cafeteria or, in some cases, an entire school. The members assert a right to collect "fees" from other students in exchange for such "privileges" as walking down the hall and being protected from assault.

2 "Our Nation's Schools—A Report Card: 'A' in School Violence and Vandalism," April 1975, p. 5.

3 "Violence by Youth Gangs and Youth Groups in Major American Cities," summary report, April 1976, p. 8.

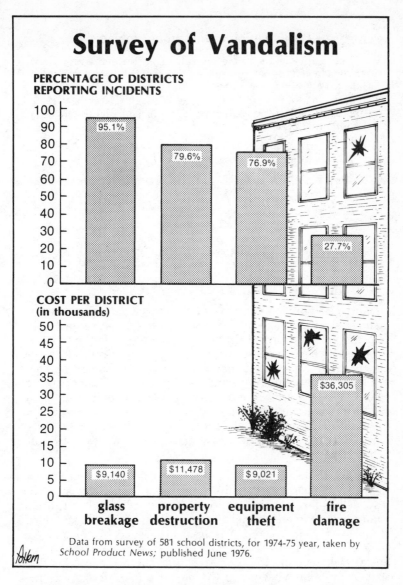

Survey of Vandalism

PERCENTAGE OF DISTRICTS REPORTING INCIDENTS

- glass breakage — 95.1%
- property destruction — 79.6%
- equipment theft — 76.9%
- fire damage — 27.7%

COST PER DISTRICT (in thousands)

- glass breakage — $9,140
- property destruction — $11,478
- equipment theft — $9,021
- fire damage — $36,305

Data from survey of 581 school districts, for 1974-75 year, taken by *School Product News;* published June 1976.

In Philadelphia, Miller reported, several high schools were forced to close their cafeterias because gangs had claimed the right to control access and seating arrangements. He was told that some schools in New York City had "sold out" to the gangs; they could recruit members openly in return for promises to refrain from violence.

Varied Explanations for Anti-Social Behavior

What are the causes of violence and vandalism among American young people? No one knows for certain, although there are several standard explanations. Some blame the

175

Public Opinion on School Problems

Lack of discipline has been named as the most important problem facing the nation's schools, in six of the last seven annual Gallup Poll surveys of public attitudes toward education. According to the latest survey, released in December 1975, Americans ranked the leading problems faced by local schools in the following order:

1. Lack of discipline
2. Integration and segregation
3. Lack of proper financial support
4. Difficulty of getting good teachers
5. Use of drugs
6. Size of the school and classes
7. Crime, vandalism and stealing
8. Poor curriculum and pupils' lack of interest
9. Parents' lack of interest and lack of proper facilities
10. School board policies

glamorization of violence on television,[4] lack of student involvement in setting school policy, overcrowded facilities, or the increasing politicization of the schools. Others blame the ineffectiveness of the juvenile court system and the resulting feeling among many youths that they will escape punishment for their misdeeds. The breakdown of the family plus the lack of personal values in society are also cited as reasons for juvenile delinquency. "We're not transmitting to our young people the respect for the rights and property of others that we did in years past," Larry Burgan, chief of security for the Baltimore City Public Schools, has said.[5]

In 1969, the National Commission on the Causes and Prevention of Violence stated in its final report that television was responsible for teaching children "a set of moral and social values about violence which are inconsistent with the standards of civilized society." But a later study issued by the Surgeon General's Scientific Advisory Committee on Television and Social Behavior in 1972, reported that the evidence was "not conclusive" that violence in the media produced aggression.

Some psychologists and sociologists believe violent and disruptive students are motivated by their fear, anxiety and unhappiness in the school system. If students are doing poorly, they may resent "being compelled to sit in school in an atmosphere that reminds them of failure," said Albert Shanker, president of the American Federation of Teachers.[6] Often they

---

[4] See "Violence in the Media," *E.R.R.*, Vol. I, pp. 377-394.
[5] Quoted by Myron Brenton, "School Vandalism," *Today's Education*, March-April 1975, p. 84.
[6] Testimony before the Senate Subcommittee to Investigate Juvenile Delinquency, April 16, 1975.

may perform acts of vandalism or violence to get attention or win the approval of other kids. "For the child who falls behind, who hears such words as 'dumb' or 'retarded,' 'non-reader' and 'failure'...the damage to his self-esteem is almost certainly irreversible," Kenneth Wooden has written in his book *Weeping in the Playtime of Others* (1976). "These years of educational failure shatter the self-confidence of the child. Failure leads to frustration and hopelessness, which in turn can lead to aggressiveness."

Racial tensions and antagonisms, particularly those arising from the busing issue,[7] have also been cited as causes of violence in schools. However, according to Benjamin F. Holman, director of the Justice Department's Community Relations Service, busing violence is caused far more often   by adults than by students. "Parents and proponents of causes are the culprits in these conflict situations," he wrote in response to an inquiry from Sens. Edward W. Brooke (R Mass.) and Jacob K. Javits (R N.Y.). "Even those situations that originate among students usually do not grow into major conflicts unless parents and other adults are drawn into them."[8]

Suspension and Expulsions Under Question

It is as difficult to curb school crime as it is to pinpoint its causes. The suspension or expulsion of disruptive students, according to some experts, generally fails to stop school violence and vandalism and may worsen the problem. Robert E. Phay, professor of public law and government at the University of North Carolina, told the Senate subcommittee at further hearings in September 1975: "It just removes it [violence] from the school to another place. In fact, I suspect that the misconduct increases when students are out of the jurisdiction of the school." The National Association of School Security Directors reports that a substantial amount of school crime is caused by dropouts, truants and suspended or expelled students.

In a study of school suspensions completed last year, the Children's Defense Fund, a non-profit children's rights group based in Cambridge, Mass., concluded: "The solution to school violence does not lie in more suspensions but less, for its causes are to be found more on the streets, where dropouts, pushouts, and suspended students pass the time among delinquent gangs in arms or drug trade; in the lack of preparation for decent jobs... and in the rates of illiteracy and its attendant frustration and anger."[9]

---

[7] See "Busing Reappraisal," *E.R.R.*, 1975 Vol. II, pp. 945-964.
[8] Holman letter to Sens. Brooke and Javits reprinted in the *Congressional Record*, June 26, 1976.
[9] "School Suspensions: Are They Helping Children?" September 1975, p. 20. A "pushout" is a student who is dissuaded from attending school by parents or administrators.

In analyzing official data[10] for 1972-73, the Children's Defense Fund found that the vast majority of school suspensions were for non-violent offenses such as tardiness, truancy, pregnancy, smoking, dress code violations or failure to purchase required equipment. Less than 3 per cent of the suspensions were for destruction of property, the illegal use of drugs or alcohol or other criminal activity.

Black students were suspended at twice the rate of any other racial group, the report added. "We have found what black parents, children, and civil rights groups have charged for years—that there is racial discrimination and insensitivity in the use of disciplinary sanctions," Marian Edelman, head of the Children's Defense Fund, testified before the Senate subcommittee at its September hearings. She noted that some offenses, such as carrying a metal pick used to comb Afro hairstyles or wearing a headscarf, could lead to the suspension of black youngsters.

"The fact is simple but stark: vandalism and violence have become one of the foremost problems of the nation's schools during the past five years."

National School Public
Relations Association

The Children's Defense Fund's report recommended that only students who pose a direct and serious threat to property or people be suspended from school. In addition, it said, school disciplinary rules should be made available to students and parents in writing at the beginning of each school year. "At the very minimum, schools must provide immediate and adequate due process safeguards for students before they are excluded from school," the report said.

The Supreme Court in January 1975 ruled that every school child has an "entitlement" to education that cannot be taken away, even for a short time, without due process of law. In suspensions of less than 10 days, the Court said, students must be given a written or oral notice of the charges against them. They must also be given a chance to present their side of the story. The Court stopped short of saying students had the right to legal counsel and a formal hearing, but it did say that they

---

[10] Compiled by the Office for Civil Rights, Department of Health, Education, and Welfare.

were entitled to "rudimentary precautions against unfair findings of misconduct and arbitrary exclusions from school."[11]

One month later, the Court held in another case[12] that a school board member could be sued for personal damages "if he knew or reasonably should have known that the action he took...would violate the constitutional rights of the student affected..." The case involved three tenth-grade girls who admitted "spiking the punch" at a school party. The principal suspended them for two weeks and the school board increased the suspension to three months. The U.S. Court of Appeals for the Eighth Circuit (Kansas City, Mo.) ruled that the suspensions violated the students' right to due process since no evidence, other than their admission, had been submitted to show they had violated the school rule against the use of intoxicating beverages.

Changed Concepts of Juvenile Rights

T HE CURRENT age of student rights presents a marked contrast to the early years of American education, when the birch rod dominated the classroom. American colonists, coming from a land where flogging was a time-honored punishment, carried on the tradition. Not only were colonial children whipped by authoritarian schoolmasters, they were tormented from the pulpit by the threat of eternal damnation for their misbehavior. "This repressive attitude toward life," Herbert Arnold Falk has written, "this insistence on conformity to a moral and ethical code based on purely religious sanction, was naturally reflected in colonial schools and in the discipline of the children."[13] Through the later use of the famous *McGuffey Eclectic Readers,*[14] school children were taught to respect the moral virtues of individual enterprise and to avoid the excess of self-indulgence.

Whipping posts gradually disappeared but the tradition of punishing children with the rod remained throughout the 19th century and well into the 20th. The prevailing view was that students were inferior and should be obedient. Even Horace Mann, who crusaded against excessive corporal punishment during the 1830s, did not approve of abolishing it altogether. As

---

[11] *Goss v. Lopez,* 419 U.S. 565.

[12] *Wood v. Strickland,* 420 U.S. 308.

[13] Herbert Arnold Falk, *Corporate Punishment: A Social Interpretation of Its Theory and Practice in the Schools of the United States* (1941), p. 42.

[14] Named for the author, William Holmes McGuffey. His first reader was introduced in 1836; it went through successive printings and revisions.

late as 1899, Boston recorded 11,768 cases of physical punishment in boys' grammar schools whose enrollments totaled 16,198. Nineteenth-century literature is replete with schoolroom scenes of ears boxed, noses pinched and skulls rapped for offenses that would be considered trivial today—squirming, giggling, whispering, and slowness to answer questions.

Social changes in the early decades of the 20th century modified this authoritarian atmosphere. The teacher was still boss but the emphasis was more on cultivating student self-discipline rather than a rigid conformity to rules of conduct. During this period, the study of child psychology advanced and the Puritan influence declined. Student governments, elective courses and recreational facilities became prominent. New guidelines on student discipline were embodied in the progressive education movement, which said: "The conduct of the pupil should be governed by himself according to the social needs of his community, rather than by arbitrary laws. Full opportunity for initiative and self-expression should be provided."[15]

Inapplicability of Old Disciplinary Rules Today

A rise in juvenile delinquency in the decade following World War II revived public support for corporal punishment. A scholarly study in the early 1960s said it was "still a factor in the schools" and "is still practiced even in areas where regulations forbid it." The author found a "strong trend" in public opinion "away from the permissive and toward the authoritarian point of view in discipline of pupils in the public schools." This was due, he wrote, to concern over "ever-mounting unruliness and disorder in the schools."[16]

In 1975 came a legal victory for corporal punishment. The Supreme Court refused on Oct. 20 to review, and thus let stand, a lower court ruling that corporal punishment in the public schools was not a violation of the constitutional rights of parents. The three-judge federal court had ruled that the student must be given fair warning and that corporal punishment should be used only as a last resort. The National Education Association, the American Civil Liberties Union and the American Psychological Association all have opposed corporal punishment in the public schools, and few people consider it the answer to the discipline and crime problems today.

In many instances, school administrators are dealing with delinquent juveniles who have committed serious crimes. Their cases must be handled by the juvenile justice system, not by a

---

[15] From *Progressive Education,* April 1924, reprinted in *Readings in American Educational History* (1951), Edgar W. Knight and Clifton L. Hall, eds. p. 528.
[16] Keith Franklin James, *Corporal Punishment in the Public Schools* (1963), pp. 88-89.

teacher and a paddle. Harvard criminologist James Q. Wilson said in a speech before the 1975 conference of the Council for Educational Development and Research: "Much of what is termed 'crime in the schools' is crime that involves school children or school personnel, but it no more deserves to be called 'school crime' than ordinary crime deserves to be called 'family crime' because families are so often involved in it."[17]

Juvenile crime has grown steadily in recent years. In 1974, the latest year for which the FBI has compiled national statistics, youths under 18 accounted for 51 per cent of the arrests for property crimes, 23 per cent of the arrests for violent crimes and 27 per cent of all arrests *(see box, p. 182)*. As juvenile crime has increased, the juvenile criminal system has been heavily criticized. "It has become increasingly apparent that our traditional system of juvenile justice is a failure," Judge Irving R. Kaufman, chief judge of the U.S. Court of Appeals for the Second Circuit (New York), said recently. "It neither safeguards our society from violent juveniles nor provides adequate protection for the alarmingly large number of children reared in brutal environments...which breed hostility and failure."[18] Kaufman has served as chairman of the Joint Commission on Juvenile Standards, sponsored by the Institute of Judicial Administration and the American Bar Association, which has been working on reform of the juvenile justice system since 1971 *(see p. 184)*.

Emergence of Concept of Juvenile Delinquency

The concept of juvenile delinquency—as opposed to a general concept of crime to be dealt with irrespective of age—emerged in the 19th century, when interest in deterring and punishing young offenders gradually shifted to a concern for reforming and rehabilitating them. At first, the task of rehabilitating delinquents was carried out almost exclusively by voluntary groups. The first Ragged Schools for destitute or abandoned children were established in England in 1818. The Reformatory Schools Act of 1854 made it possible for English judges to commit offenders under age 16 to reformatories, which were then in private hands.

In the United States, the "child-saving" movement led to the establishment of training schools designed to keep minors out of jail. The first institution of this kind was the House of Refuge, founded in New York City in 1825 by the Society for the Reformation of Juvenile Delinquents. The children, some of them waifs off the streets, were housed in a grim building that had been a troop barracks. The first publicly supported school for delinquents was established in 1847 in Massachusetts.

---

[17] Excerpt reprinted in *Educational Researcher,* published by the American Educational Research Association, May 1976, pp. 3-6.
[18] Quoted in *U.S. News & World Report,* June 7, 1976, p. 65.

Juvenile Crime in the United States

Year	Arrests* All Ages	Per Cent Under Age 15	Per Cent Under Age 18
1974	6,179,406	9.8	27.2
1973	6,499,864	9.5	26.4
1972	7,130,194	9.5	25.6
1971	6,966,822	9.5	25.8
1970	6,570,473	9.2	25.3
1969	5,862,246	9.7	25.6
1968	5,616,839	10.0	25.9
1967	5,518,420	9.6	24.3
1966	5,016,407	9.2	22.9
1965	5,031,393	8.5	21.4

*For all reported offenses except traffic violations

Source: FBI Uniform Crime Reports

The philosophy behind the programs of American reform schools underwent little change for years. Their primary purpose was to guard delinquents from the influences that had led them astray, to instill in them a respect for authority and to teach them a trade. Rigid discipline, religious instruction and "busy work" were the chief ingredients of the program. During the 1850s, the idea was promoted that children and youth could be rehabilitated more easily if placed in a rural setting. It was believed that urban environments bred delinquency and that country living would put juveniles in a healthier frame of mind.

One of the early state institutions, established in Lancaster, Ohio, in 1858, consisted of a group of log cabins, each housing 40 boys and a custodian, who was known as an "elder brother." The youths worked on a farm eight and a half hours a day. Recaptured runaways were punished by confinement in a dark cell for two weeks or by transfer to a penitentiary. Children were usually committed to an institution for an indefinite term, and even the best-managed reform schools were essentially prisons for the young.

Other efforts to separate incarcerated children and adult criminals were gradually initiated. In 1861 the mayor of Chicago appointed a commissioner to hear and decide minor charges against boys 6 to 17 years old and to place them on probation or in a reformatory. An 1870 law required that children's cases in Suffolk County (Boston) be heard separately from adult cases, and it authorized a representative of the commonwealth to investigate cases, attend trials and protect children's interests. The statute was extended throughout Massachusetts in 1872. In

1877, separate dockets and court records were provided in juvenile cases. New York adopted similar provisions in 1892, as did Rhode Island in 1898.

It was Illinois, however, that established the first statewide court especially for children when it passed its Juvenile Court Act of 1899. This law included most of the features that have since come to distinguish the juvenile court system. It formally codified the concept of *parens patriae*[19] and gave the state discretionary power over the welfare of children.[20] The court, in effect, became a substitute parent. Other states quickly enacted similar laws—Wisconsin and New York in 1901, Ohio and Maryland in 1902, and Colorado in 1903.

The object of the new juvenile court system was not to punish or apportion guilt, but to save children from the corrupt influences of urban life and steer them on the road to recovery by giving them care, treatment, discipline and responsible supervision. The judge was to sit at a desk or table instead of behind a bench, fatherly and sympathetic while still authoritative and sobering. A new vocabulary symbolized the new philosophy behind the court system. A child was not sentenced but assigned to a "dispositional alternative" such as a state training school. He or she was not "imprisoned" in a penal institution, but rather was "remanded" to a reformatory for "rehabilitation" and "supervision."

The individual's background was more important than the facts of a given incident. Because it was important that the children be protected from the ordeal of criminal courts, there was to be no adversary proceeding in the new juvenile court system. For a long time, in fact, the courts were run primarily by social workers and others with no legal training. Lawyers were seldom present in the court and many juvenile court judges were not lawyers.

Court Decisions to Protect Youthful Defendants

All that was turned around by the Supreme Court in 1967. It held[21] that children brought before a juvenile court were entitled to the same procedural protections afforded by the Bill of Rights in trials of adults. The Court ruled that the following due process requirements must be provided in juvenile cases: (1) timely and adequate notice of charges; (2) the right to be represented by counsel, court-appointed if necessary, in any case that could result in incarceration of the child; (3) the right

---

[19] Literally "father of the country," the Latin phrase conveys the legal concept of a state official paternally taking charge of the interests of persons without parents or guardians or of those incapable of conducting their affairs.

[20] See Jean B. Chalmers, "Rejuvenating Juvenile Courts," *Trial*, July-August 1975.

[21] *In Re Gault,* 387 U.S. 1.

to confront and to cross-examine witnesses and complainants; and (4) a warning of the right to remain silent and the privilege against self-incrimination. "Under our Constitution," the Court said, "the condition of being a boy does not justify a kangaroo court."

Changes that have been made to protect the interest of children and adolescents in the juvenile court system have had no visible effect on juvenile crime itself. The ideals and rhetoric of the architects of the first juvenile courts seem never to have been properly translated into reality. "Perhaps they never could have...," Jean Chalmers has written. "The courts have never had the necessary staffs, operating funds, auxiliary services or facilities to successfully achieve the goals."[22] In addition, the original aim of the juvenile justice system—the individual rehabilitation of each offender—appears outmoded in today's society. Adolescents are a much different breed than they were at the turn of the century, and finding a "cure" for each juvenile offender is a difficult task.

Yet the search continues for ways to make the juvenile justice system work more effectively. In some communities there has been a shift away from helping "disturbed" young people and toward protecting the victimized citizenry. This reflects a "get tough" policy which is often characterized by attempts to deal with youthful perpetrators of violent crime as adults. An educator and psychoanalyst, Ernest van den Haag, perhaps summed up the feeling of many adults when he wrote in his book *Punishing Criminals* (1975): "The victim of a fifteen-year-old mugger is as much mugged as the victim of a twenty-one-year-old mugger, the victim of a fourteen-year-old murderer or rapist is as dead or as raped as the victim of an older one. The need for social defense or protection is the same."

Study by Commission on Juvenile Standards

After a four-year study of the juvenile justice system, the Joint Commission on Juvenile Standards, made up of prominent psychiatrists, sociologists, penologists, educators, lawyers and judges, has approved a comprehensive set of recommendations for improving the system. Eventually, the commission's 23 volumes of recommendations will be offered as models for new state legislation.

Specifically, the commission has proposed an end to "indeterminate sentencing" of juvenile criminals—a procedure that is slowly losing appeal among criminologists and penologists and has been criticized for being unfair and ineffective.[23] Current juvenile sentencing procedures would be

---

[22] Chalmers, *op. cit.*, p. 66.
[23] See "Reappraisal of Prison Policy," *E.R.R.*, 1976 Vol. I, p. 185.

overhauled to provide definite and strict sentencing for the most serious juvenile offenders. Non-criminal behavior—the so-called "status offenses" like incorrigibility, immoral conduct and truancy—would be removed from the jurisdiction of the juvenile court altogether and would be handled by social agencies instead. Another major recommendation of the commission is that the current secret juvenile proceedings be opened up and made more public. All decisions affecting a juvenile's future would have to be explained in writing.

Action to Make Schools More Secure

WHILE LEGISLATORS are trying to improve juvenile justice and reduce juvenile crime, school officials are looking for ways to curb violence and vandalism in their schools. A novel idea for protecting school property is that of "watchmobiles" or school "sitters." In many communities, a local family is allowed to move its mobile home onto the school grounds to deter vandalism. Generally, the "sitters" live rent free in exchange for reporting any suspicious behavior to local authorities. In Elk Grove, Calif., where the idea originated, the school district experienced only two break-ins during the 1974-75 school year, in contrast to 40 or 50 a year before the program began in 1967.

Many school districts also have added more security forces and equipment. Floodlights, closed-circuit television and intricate burglar alarms have been installed. Electronic surveillance is becoming very popular. At the 1976 conference of the National Association of School Security Directors in Alexandria, Va., delegates were shown such new products as microwave intruder detectors for school hallways and ultrasonic alerters that warn of possible theft. A communications device disguised as a fountain pen can be triggered by a teacher who is in danger.

A booklet issued by the United Federation of Teachers, the teachers union of New York City, advised teachers not to be alone for long. "Teachers may feel safe because they lock their classroom doors," the "Security in the Schools" booklet stated. "But locks can be picked fairly easily. More than that, experience and assault records show that when someone knocks, teachers open their doors." The booklet further warned teachers not to be alone in the faculty lounge, and it advised them to arrive at school no more than 30 minutes before classes begin.

The booklet also observed: "Too many schools are hazardous for entirely unnecessary reasons...simply because the people responsible for designing schools often have no understanding of children." The booklet cited the example of circular corridors that have been built in some modern schools. These corridors may win praise from architects but they obstruct vision beyond a few feet. Other examples of dangerous school architecture are low, sloping roofs that allow burglars to climb up, and suspended tile ceilings that can be punched out and made into lethal missiles.

According to John Zeisel of the Harvard Graduate School of Design, school vandalism could be reduced by better school design. His suggestions for better school design, published in the March 1974 issue of "Schoolhouse," newsletter of the Educational Facilities Laboratories, included these:

Ensure that there are no footholds on exterior walls.

Keep climbable plants away from the walls.

Use pull-down or sliding grills to cover transparent doorways when the building is closed.

Avoid wall and ceiling materials that can be damaged easily.

Place administrative offices near entrances so that the staff can see who is going in and out of the building.

Use washable materials on surfaces that children can reach.

Plan walls that are too high to climb with accessible "ladder substitutes," such as long pieces of lumber.

Design secondary exit doors so they are not accessible from the outside.

Avoid placing large areas of glass on entrance doors.

Minimize the amount of glass around play areas.

Repair damages as quickly as possible to discourage vandalism.

Since glass breakage is one of the most common forms of school vandalism, many schools around the country have replaced their glass windows with various new types of tempered glass and plastics. But even these substitute materials have been abused. In Baltimore, new polycarbonate windows, about 250 times the strength of glass, were installed in the public schools. But young offenders learned to remove the glazing compound before it had hardened. School administrators tried to counteract this by fastening the glazing strips with sheetmetal screws, but then the vandals simply unscrewed these with screwdrivers. The schools then tried pop rivets, which seemed to work, until the youths learned to squirt the new windows with lighter fluid and melt them.

Success of Student Patrols in Maryland Schools

Many administrators believe that getting students involved in anti-vandalism campaigns and instilling them with school pride is the best way to stop school crime. In Prince George's County, Md., school officials have instituted a highly successful Student Security Advisory Council involving several hundred students in the junior and senior high schools. The council serves as an advisory group to the principal and meets regularly to develop school security plans.

During their free time, teams of students patrol school parking lots and monitor locker areas. They also run a rumor control center, manage a school cleanup day, serve as student security teams during dances, and keep their homerooms informed of student responsibilities in maintaining security. The students do not confront others when they see them committing an offense, but report them to school authorities.

Robert Phay, the University of North Carolina professor, has urged that students be allowed to participate in drawing up codes of conduct. "This is an important way to communicate to students that their support and assistance is needed to make school a worthwhile experience," he said in his appearance before the Senate subcommittee. "Students need to know that they are the primary beneficiary of an orderly school operation and the primary loser when school is not orderly. They must understand that they have a major responsibility to contribute to the orderly operation." Phay said student conduct codes should include a written statement of the basic constitutional rights of students and a clear outline of the ground rules of school discipline.

Another witness before the subcommittee at its September hearings, Alan H. Levine of the New York Civil Liberties Union, called for passage of federal legislation to protect student rights. "[H]ow people behave is substantially affected by how they are treated," he said. "If students are treated more fairly, one source of their anger and frustration will be eliminated." Reminding the subcommittee that the Supreme Court in *Goss v. Lopez (see footnote 11)* guaranteed students the right to a hearing before being punished, Levine suggested that other student rights should also be guaranteed, including the right to privacy and protection against arbitrary searches. He asked that corporal punishment be abolished and that procedures for airing grievances about school policies be established.

"The primary concern in many American schools today is no longer education but preservation."

Sen. Birch Bayh (D Ind.), chairman,
Senate Subcommittee to Investigate
Juvenile Delinquency

James Q. Wilson, the Harvard criminologist, takes issue with the argument that giving children more rights is an important way to cope with school crime. He said in his speech to the Council for Educational Development and Research: "I think the issue of the kind of rights school children should have is separable from the issue of what to do to protect the possibility of carrying out education within the schools, free of the threat of violence, disorder and theft. Furthermore, there is absolutely no reason to believe that extending rights will reduce violence. Indeed, there is as much evidence against as in support of that proposition."

Although Wilson maintained that "we are facing a problem...we do not understand...and probably cannot eliminate in a generation or two," he did offer suggestions for coping with the increase in criminal behavior among youth. One proposal was that society consider offering alternative routes into the work force other than high school, such as apprenticeships to craftsmen or to employers. He advised that society should get away from the notion that all young people must be channeled through high school in uniform fashion.

Jesse Jackson's Campaign Among Black Youth

Many educators have urged that troubled and disruptive young persons be taken out of the regular school environment and placed in other educational settings. They argue that perhaps in a school better tailored to his or her learning abilities, a child would feel more at home, would perform better, and would be happier. Teachers are continually looking for ways to encourage rebellious students to enjoy school. "The nation does not need laws that force adolescents to go to school," the National Commission on the Reform of Secondary Education observed a few years ago. "It needs schools and school-related programs that make adolescents wish to come."[24]

Convincing students of the need for education is no small task. But one man who has taken on the job is the Rev. Jesse Jackson, the black head of Operation PUSH (People United to Save Humanity) in Chicago. Jackson believes that many black high schools around the nation are in a state of decay, and that if student discipline does not improve soon, the future of the black race may be at stake. "Respect, responsibility and morality must be brought back into the school...," he said recently. "Parents should provide children with motivation, discipline, care, love and chastisement."[25]

In his evangelical Push for Excellence campaign, which he has brought to several large cities around the country, Jackson exhorts young students to pay attention to moral authority and to study hard. He is appalled at the lack of discipline in the public schools, and urges administrators to prohibit students from carrying radios and tape players during school hours. He advocates a strict dress code, and an end to the use of street language by young blacks. "I'm convinced that if we begin to instill discipline and responsibility and self-respect," he said recently, "there will be better conduct."[26]

Many persons are dubious that Jackson's self-disciplinary approach to black pride and excellence will succeed. But his message appears to have caught on among many black students in the high schools he has visited so far. If his approach could somehow be broadened to apply to all students, it could represent a start toward solving the problems of adolescent restlessness and juvenile crime.

---

[24] Cited by Frank Brown, chairman of the commission, in *Phi Delta Kappan*, December 1973, p. 229.
[25] Quoted by Paul Delaney in *The New York Times*, June 8, 1976.
[26] Quoted by Michael Putney, *The National Observer*, May 8, 1976.

▼▼▼

Selected Bibliography
Books

Coffey, Alan, *Juvenile Justice as a System*, Prentice-Hall, 1974.

Eldefonso, Edward, *Law Enforcement and the Youthful Offender*, Wiley, 1973.

Falk, Herbert A., *Corporal Punishment: A Social Interpretation of Its Theory and Practice in the Schools of the United States*, AMS Press, 1941.

Gibbons, Don C., *Delinquent Behavior*, Prentice-Hall, 1976.

James, Keith F., *Corporal Punishment in the Public Schools*, University of Southern California Press, 1963.

van den Haag, Ernest, *Punishing Criminals*, Basic Books, 1975.

Wooden, Kenneth, *Weeping in the Playtime of Others*, McGraw-Hill, 1976.

Articles

Brenton, Myron, "School Vandalism," *Today's Education*, March-April 1975.

Chalmers, Jean B., "Rejuvenating Juvenile Courts," *Trial*, July-August 1975.

Jackson, Jesse L., "Give the People a Vision," *The New York Times Magazine*, April 18, 1976.

Kirk, William J., "Juvenile Justice and Delinquency," *Phi Delta Kappan*, February 1976.

Rector, Milton G. and David Gilman, "How Did We Get Here and Where are We Going—The Future of the Juvenile Court System," *Criminal Justice Review*, Spring 1976.

Slaybaugh, David J., "School Security Survey," *School Product News*, June 1976.

"Schoolhouse," Educational Facilities Laboratories Newsletter, March 1974.

"Terror in the Schools," *U.S. News & World Report*, Jan. 26, 1976.

Wilson, James Q., "Crime in Society and Schools," *Educational Researcher*, May 1976.

Studies and Reports

Berger, Michael, "Violence in the Schools: Causes and Remedies," Phi Delta Kappa Educational Foundation, 1974.

Children's Defense Fund, "School Suspensions: Are They Helping Children?" September 1975.

Editorial Research Reports, "Education's Return to Basics," 1975 Vol. II, p. 665; "Juvenile Offenders," 1970 Vol. I, p. 99; "Discipline in Public Schools," 1969 Vol. II, p. 633.

Flygare, Thomas, "The Legal Rights of Students," Phi Delta Kappa Educational Foundation, 1975.

Miller, Walter B., "Violence by Youth Gangs in Major American Cities," Law Enforcement Assistance Administration, U.S. Department of Justice, summary report, April 1976.

National School Public Relations Association, "Violence and Vandalism," 1975.

Research for Better Schools, Inc., "Planning Assistance Programs to Reduce School Violence and Disruption," Law Enforcement Assistance Administration, Department of Justice, January 1976.

U.S. Congress, Senate Subcommittee to Investigate Juvenile Delinquency, published hearings of April 16, June 17 and Sept. 17, 1975.

INDEX

D

K

Kelley, Clarence M. - 3
Kennedy, Edward M. (D Mass.)
 Criminal code - 19, 70
 Federal judge selection - 116
 Mandatory sentencing - 101

L

Law Enforcement Assistance Administration (LEAA)
 "Career criminal program" - 104, 105
 Omnibus Crime Control and Safe Streets Act of 1968 - 95
 Performance studies - 17, 18
 Probation programs - 95
 Prosecuting repeat offenders - 4-6
 School violence studies - 173, 174
Lawyers. See Attorneys.
LEAA. See Law Enforcement Assistance Administration
Legal Services
 Attorney advertising - 137-139
 Citizen law movement - 143-146
 Legal aid societies - 140
 Legal clinics - 136, 137
 Legal Services Corporation Act - 142, 143
 Paralegals - 137, *(box) 138*
 Pre-paid insurance - 134-136
Levi, Edward H. - 102
Lombroso, Cesare - 10

M

Marijuana
 Decriminilization - 155, 156, 166, 167
 Domestic Council Task Force - 153
 Primary drugs of abuse *(box)* - 157
McClellan, John L. (D-Ark.) - 19
Miranda v. Arizona - 112, *(box)* 113
Montreal Convention of 1971 - 36
Murphy, Patrick V. - 7

N

Nader, Ralph
 Citizen Law movement - 143, 144
Narodnaya Volya gang - 32
New World Liberation Front - 28
Nixon, Richard M.
 Burger appointment - 112, 124
 Crime policy - 13, 14
 District of Columbia Crime Act (box) - 104
 Drug policy - 153, 167
 Federal judge selection - 112

Terrorism policy - 38

O

Office of Economic Opportunity - 141-143

P

Parker, Donn B. - 47, 55, 58, 62
Parole. See *also* Criminal Release System
 Abolition - 69
 Criticisms - 94-96, 100, 101
 Definition *(box)* - 72
 Origins - 98
People United to Save Humanity (PUSH) - 188, 189
Powell v. Alabama - 121
Powell, Lewis F. Jr. - 112, 138
President's Commission on Law Enforcement and Administration of Justice
 Bail - 94
 Probation - 95
Pre-Trial Detention - 8
Prison Facilities
 American prison population *(box)* - 71
 Model prison - 10, 82, 83
 Overcrowding - 70-73, 103-105
Probation. See *also* Criminal Release System
 Abolition - 68, 69, 81
 Crime Commission report - 95
 Criticisms - 94-96
 Definition *(box)* - 72
 Juveniles - 97, 98
Prosecutor's Management Information System (Promis) - 5, 6
Punishment
 Computer criminals - 59-62
 Corporal - *(box)* 11, 74, 179-181
 Indeterminate sentencing - 69, 70, 80-82, 100, 101
 Proposed sentencing guidelines - 19
 Reformatories - 9, 76
 Solitary confinement - 75

R

Recidivism
 Emphasis on prosecution - 4-6
 Rehabilitation - 82
 Repeat crimes *(graph)* - 5
Rehabilitation
 Drug abuse treatment - 161, 162
 "Medical model" - 68, 77, 83
 Recidivism - 82
 Reformatory "cures" - 76, 77
 Voluntary programs - 69
Rehnquist, William H. - 112